MEDITERRANEAN
SEA

Rosetta

Damietta

Alexandria

Sebennytos

Tanis

Sais

Qantir

Mendes

Avaris

Tell Basta

Tell el-Yahudiyah

Giza • Heliopolis

Abusir • Tura

Memphis

Saqqara

The Fayoum Lisht

Medum

Hawara

Gurob • Lahun

Kahun

el-Ashmunein • Beni Hasan

Tuna el-Gebel

Meir • Tell el-Amarna

Deir el-Gebrawi

Assiut

River Nile

Rifeh

Abydos

Denderah

Nagada

EGYPT

Armant • Thebes

Esna

Hieraconpolis • el-Kab

Edfu

RED
SEA

Kom Ombo

Elephantine • Aswan

A Year in the Life of
Ancient Egypt

Rosalie David

ARCHAEOLOGY

PEN &
SWORD

First published in Great Britain in 2015 by
PEN & SWORD ARCHAEOLOGY
an imprint of
Pen and Sword Books Ltd
47 Church Street
Barnsley
South Yorkshire S70 2AS

ISBN 978 1 47382 239 9

A CIP record for this book is available from the British Library

Printed and bound in India
by Replika Press Pvt. Ltd.

Typeset in Times New Roman by
CHIC GRAPHICS

Pen & Sword Books Ltd incorporates the imprints of
Pen & Sword Archaeology, Atlas, Aviation, Battleground, Discovery,
Family History, History, Maritime, Military, Naval, Politics, Railways,
Select, Social History, Transport, True Crime, Claymore Press,
Frontline Books, Leo Cooper, Praetorian Press, Remember When,
Seaforth Publishing and Wharncliffe.

For a complete list of Pen and Sword titles please contact
Pen and Sword Books Limited
47 Church Street, Barnsley, South Yorkshire, S70 2AS, England
E-mail: enquiries@pen-and-sword.co.uk
Website: www.pen-and-sword.co.uk

Contents

Acknowledgements

I am very grateful to Pen and Sword Books, and particularly Eloise Hansen, for advice and support given throughout the production of this book. I would also like to thank the following individuals and institutions. For copyright permission to use various images: The Manchester Museum; The University of Manchester (including The John Rylands University of Manchester Library); and my husband, Antony, for all images not otherwise accredited. For practical help and advice in producing the manuscript I am again grateful to my husband, and to Cosmo Graphis Imaging Ltd of Altrincham. Finally, I should like to express my gratitude to Dr Campbell Price, Curator of Egypt and the Sudan at The Manchester Museum, for all his encouragement and support, and especially for contributing the Preface to this book.

Rosalie David
Manchester

Preface

We have a seemingly endless fascination with the lives of the ancient Egyptians. Although it is the elite – the pharaoh, royal family, and powerful officials – that captivate most popular interest, the more humble daily existence of the majority of the Egyptian population exerts its own special appeal. Despite the modern tendency to focus on celebrity lifestyles, museum visitors frequently express an interest in knowing what their own lives would have been like had they been born in the time of the pharaohs.

We are uniquely privileged to have so many sources with which to get to know the inhabitants of the ancient Nile valley. Few other ancient civilizations preserve such a wealth of objects, written records or depictions of life as they hoped it would continue for eternity. From the priestly statue-owner, who buys his right to an offering service with a donation to the temple, to the charioteer who left a boastful account of his bravery in the king's service, we are afforded bright but fleeting glimpses into everyday activities. Of course, the Egyptians did not act with future Egyptologists in mind – although I suspect that they would be touched to know of our abiding interest in them. The picture we have of life – and even expectations after death – is partial. We must use our imagination – albeit informed by familiarity with other, relevant sources – to fill in the gaps, but it is always tempting to imagine ancient Egypt as it was experienced by its inhabitants.

The Manchester Museum, home to one of Europe's most significant Egyptology collections, contains a unique series of objects that give a special perspective into day-to-day life. These derive principally from the excavations of the 'Father of Egyptian Archaeology', William Matthew Flinders Petrie (1853–1942), at the site of the pyramid builders' town of Kahun and the royal harem palace at Gurob. Unlike the majority of items in museums, which come from tombs and temples, these objects were for the most part not deliberately deposited and therefore give an incidental insight into everyday activities and concerns.

Professor Rosalie David knows this material better than most, having been Keeper of Egyptology at the Museum for thirty years. Her deep familiarity with the country of Egypt has helped the author produce an authentic feel for life on the banks of the Nile so long ago, perhaps not so very different from rural parts of Egypt today. By arranging her narrative around the three seasons of the Egyptian year, Rosalie adopts a framework that would have governed most ancient Egyptian life and in doing so, with typically lucid style, imparts a great deal of information derived from preserved sources.

Rosalie has chosen several names for her *dramatis personae* that belong to mummies in Manchester. Her own ground-breaking work on the mummies has brought them to life through the lens of modern science, yielding insights into ancient diet, disease and lifestyle. It is therefore appropriate that the names of some of the mummies have been used in an imagined setting here – for, according to the ancient funerary wish, remembering the name of the deceased enables them to live again.

Campbell Price
(Dr Campbell Price, Curator of Ancient Egypt and the Sudan, Manchester Museum, The University of Manchester)

Introduction

The Historical and Geographical Setting

Geographical Factors

The civilization of ancient Egypt was created by the country's geography and climate. The resultant agriculture influenced the form and development of the calendar, which was divided into three seasons: Inundation, Planting and Harvesting. This book will consider the daily life and activities of various social classes – royalty, nobility, officials, craftsmen and peasants – within the framework of this agricultural pattern.

A glance at a map of modern Egypt will show that, as in antiquity, most of the country is desert, but the Delta (the inverted triangle where the Nile meets the Mediterranean), the Nile Valley, and the scattered oases in the Western Desert are fertile.[1] Over millennia, this landscape has been created by the actions of Egypt's great river, the Nile, for although the country has a negligible rainfall, these fertile areas have come into existence because of the phenomenon of the river's inundation. Indeed, no other civilization has ever been so dependent on the regular occurrence of one natural event.

The Nile's course within Egypt covers a distance of some 600 miles between Aswan in the south and the Delta, where its two main branches enter the Mediterranean through the towns of Rosetta in the west and Damietta in the east. However, this great river – the longest in Africa – starts its journey far to the south of Egypt, three degrees south of the Equator in the region of the Great Lakes.

Until recent years, the natural effects of the inundation were experienced throughout Egypt. However, since the nineteenth century

CE, a series of dams has been constructed across the river at various points (the most famous is the High Dam at Aswan), and these now allow the volume of water to be held back and subsequently released through a network of canals, as required for irrigation and other purposes. Behind the Aswan High Dam, the retained water has created Lake Nasser.

In antiquity, the level of the inundation was capricious and uncontrollable. Each year in May, the summer monsoon begins in Ethiopia, and this rain increases the waters of the Nile with the result that the river becomes swollen. In earlier historical periods, the river flooded out over its banks and deposited its rich black silt on the banks and across the Delta. Between Khartoum (the capital of modern Sudan) and Aswan (Egypt's southernmost city) the course of the river is interrupted by six cataracts. These have no dramatic features but simply consist of scattered groups of rocks which partially obstruct the flow of the river. In ancient Egypt, the effects of the inundation would be first experienced in June at the First Cataract (situated just south of modern Aswan). Then, the inundation would gradually continue northwards, until the flood reached its peak in the Delta in September. Thereafter the flood-waters gradually receded, and reached their lowest level the following April, leaving the riverbanks covered with a rich deposit of black silt which provided the basic conditions for intensive cultivation. The inundation was regarded as an annual miracle which restored life and fertility to the parched land. The water levels were measured and recorded on devices known as Nilometers, which were positioned along the river, and the people celebrated religious rituals to ensure that the river rose and brought them its benefits.

However, there was always the fear that the inundation would not happen. This would have brought death and destruction to the land and its people; and although there is no evidence that this disaster ever occurred, the flood level was unpredictable and uncontrollable, and this had a profound impact on people's safety and prosperity. An excessively high Nile could flood the land and bring devastation to dwellings and their inhabitants, while an insufficient flood resulted in famine. The inundation could result either in fertility and prosperity or in death and devastation, and the Nile and the sun were correctly regarded as the two great life-giving forces that created and moulded the Egyptian civilization.

The Irrigation System

From earliest times, the Egyptians were aware of the need to develop an efficient irrigation system which would utilize the bounties conferred by the inundation, and bring benefit to all the scattered communities along the Nile Valley and in the Delta.[2] This common goal undoubtedly gave the people a sense of unified identity, and laid the foundation for the ultimate unification of Egypt as a State in *c.*3100 BCE. Thus, a geographical area that lacked physical cohesion and was intrinsically difficult to rule was united by a natural phenomenon and the need to harness its benefits. A limestone macehead discovered at the predynastic city of Hieraconpolis in 1898 CE is carved with scenes that include a depiction of an early ruler, Scorpion, enacting ceremonial rites associated with irrigation; by the time one of his successors, King Menes (Narmer), unified Egypt in *c.*3100 BCE, a countrywide irrigation system was already in place.

The State-organized irrigation system had the main aim of using the Nile flood, and the black silt which accompanied it, to cultivate as much land as possible on either side of the river. This system, probably established as early as the fourth millennium BCE, involved a technology known as simple basin irrigation, which continued in use until the construction of dams and barrages in the nineteenth century CE, when Egypt moved into the industrial age. This early technique utilized existing natural conditions: alluvial flats (which were naturally divided into a maze of irregular basins of different sizes by means of levee ridges), small distributory branches, and abandoned stream channels, formed the basis of the system.

As the floods receded, these natural basins would drain off, leaving a deposit of rich black silt. However, human effort could very effectively extend this natural system: earth dykes were built to divide the land into compartments of different sizes, and water was diverted into these basins through a series of canals when the Nile water rose; when the river level fell again, any remaining water was drained off, and the deposit of rich soil could be used for sowing crops. Even in the dry season, it was possible to create artificial reservoirs by breaching the levels so that local flooding occurred. The water could then be retained in the basins by damming-in the flow, and later this could be released as required and used to water the fields. Thus, by developing and enhancing their natural environmental conditions, the early Egyptians were able to produce the necessary conditions for an intensively cultivated landscape.

Most of the population worked on the land, producing food for their own needs, and also for the State. Cereals were the main crop.[3] Two kinds of wheat (spelt and emmer) were grown and, together with the barley crop, they provided the basic ingredients for the staple diet of bread and beer. Peasants, who either worked in family groups or a gang, were responsible to State officials; they acted on behalf of the king who, at least in theory, owned all the land, its resources, and people. The officials were responsible for the organization of the irrigation system, and for collecting and storing the produce which was ultimately redistributed to feed those sectors of the population who did not grow their own food because they were otherwise employed.

The Egyptian Calendar
The height of the flood obviously differed from one district to another, dictating when various agricultural operations could be carried out. However, the Nile's regular actions and the resultant agriculture formed the basis of ancient Egyptian civilization, and a calendar was developed in which the character of each season was defined by these periodic agricultural functions. In antiquity, the agricultural year was divided into three equal seasons, each consisting of four months; thus, each year had twelve months, and each month consisted of thirty days, made up of three periods of ten days. These seasons were known as *Akhet* (Inundation), *Peret* (Planting and Growing), and *Shemu* (Harvesting). This system gave a total of 360 days each year, but the Egyptians soon recognized the imperfection of their calendar system, which could not provide permanent synchronization between the seasons, the months and the agricultural activities. To remedy this, at a very early date they added five additional days (epagomenal days) at the end of the twelfth month, so that the seasons returned to their

fixed periods. In addition, they added a quarter day which gave every fourth year a length of 366 days.

Despite its drawbacks, the Egyptian calendar was simple and straightforward, and unlike our own system, did not have any months of unequal length. However, although this system produced three seasons which reflected the country's agricultural activities, the climate of Egypt actually divides the year into two seasons – a hot period which lasts from May until September, and a cooler time from November to March; October and April are regarded as transitional months.

Benefits of the Irrigation System

The inundation started around 20 July, which was officially known as New Year's Day. There was a period of intensive preparation at the end of the summer, during which holes were made in the dykes at the highest points and the required amount of water was released into the basins before the openings were dammed up. Then, when the Nile waters finally receded, the seed could be planted and, once the crops had grown, they were harvested and the grain was stored.

The key to this fertility and abundance of plant life was the continuous, unrelenting need to have mastery of the irrigation system. This eventually enabled the Egyptians to turn the natural phenomenon, which flooded the lower ground but left the high ground dry each summer, into a system which allowed two annual crops to be produced. The irrigation system involved coordinating the thousands of workers who distributed water to every part of the country. Additionally, the organizers also had to ensure that dykes were constructed, and the land reclaimed by levelling the mounds and filling up the depressions in the ground. Also, canals had to be planned, dug and maintained, so that as many areas as possible could be irrigated, and the irrigation basins, with their surrounding earth banks, had to be created so that the arable land could be covered with water and silt to a maximum extent. Constant vigilance and continuous maintenance were required throughout the country to ensure that the system worked, and this could only be achieved when the political system functioned efficiently. In times of national crisis when ruling power became decentralized, the irrigation system usually collapsed, with the result that society and the economy suffered and sometimes disintegrated.

Sources of Evidence

Egypt's unique geographical background profoundly influenced the material development of the civilization.[4] With only limited cultivated land available for agriculture, horticulture, animal husbandry and the construction of domestic dwellings, it was customary from earliest times to find an alternative location for the burial of the dead. Graves, and later tombs and pyramids, were located on the edges of the desert where the hot, dry sand has provided ideal environmental conditions to preserve these buildings and their contents – bodies and religious artifacts – until the present day.

By contrast, the towns (settlement sites) and villages, built in the cultivated area, have survived less well; in addition, whereas tombs and temples (which often formed the nucleus of a town) were built of stone to last for eternity, the civic, military, and domestic buildings (including palaces) were constructed from mudbricks, a far less robust building material which was frequently damaged by the alluvial mud brought down by the annual inundation. Situated on the irrigation

Step Pyramid of Djoser. Imhotep, the architect of this building, was later worshipped as a god of medicine. From Saqqara. Dynasty 3.

dykes and on the mounds and hillocks formed by the alluvial deposits, the towns were usually rebuilt on former habitations at sites which had been demolished and levelled many times. Therefore, it is very difficult for archaeologists to trace any underlying order or attempted town-planning in cities and towns that existed for thousands of years. In addition, in more recent times, generations of local villagers have removed mudbricks from these ancient sites to use as fertilizer.

Settlement sites are therefore vulnerable and relatively poorly preserved, with the result that they have not been studied as extensively as tombs and temples.[5] This has sometimes led to a somewhat biased interpretation of Egyptian civilization, placing undue emphasis on religion and funerary beliefs and neglecting various aspects of social history and daily life. Nevertheless, despite the limitations imposed by archaeology, a wealth of evidence remains which demonstrates the main developments in ancient Egypt, and current scholarship is now trying to produce a more balanced appraisal of the civilization. The remains of monumental buildings in Egypt are among the most impressive in the world, and although some (such as the pyramids) have always been visible above ground, others have only been revealed through archaeological excavation over the past 200 years. In addition to the settlement sites, which include cities, towns, villages and fortresses, there are cemeteries (*necropolis*; pl. *necropolises*) which once accommodated the burials of royalty (in tombs or pyramids), 'private' tombs for nobles and officials, the graves of craftsmen and peasants, and catacombs or cemeteries for animal burials. Magnificent temples, originally either attached to royal burial places or located in cities and towns, have also survived.

Archaeologists have uncovered extensive collections of artifacts (man-made objects) in the tombs or left behind by their owners in domestic contexts. Better environmental conditions in tombs than at domestic sites have ensured that tomb goods are generally much more plentiful than those found in houses. A belief in a life after death encouraged the Egyptians to place a range of objects within the tombs. These included funerary goods such as coffins and articles directly associated with the burial of the dead; there were also items of everyday use – pottery, tools, weapons, clothing, jewellery, cosmetics and food – intended for the deceased owner's use in the next world.

Additionally, the interior walls of the private tombs were decorated with scenes which depict some of the everyday activities that the owner hoped to enjoy in the next life. Therefore, although more evidence has survived about funerary and religious beliefs and customs than everyday practices, wall-scenes and tomb goods relating to daily activities provide ample information about lifestyle and technological advances.

From the Old Kingdom onwards, the Egyptians intentionally preserved the bodies of royalty and the elite by using a technique known today as 'mummification'. The main incentive for this development was religious, and the custom continued for some 3,000 years. Today, scientific examination of these mummified remains can reveal information not only about their funerary practices and mummification procedures, but also about diseases prevalent at that time.

Despite the wealth of this material evidence, archaeological discoveries can only provide a limited view of any civilization, and in order to enter the Egyptians' minds, to attempt to understand their beliefs, and to appreciate their wit, humour, joy and sorrow, it is necessary to turn to complementary literary sources. Although historians can never fully interpret the experiences of another age, they are able to understand ancient Egypt more than many other early societies because of the wealth of surviving archaeological and documentary evidence.

Slate palette showing a man hunting ostriches. Small palettes were originally produced for grinding eye make-up minerals, but the design evolved into large ceremonial palettes that were placed in tombs or temple deposits. Some depict hunting scenes; it was believed that these could be magically 'brought to life' so that the owner would be able to enjoy this activity, and the resultant food, in the afterlife. Unprovenanced. Predynastic Period. Manchester Museum.

16

The Decipherment of Hieroglyphs and the Importance of Textual Evidence

The earliest written sources date to the beginning of the historical period (*c*.3100 BCE), and continue for over 3,000 years. In addition to these indigenous records, inscribed on papyri, *stelae* (stone slabs decorated with religious scenes and texts), *ostraca* (limestone flakes or pottery sherds), and tomb and temple walls, there are later accounts by Classical travellers who visited the country and observed the Egyptians and their customs in the twilight of this once-great civilization. Egyptian hieroglyphs were deciphered by the Frenchman Champollion in 1822 CE, enabling an extensive secular and religious literature to be translated and understood.[6] He and other scholars demonstrated that although the Egyptians believed that writing had its own potent spiritual force (and for this reason was used to decorate buildings and artifacts), the basic purpose of the hieroglyphic script was to convey a fully comprehensible language which had its own grammar and vocabulary. Essentially, hieroglyphs were signs that conveyed a language, in the same way that we use the alphabet to express in writing the sound-values of our own words and sentences.

Before Champollion's discoveries, medieval and Renaissance scholars had been forced to rely on travellers' accounts and on their own erroneous observations. Consequently, many of these early studies produced inaccurate and often ludicrous interpretations of monuments, beliefs and customs, and scholars could only begin to gain a clear understanding of the meaning of the monuments and artifacts once they were able to read the texts. Even the best-preserved examples of tombs, temples and pyramids cannot be interpreted solely from their layout and architectural forms: the ability to read and translate the inscriptions that adorn their walls is essential if a monument's true significance is to be understood.

For example, before hieroglyphs were deciphered, early travellers proposed some remarkable theories to explain the meaning and purpose of the pyramids, based on their erroneous conclusion that the hieroglyphs inscribed on the walls of some pyramids were there for purely symbolic and magical reasons. It was only after Champollion discovered how to decipher hieroglyphs that these *Pyramid Texts* could be properly translated, providing convincing evidence that a pyramid's main purpose and function was to accommodate the royal burial.

Similarly, inscriptions covering the external and internal walls of temples provide detailed information about the rituals which were once performed there, and convey additional knowledge about Egyptian mythology, religion and political history. The inscriptions on the internal walls of tombs not only augment and explain the content of the associated painted or carved wall-scenes, these texts, as well as those found on tomb furniture and funerary goods, also provide a wealth of information about religious and funerary beliefs, genealogies, social and economic systems, arts and crafts, and everyday life. In fact, inscriptional evidence is crucial in helping scholars to understand and interpret even the most complete and well-preserved monuments.

Without the unique insight provided by some literary sources, the true significance of some aspects of Egyptian thought or belief would remain obscured or misunderstood. Examples include the *Wisdom Texts* which preserve the ancient Egyptian concepts of wisdom, piety and ethics, and the Aten hymns which preserve the main tenets of Atenism – a doctrine of solar monotheism which briefly dominated Egyptian religion. Again, documents relating to the law, medicine and education preserve information about aspects of society which would otherwise have been lost. Some texts provide invaluable information about the political history of Egypt, its chronology, and the correct sequence of rulers. These include the historical inscriptions found on temple walls: detailed descriptions of royal military exploits, and king-lists, intended to ensure that the named kings were present, as 'royal ancestors', to receive the sacred food offered during the temple rituals.

However, not all texts are important because they augment existing archaeological evidence: one group of documents, known collectively as the *Pessimistic Literature*, questions some of the most basic tenets of Egyptian religion, including the existence of an afterlife, although the certainty of personal eternal existence is assiduously promoted elsewhere in traditional literary accounts and the elaborate tombs and burial assemblages. The *Pessimistic Literature* presents an alternative, sceptical viewpoint which focuses on the delights of life in contrast to the uncertainty and despair associated with death. We are afforded this rare insight into contradictory religious beliefs only because these texts have been preserved and translated.

No textual evidence survives from the predynastic cultures which existed before the historical period (prior to *c*.3100 BCE), although occasionally the literature of later times can help to clarify some aspects of this obscure period. Essentially, archaeological excavation has revealed the material remains of these early communities, and provided us with clues about their political and social structures and religious beliefs and practices.

Egyptian Chronology

Ancient Egyptian history covers a period from *c*.3100 BCE to the conquest of the country by Alexander the Great in 332 BCE. During the centuries before the Dynastic Period (which started in *c*.3100 BCE), in an era which Egyptologists have designated the 'Predynastic Period' (*c*.5000 BCE–3100 BCE), early communities developed ideas and beliefs which laid the foundations for later political and cultural developments. After 332 BCE, Egypt was ruled by a line of Macedonian Greeks, the descendants of Alexander the Great's general, Ptolemy, who, as Ptolemy I, inaugurated the Ptolemaic Period. This culminated in 30 BCE when the last of this dynasty, Queen Cleopatra VII, failed to retain control of Egypt, which was subsequently absorbed into the Roman Empire.

An Egyptian priest, Manetho (*c*.305 BCE–246 BCE), wrote a chronicle of Egyptian rulers, and divided this king-list into thirty dynasties. A later chronographer added a thirty-first dynasty. As a priest at the temple of Sebennytos in the Delta, Manetho would have had knowledge of Egyptian hieroglyphs and Greek, and first-hand experience of religious beliefs and customs; also, he would have had access to king-lists and registers kept in the temples. His work, entitled the *Aegyptiaca* ('History of Egypt'), remains our most important contemporary Egyptian source; although it has not survived intact, it is preserved in edited extracts in the writings of four other early writers. Although the details given in these accounts sometimes vary and the reliability of some of Manetho's 'facts' has been questioned, his work nevertheless remains the most comprehensive ancient source for the sequence of Egyptian rulers and dynasties.

Manetho provides no explanation of why he divided the list of rulers into dynasties, and there is no clear indication of what a 'dynasty' actually signifies. In some instances, for example, it included a line of rulers related by family ties, and when there were no direct descendants or if another family seized power, then the dynasty changed. Sometimes, however, one family spanned more than one dynasty and there was a smooth and apparently amicable transfer from one dynasty to the next.

Today, historians still retain the thirty-one dynasties, grouping them into several major periods or 'Kingdoms', which are characterized by particular historical, political and religious features. These are: the Archaic Period (Dynasties 1 and 2); the Old Kingdom (Dynasties 3 to 6); the First Intermediate Period (Dynasties 7 to 11); the Middle Kingdom (Dynasty 12); the Second Intermediate Period (Dynasties 13 to 17); the New Kingdom (Dynasties 18 to 20); the Third Intermediate Period (Dynasties 21 to 25); and the Late Period (Dynasties 26 to 31).

A Brief History
During the Predynastic Period (*c.*5000 BCE–3100 BCE), neolithic communities gradually came into existence in the Nile Valley and Delta. Lack of written evidence and scarcity of artifacts from domestic sites of this period (most material comes from the cemeteries) limits our knowledge of these societies, but they appear to have shared certain features. They had a similar social organization, and gradually replaced hunting with farming and agriculture. They produced fine quality pottery, tools, weapons and domestic utensils, and there were already clear indications that they revered the dead and buried them with respect, perhaps because they believed that there was a life after death.

Gradually, these early communities came to form larger political and social units, which each had its own area capital, chieftain and major deity. Eventually (*c.*3400 BCE) two kingdoms were established as the people drew together to protect themselves against external attack, and to respond to a common need to irrigate the land and increase food production. The northern kingdom (the 'Red Land') was situated in the Delta, while the southern one (the 'White Land') occupied part of the Nile Valley. Although they were politically

20

independent with their own capitals and rulers, the two kingdoms clearly shared a common culture and provided the impetus for new ideas. For example, writing may now have started to develop in Egypt, and there were advances in the arts and crafts; monumental brick architecture was also introduced to provide a new type of burial place (known today as a *mastaba*-tomb) for the leaders of the society. Ultimately, the southern rulers set out to conquer the north, a goal finally achieved by King Menes in *c*.3100 BCE when he unified the two lands.

In the Archaic Period (*c*.3100 BCE–2686 BCE) which followed, Menes and his descendants established a unified state which they ruled from the capital city, Memphis. The foundations of the kingdom's political and social organization were laid down, and there were significant advances in technology, building techniques, and in arts and crafts.

The Old Kingdom (*c*.2686 BCE–2181 BCE) is regarded as the first great period of Egyptian history. According to some Egyptologists, the developments in architecture, art, religion and literature witnessed during this period were never surpassed in later times. The architectural style of substantial mudbrick *mastaba*-tombs constructed for the rulers and the nobility in the Archaic Period was continued for the nobles, but these monuments were now built of stone rather than mudbrick, and the internal walls of the tomb-chapel (where offerings were placed for the deceased tomb-owner) were decorated with registers of scenes that depicted many aspects of everyday life. The tombs were also lavishly equipped with funerary goods and articles for use in the next life.

The Old Kingdom was characterized by a new type of burial place – the pyramid – which was introduced for the kings. The earliest one, designed as a stepped pyramid by Imhotep, the First Minister and architect of King Djoser, still forms part of an elaborate funerary complex at Saqqara. In Dynasty 4, the finest examples of pyramids were built at Giza for Cheops, Chephren and Mycerinus. The pyramid form, probably an integral element of the worship of the sun-god Re which predominated at that time, clearly demonstrated the king's divine status and the chasm which existed between him and his subjects. He was regarded as the god's son, with special rights and

Pyramid of Chephren, with remains of its causeway and valley temple. The original limestone casing can be seen on the apex of the pyramid. The Great Sphinx, which dominates the foreground, is believed to date to the same reign and may portray Chephren's facial features. Giza. Dynasty 4.

privileges, and he alone could aspire to an individual immortality which would be spent in the heavens, in the company of the gods.

The king headed a rigid social hierarchy which included the nobles (who were often the king's relatives), State officials, craftsmen, and peasants. The king's subjects did not expect to experience individual eternity: they could only hope for vicarious immortality, granted through the king's beneficence because they had assisted in some way towards his personal resurrection.

However, construction and maintenance of the pyramids and the employment of staff to serve in the associated temples proved to be an insupportable drain on the country's resources. By Dynasty 5, the size and quality of the pyramids had been reduced, and after Dynasty 6, a combination of economic, political, religious and social factors led to the collapse of centralized government.

During the following First Intermediate Period (*c.*2181 BCE–1991 BCE), the political system unravelled and the conditions of the

Predynastic Period reappeared: centralized government disintegrated, and local chieftains seized power, dominating their own areas and engaging in civil warfare. Irrigation suffered as the result of this political collapse, resulting in widespread famine, poverty, disease, and social upheaval. Eventually, in Dynasty 11, the Mentuhotep family managed to restore order throughout much of the country and to re-establish more settled conditions. They ruled from their power base at Thebes, but as in the preceding dynasties, many provincial leaders continued to wield considerable power in their own districts where they were buried in magnificent painted tombs cut deep into the cliff-side near their local towns.

The Middle Kingdom (1991 BCE–1786 BCE) was Egypt's second great historical period. Again, a strong line of kings occupied the throne; they were the descendants of Amenemhet I, a commoner (probably the First Minister of the last Mentuhotep) who had seized power. He moved the capital from Thebes to el-Lisht in the north, and reinstated the construction of pyramid complexes. The kings of this dynasty, ever mindful of their tenuous claim to rule Egypt, introduced various political measures such as co-regencies, whereby the king could ensure a smooth succession by sharing the throne with his chosen heir.

These rulers also re-established the contacts with other countries that had lapsed during the First Intermediate Period. In Nubia (which lay to the south of Egypt) they restored their dominion so that they could ensure access to the region's hard stone, which they needed for major building projects, and they set up a string of fortresses to impose their rule over the local population. The Egyptians adopted a different approach with their northern neighbours, developing trading contacts with the inhabitants of the Aegean islands and the city of Byblos on the Syrian coast.

A major development in the Middle Kingdom was the popular ascendancy of the god Osiris, who now became a successful rival to Re, the royal patron deity of the Old Kingdom. Regarded as a dead, deified king who had been murdered but was subsequently resurrected, Osiris gained widespread support because of his promise of individual eternity, not just for the king, but for all worshippers who led pious and worthy lives.

descending passageways. Sixty-odd tombs have so far been discovered there, but despite various attempts to conceal the burials and defeat the tomb-robbers, all – with the exception of Tutankhamun's burial place – were extensively ransacked in antiquity. Caches discovered in the nineteenth century CE contained the bodies of the royal dead which the priests of Dynasty 21 had collected from the plundered tombs and reburied, in an attempt to prevent further desecration.

The internal walls of tombs in the Valley of the Kings are decorated with sculpted and painted scenes based on illustrations found in the funerary books. These scenes and accompanying inscriptions were expected to provide the king with magical protection and assist his passage into the next world. In a neighbouring area, known today as the Valley of the Queens, there are other decorated rock-cut tombs which once accommodated the burials of some royal wives and princes.

Elsewhere in the same district, rock-cut tombs were prepared for the courtiers and officials, but in contrast to the scenes found in the

Part of the ceiling decoration in the tomb of Siptah, showing the vulture goddess Nekhbet with outstretched wings that protect the tomb and its contents. The king's name (Akh-en-(Re) setep-en-Re) is inscribed inside the golden cartouches (ovals). Valley of the Kings, Thebes. Dynasty 19.

royal burials, the walls of these tombs were decorated with scenes of everyday activities which, through the power of magical rituals, the owner expected to experience and enjoy in the next world. This evidence provides an unparalleled opportunity to study the contemporary lives of the rich and poor during this period.

Towards the end of Dynasty 18, the inherent rivalry between the kings and the priests of Amen-Re reached a climax when Amenhotep III and his son, Amenhotep IV (Akhenaten), attempted to limit the god's power. Akhenaten promoted the monotheistic cult of another deity, the Aten (sun's disc), closed the temples of all other gods, and disbanded their priesthoods. There followed an interlude of political and religious upheaval known today as the Amarna Period, when Akhenaten, his wife Nefertiti, and their six daughters moved the royal court from Thebes to the new site of Akhetaten (Tell el-Amarna). However, when this experiment failed, Akhenaten's successors reversed his policies and reinstated the traditional deities.

In Dynasty 19, a new family of rulers sought to restore Egypt's prestige abroad, and kings Sethos I, Ramesses II and Ramesses III all recorded their great military exploits on temple walls. In contrast to these detailed historical accounts, no references to the biblical Exodus have yet been found in Egyptian texts, although some scholars have suggested that the event may have taken place in the reign of Ramesses II.

During Dynasties 19 and 20, Egypt faced a new threat on her western front, where Libyan tribes were beginning to infiltrate and settle. Merneptah and Ramesses III fought vigorously against coalitions of these Libyans who joined forces with the so-called Sea-peoples, itinerant groups who were moving southwards in search of a new homeland in Egypt. Despite initial defeat, the descendants of these Libyan attackers eventually settled in the Delta where they prospered, and finally became the rulers of Egypt in Dynasties 22 and 23.

The Third Intermediate Period (1085 BCE–668 BCE) witnessed the start of Egypt's gradual but irreversible decline. In Dynasty 21, the rivalry between kings and priests again had a major impact upon political arrangements in the country. The kingdom was now divided, with the legitimate line of kings ruling from a new capital city, Tanis, in the Delta, while a family of High-priests of Amen-Re took control of Thebes and the surrounding district in the south. The two lines were eventually joined by marriages between the Tanite princesses and Theban High-priests, and when the last ruler of the Tanite dynasty died without a male heir, the throne passed to his son-in-law, Shoshenk, the descendant of Libyan chiefs. He established Dynasty 22, and ruled the country either from Tanis or Bubastis in the Delta. He was the most able ruler of this line and attempted to revive Egypt's internal and external authority, but the centralized power of the kingship was already in decline. In Dynasty 25 (the so-called 'Ethiopian Dynasty'), a line of rulers of foreign origin emerged from southern Nubia where they had already established their power-base. They worshipped Amen-Re and promoted Egyptian culture, and managed to extend their control northwards throughout the country. However, they were eventually driven back to their southern homeland by the Assyrians who, having established their own empire, now invaded Egypt from the north.

The Late Period (664 BCE–332 BCE) witnessed further disintegration and loss of native control over Egypt. The Ethiopians and Assyrians finally departed from Egypt, and a line of native rulers emerged who, as Dynasty 26, governed the country from Sais in the Delta. However, this brief interlude, in which national pride and excellence were marked by a revival in arts and crafts, was short-lived, and in Dynasties 27 and 31, Egypt once again became subject to foreign domination, now as part of the Persian Empire.

Mummy of a child, wrapped in linen and decorated with scenes including the 'Weighing of the Heart'. The mummy incorporates a gilded/painted cartonnage foot cover, and a gilded cartonnage head/chest cover which has inlaid eyes and stones/glass set into moulded representations of jewellery. From Hawara. Roman Period. Manchester Museum.

Mummy of a man incorporating a painted portrait. Unlike earlier stylized funerary images, these portraits (introduced in the Roman Period) represent individual likenesses. They may have been painted as portraits when the owners were alive, and ultimately included in their mummies. From Hawara. Roman Period. Manchester Museum.

29

The influence of both the Assyrians and the Persians on Egypt was probably minimal, but the impact of the Greeks and Romans, who next took control of the country, was considerable. Under the Ptolemaic rulers (332 BCE–30 BCE), large numbers of Greeks settled in various parts of Egypt. The magnificent city of Alexandria, founded by Alexander the Great on the Mediterranean coast, now became Egypt's capital; it was a great centre of learning, and a focus for the process of Hellenization (the promotion of Greek customs and culture) which now prevailed throughout the country.

The Ptolemaic rulers ensured that Hellenistic culture predominated: Greek became the official language, and Greek customs, religion and the legal system were firmly established. However, although the country had been effectively colonized by the Greeks, the Egyptians continued to use their own language, customs and laws. In order to exert their rights as Egyptian pharaohs, the Ptolemaic rulers built new Egyptian temples so that they would be accepted by the Egyptian gods as legitimate kings, and the old State cults were continued. Ultimately, heavy taxes and general popular dissatisfaction prompted the Egyptians to riot in 30 BCE, and with the death of Cleopatra VII and her young heirs, the country was now conquered by the Roman Emperor Augustus. He designated Egypt as his personal possession, and it became a province of the Roman Empire.

The Romans retained many features of the administrative system set up by the Ptolemies, and the Roman emperors perpetuated the custom of representing themselves as Egyptian rulers so that they could claim divine authority to govern Egypt and exact taxes from the population. In support of this concept, they completed and made additions to several of the Egyptian temples that had been founded by the Ptolemies. Egypt was now merely regarded as the main grain producer of the Roman Empire, and the indigenous population suffered from heavy taxation and reduced living standards.

Section 1

Inundation

The following chapters will provide an outline of some everyday activities experienced by different social classes throughout the course of one year. In order to explore this theme as fully as possible, but also to place it within a defined historical setting and context, these events will be described as if they were part of the life of an imaginary ancient Egyptian family who lived in the New Kingdom, one of the greatest periods of Egyptian civilization.

For this purpose, it has been assumed that the head of this household, a government official named Khary, lived at Thebes in Dynasty 18. As members of the upper classes, he and his family enjoyed an affluent lifestyle. In addition to his townhouse in the city on the east bank of the river, Khary possessed a fine country estate, where we shall follow his everyday activities and those of his family and servants throughout the course of a year. This imaginary family also included Khary's wife, Perenbast, who owned property in her own right and carried a title, 'Chantress of Amun', which reflected her high social standing; and the couple's two elder sons, Nakht, a lawyer who also held a priesthood and was married to Merenmut, and Amenemhet who fought as an army officer in the military expeditions which the king led to Nubia and Syria/Palestine. In addition, there was a daughter, Meryamun, who was married to a doctor, Amenmose, and Khary's youngest son, Ipy, who was still at school. Perenbast's elderly mother, Nefert, also lived with the family. Wealth and social position enabled these people to provide themselves with relatively elaborate burials at Thebes, and their preparations for the afterlife will also be described.

Chapter 1

The Land and its People

Structure of the Society

During the New Kingdom, Egypt became a great military power, and possessed an empire which stretched from Nubia to Asia; however, the main structure of the society still reflected the pattern which had been established in the Old Kingdom.[1] At the top, and central to the whole scheme, was the god-king. Chosen by the gods, the king was himself regarded as a god represented in human form. However, he was not the gods' equal, and although he acted as their agent on earth, he retained many human characteristics and was subject to the laws of Egypt. Each king was believed to be the physical offspring of the leading god of the dynasty, born to the chief wife of the previous ruler, a unique status which enabled him to mediate between the gods and mankind, and which also placed an impassable chasm between the king and his subjects. By *c.*3100 BCE, a line of kings who ruled a united Egypt had emerged from the most powerful tribal chieftains of the Predynastic Period, but as their royal duties in religion, law and justice, politics and warfare increased, they delegated certain aspects of these roles to royal officials.

In the Old Kingdom, the king was already surrounded by a powerful Court, which included the royal wives and adult royal children. It was probably customary for the king to marry the chief royal heiress (the eldest daughter of the previous king and queen, frequently the ruling king's own sister) to ensure his succession to the throne, but there were many siblings by secondary wives who sometimes disputed an heir's claim. These royal relatives comprised the nobility during the Old Kingdom, and in a futile attempt to secure

Pottery jar decorated with the scene of a religious festival. A river-boat with banks of oars is shown transporting two divine shrines along the Nile. From Naqada. Predynastic Period. Manchester Museum.

their unconditional support, the king gave them the most powerful and influential positions in government.

At first, they only held these posts for life, but by the end of the Old Kingdom, the king had appointed men from outside his own family circle to senior positions, and increasingly he began to make

33

An alabaster offering-tray from a tomb. These were part of the funerary cult of presenting food to the deceased tomb-owner to ensure that he had eternal nourishment. From Medum. Dynasty 3. Manchester Museum.

these appointments hereditary, to try to ensure these governors' loyalty. His divine authority, however, was ever more challenged and undermined by political, economic and religious developments, and these men eventually usurped power and ruled almost independently in their own districts.

In the later Old Kingdom, the First Intermediate Period, and even the earlier part of the Middle Kingdom when the status of royalty had been re-established, the king continued to encounter the nobles' rivalry. This situation was not rectified until Dynasty 12, when one king took steps to curtail their powers, and by the New Kingdom these great landowners had been replaced by a hierarchy of officials who were responsible to the king. Our imaginary official, Khary, held one of these posts. However, there were two other groups of officials who played a significant role in the balance of power – senior officers in the army and the priests; over the centuries, various rulers used different ploys to attempt to control their influence.

In the Old Kingdom, the king and his great administrators and governors were supported by an extensive bureaucracy of minor officials and clerks who made up the middle layer of society. In the New Kingdom, a similar structure of minor bureaucrats managed the government and all matters relating to Egypt's empire. Some supervised the artisans and craftsmen who produced the funerary monuments and equipment for funerary and domestic use. By the New Kingdom, there would have been flourishing communities of craftsmen at Thebes and other major cities, as well as in the town (known today as Deir el-Medina), specially built to house the workmen engaged in building and equipping the royal tombs.

However, despite the establishment of some major urban centres in Egypt, the agricultural workforce (perhaps eighty percent of the total population), which grew the food for the whole society, was the mainstay of the country throughout all historical periods.[2] These people were peasants rather than 'slaves', since they were not owned by one master, although their lives and opportunities were very limited.

Although all land officially belonged to the king, in practice it was distributed between various owners. By the New Kingdom, these owners included temples, government officials, and army officers who had replaced the provincial governors and great officials of earlier times. Sometimes, the land was administered by a royal agent who, in turn, rented out small areas to the peasants in return for payment. When the estate was owned by an official, he usually employed a steward to supervise the land and the peasants who cultivated it.

In earlier times, the provincial governors had been obliged to raise taxes and to make provision against famine by building up reserve food supplies after a good harvest. In the New Kingdom, landowners were still expected to pay their dues to the State, and these were exacted from the peasants who worked the land. Therefore, in addition to meeting the needs of their own families, the peasants were constantly required to pay their taxes to the estate owner in the form of surplus food produce. These taxes paid to the Crown ultimately fed the rest of society and provided the offerings that were presented in the temples and tombs; they were also used as exchange commodities in foreign commerce. Some people acquired their land through inheritance, while others received it as a gift from the king, and from the New Kingdom onwards land was also given to professional soldiers as a reward for their service to the country. This land would remain in the ownership of the soldier's family for as long as its members continued to serve in the army.

The peasants were unable to cultivate the land for three months each year because the fields became waterlogged as a result of the inundation. During this time they undertook other duties, which may have included work at royal building sites: during the Old Kingdom, this probably included pyramid construction, while in the New Kingdom they may have built new towns. As a means of payment, the State provided food rations for these men and their families. Such schemes may have been initiated to support the peasants during the inundation, and also to ensure that a large, unemployed workforce never had the time and opportunity to foster insurrection.

The peasants were also liable to undertake *corvée* duty. They could be requested to work in the mines, the quarries, and on building sites, and before a professional army was established in the New Kingdom, they were obliged to fight as soldiers. *Corvée*-duty was an obligation which all the king's subjects were expected to fulfil, but the wealthy circumvented the problem by employing substitutes to work on their behalf.

The landowners had the freedom to choose which crops they would grow, provided they met their tax obligations, and when there was a surplus at the harvest, they probably sold this to the State. However, only the government could sell or export superfluous national produce to other countries. An extensive government bureaucracy exacted heavy taxes which almost everyone was expected to pay. From the Old Kingdom onwards, a regular census of the fields, herds, and gold supplies was undertaken, so that the obligations of each district could be established. Some taxes were paid to the Crown in gold, which was used to provide subsidies for conducting foreign diplomacy and to pay the salaries of senior government officials. The State's most important commitments, which involved the payment of its large bureaucratic staff and the provision of a food reserve for times of famine, were met through the taxes collected in the form of agricultural produce.

Central government had the responsibility for assessing and fixing taxes. In order to predict the potential harvest (and the taxes which would be paid on this produce) in any one year, officials carried out an agricultural census, measuring the arable land and recording the names of the institutions (such as temples) and private individuals who owned it; they also had to ascertain the height of the Nile flood in order to calculate the year's crop and the probable tax yield. Details of the water level were obtained from Nilometers situated along the river banks.

Each Nilometer consisted of a stone staircase, encased between two walls, which descended to the Nile. On one wall of the Nilometer, a succession of graduated scales was inscribed; this was accompanied by a record of the heights to which the river had risen at different times. The information enabled the officials to calculate the gradual rise and fall of the river and thus assess the potential harvest and the optimum time for opening the canals and allowing the water to flow into the irrigation system. In this way, the inundation was a vital component of the government's taxation and revenue policy; it directly indicated and influenced the level of annual profits that could be expected, which would result from the export of grain and other commodities.

Another inspection was carried out when the crops began to grow, in order to fix a final tax assessment, and agents sometimes employed harsh measures to exact these taxes, particularly from the peasants who worked on the estates. During the New Kingdom, the peasants continued to pay their dues in agricultural produce, while the State collected taxes from artisans and craftsmen in the form of a proportion of their manufactured goods. All taxes were stored in government depots and treasuries, and then redistributed to meet State expenses.

The Start of the Agricultural Year
The story of Khary and his family centres around their imaginary estate situated in the countryside near Thebes. In ancient times, wealthy families enjoyed spending their leisure time on such estates, which included a well-appointed house and surrounding lands; the owner would supervise the management of the land, its herds, and agricultural and horticultural produce, although the day-to-day organization and oversight of the property was left in the capable hands of a Steward.

The inundation marked the start of the agricultural year. The rising waters of the Nile were experienced successively from the south of Egypt (in June) to the north (September), and had a profound effect upon the autumn season (*Akhet*) of the Egyptian calendar. In early August, when the water began to rise along the length of the river, the canals were opened to facilitate the flow of water into the fields. In the Nile Valley, where Khary's estate was situated, the area nearest the desert was inundated first because it lay at the lowest level, while the

The Nile at Aswan, once the southernmost boundary of Egypt. On the west bank (facing), the hill is crowned with a sheikh's tomb (Qubbet el-Hawa); below are rock-cut tombs of local dignitaries of the Old and Middle Kingdoms.

riverbanks – which had been gradually built up to a greater height by the annual deposit of silt – were the last stretch of land to be submerged. In the Delta, where the land levels were more equal, there was a more uniform pattern of inundation.

During an excessively high Nile, the effect of the inundation was to create isolated areas of high land which stood above the water level. Before the floodwater from the south reached Thebes, Khary's estate-workers always ensured that the flocks and herds were removed from the low-lying areas to higher ground where, during the inundation period, they were kept in stalls and fed with dried food. Every care was taken to manage the inundation system effectively, and to ensure that the dykes, embankments and canals were kept in good repair. Since the height of the land varied from one district to another, and different crops were planned for each area, Khary's workers used different approaches from farmers living elsewhere.

Everyone, however, attempted to ensure that the floodwaters passed smoothly through the irrigation system, and there was a universal concern to avoid any sudden influx that might cause severe damage to the dams.

Although a deficiency or abundance of flood-water could usually be successfully managed, sometimes there were unavoidable tragedies. The older members of Khary's family could recall exceptionally high Niles which had destroyed many villages, and a low inundation that resulted in famine. Each brought its share of human suffering and death. Also, because silt was brought down by the river every year and deposited on the land, there was a gradual but continual increase in the level of the river-bed so that, periodically, labourers had to raise the ground levels of towns and villages to ensure that they stood above the floodwaters. Once the water had been directed through the canals to cover the fields, the peasants were unable to cultivate their crops. Thus, apart from feeding the animals on the high ground with the food produced earlier in the year, or possibly taking part in State building projects, Khary's workers enjoyed a brief respite before they started sowing and reaping their crops.

Once the flood-waters had receded, the highest ground, which had remained above the water level, and the low-lying basins, which received the flood, became available once again for cultivation. The very lowest areas, however, remained inundated until November. In dynastic times (after 3100 BCE), only one annual crop was produced. Harvested as a winter crop, this consisted of flax, cereal grains (wheat and barley) and vegetables, including beans and chickpeas. If sufficient irrigation was still available after this harvest, a second crop was planted in the flood-basins in the summer, which produced more vegetables (onions and lentils) and animal fodder (fenugreek).

The Development of Agriculture

The methods of crop production employed on Khary's estate were the result of a long process of trial and development. In predynastic times, the Nile Valley did not consist entirely of dense jungles and papyrus thickets. Although there were some papyrus swamps and pools filled with reeds and lotus plants, inhabited by hippopotami, crocodiles, and aquatic fowl, the Nile Valley also accommodated seasonally flooded basins, and higher areas which supported trees such as acacia, tamarisk, sycamore and willow, where human settlements could be established. Therefore, although in later times the thickets and marshlands were substantially decreased, the main components of the landscape had already been established by this earliest period.

The early inhabitants who made their homes on the higher areas of land or the desert spurs had the opportunity, once the inundation had receded, to grow crops in the alluvial basins, where they also grazed their herds on grass and bush. These activities could be pursued for eight or nine months each year, and the people could also hunt big game in the Nile thickets and the desert. Thus, their lifestyle combined hunting and agricultural pursuits, and relied on the natural irrigation of the land resulting from the annual inundation.

Perhaps because there was such an efficient 'food-gathering' and pastoral system, and because there was probably a relatively small population, these earliest communities saw little need to utilize the land for extensive food production. They collected wild plants, hunted big game, fished, caught wild fowl, and cultivated small plantations with emmer, barley, flax and vegetables. There may also have been some domestication of animals such as cattle and goats.

However, sometime after 5200 BCE, a marked change occurred: the economy moved from limited crop cultivation and pastoralism to the production of larger quantities of food. This was probably triggered by a rapid increase in the population, prompting the need for an increased food supply. To meet this demand, it was necessary to introduce a more intensive irrigation agriculture which, according to archaeological evidence, was already functioning successfully by the time Egypt became a unified country in c.3100 BCE.

Artificial irrigation allowed the people not only to increase the land area where crops could be grown, but also to hold water in low-lying basins even when there was a deficient inundation. With this system, they could also extend their planting beyond the edges of the flood-plain, and even grow a second or third annual crop in their garden plots. Artificial irrigation greatly improved productivity by enhancing the natural irrigation features, and to some extent it could also control the catastrophes associated with natural irrigation, thus lessening the threat of political and economic disintegration.

The system of using basins and low dykes (seen here in the Delta) is still used in Egypt to retain river water which can then be diverted to irrigate the surrounding land for agricultural purposes.

A key feature of artificial irrigation was the ability to raise water manually from natural channels or remaining basins, to cultivate adjacent fields or gardens. Scenes in Old and Middle Kingdom tombs indicate that the earliest method involved the manual lifting of buckets, which the workers then carried by hand or on a shoulder-yoke to their destinations. By the New Kingdom, the *shaduf* (a pole and bucket lever) had been introduced; this device enabled estate-workers to raise water containers to a greater height. However, the *shaduf* could only be used for small-scale cultivation of horticultural crops, but not across extensive field systems.

In fact, it was the lack of suitable lifting devices that always limited the development of a major irrigation programme in pharaonic times. The situation changed when the *saqqiya* (animal-drawn water-wheel) was introduced in the Persian or Ptolemaic Periods, for the first time making it possible to almost continuously elevate quite substantial quantities of water to greater heights. This system enabled Egyptian farmers to produce an annual two-fold harvest. They could grow additional crops in the summer, and cultivate high-lying areas of land. This was a considerable improvement on the dynastic system which, although based on artificial irrigation, only enabled a single crop of wheat, barley and flax to be harvested in the winter. However, the second crop required even more intensive and strenuous labour than the first because the water level of the Nile had decreased by this time. Within a short period immediately or soon after the first harvest had been gathered, the land had to be ploughed, sown and artificially irrigated so that this second crop could be properly cultivated. This irrigation system was probably organized and operated on a local level, since it is unlikely that there was any centralized development of a canal network during this period.

A 'good Nile' produced an abundant harvest, with resultant social, political and economic stability, whereas a series of deficient inundations might result in famine and even political collapse. If poor floods and crop failures occurred at a time when there was also weak leadership, then civil unrest could easily follow. Conditions described in the *Pessimistic Literature* may reflect the historical events of the First Intermediate Period; they spell out the tragic results of political and social collapse, and one text, known as the 'Prophecy of Neferti', states:

'The land is completely perished, nothing remains. Not even the black of a nail [dirt under the fingernail] survives.' (Author's translation).

However, because of the basic predictability of the equatorial rains, the Nile flood was generally more reliable than that of any other river. Intensive artificial irrigation and improved agricultural technology and tools gave the Egyptians the opportunity to produce a food surplus, which in turn led to the establishment of urban communities. The earliest small farming groups were primarily concerned with food production, but early in Egypt's history some of these communities were gradually replaced by towns.

Instead of universal, full-time farming, there was now some differentiation of labour, with the emergence of a new class of part-time or full-time artisans and industrial workers. Some worked in the mines, while others manufactured products, and a third group took on the responsibility for distributing these goods. These people lived mainly in the towns where their work was centred. However, there was still the need for food production which was carried out by agricultural labourers. The food surplus that resulted from the new artificial irrigation system also created a product which the Egyptian government could export to other lands, in exchange for raw materials such as metals and semi-precious stones.

The new urban communities became centres for the storage and distribution of surplus food and the raw materials brought from the quarries and mines. Specialist craftsmen – potters, metalsmiths, carpenters and artists – began to live in towns where they had the advantages of a readily available supply of stored raw materials and a marketplace and distribution centre for their products. As the towns expanded, builders' skills were needed to construct houses and other urban requirements. Also, official departments and personnel were established there, to manage the granaries, food centres, raw material depots, and commercial exchanges. Eventually, an urban population emerged in which the majority were no longer engaged in agricultural pursuits.

From early times, Egypt was divided into a number of geographical and political units for which Egyptologists use the Greek term *nome*; each had a capital city which became the leading centre of the district. The local governor and his attendant bureaucrats resided in the *nome* capital, and supervised local concerns including irrigation, planting, harvesting, road and town construction, and the judiciary. Temples, with their priesthoods and secular personnel, were also located in the towns. Many of these urban developments, which formed the basis of the political system of Egypt, continued to flourish for over 3,000 years and played a significant role in the development of the civilization. Unfortunately, we still do not fully understand how the Egyptian administrative and economic systems worked, either in relation to the central government or regarding management of the surrounding agricultural land.

Life on Khary's Estate
We can imagine that life on Khary's estate involved the usual range of activities illustrated in wall-scenes or represented by tomb-models

Basketwork coffin: in predynastic and early dynastic times bodies were buried in skins, matting or these fragile coffins. Later, elite burials included rectangular wooden coffins which represented a house for the dead; by the Middle Kingdom, wealthy people included an anthropoid (body-shaped) coffin in their funerary assemblages. From Tarkhan. Dynasty 2. Manchester Museum.

funerary presentations, or were used as ingredients in medicinal treatments. No details of production procedures have survived, but the Egyptians probably experimented by adding different substances to the wine. The nature of the local soil in particular districts of the country may have facilitated the production of some especially fine wines, which are known to have received international acclaim.

The best vineyards were located in the north of Egypt but wall-scenes in tombs situated at Thebes also show wine production on local estates in the south. These representations were probably fictional, but were intended to ensure that, through magical reactivation, an eternal supply of wine was available for the tomb-owner in his afterlife. Vines were cultivated on the edges of the desert because they required only light soil, composed of a mixture of sand and clay. Grapes could be picked throughout the year to provide table grapes and grape juice;

there were also heavy vintages when the ripened grapes were picked and processed, and the wine was then poured into *amphorae* (large pottery jars with pointed bases) and left to age.

Many country estates undoubtedly included a vineyard, with a trelliswork supported by wooden forks or pillars over which the grapevines were trained, or alternatively the vines were cultivated and trimmed into small bushes which did not require any support. A mudbrick wall enclosed the vineyard, a building containing a winepress, and a reservoir of water. The estate-workers had a constant struggle to prevent birds eating the grapes, and during harvesting the young sons of the estate-workers used slings and small stones to drive them away. Once the grapes had been picked and placed in deep baskets the men carried them, either on their heads or suspended on a shoulder yoke, to the winepress.

First, they pressed out the wine using a foot-press; this consisted of a low box or trough above which there was a wooden framework. The grapes were placed in the trough, and half a dozen men trampled the fruit, supporting themselves by holding on to the framework. As the wine was pressed out, it ran through a series of openings into large vats. The sweet juice left behind in the grapes was then squeezed out by a hand-press: the grapes were placed inside a matting sack closed at either end by loops; four men twisted sticks inserted through the loops so that the juice was wrung out of the sack and accumulated in a vase placed beneath the press.

After fermentation had taken place, the wine was transferred to *amphorae*; each jar was fastened with a clay lid which carried the owner's stamped seal. Scribes recorded the number of jars that had been filled, and the jars were taken to a storage building on the estate where they were placed upright in rows; their pointed bases were either placed directly into the sandy ground, or they were supported inside stone rings or wooden stands.

Other important crops, flax and papyrus, were grown especially in the northern regions of Egypt. Flax (*Linum usitatissimum*) had been cultivated since neolithic times to produce linen, which was used to manufacture clothing, mummy bandages, domestic textiles and rope. Papyrus (*Cyperus papyrus L.*), a member of the sedge family, was a notable feature of Egypt's earliest landscape: it was originally found in huge thickets in the marshland, particularly in the Delta. In historical times, it was cultivated in the fields to provide the basic material to manufacture paper, ropes, sails, baskets, mats and sandals.

Hunting and Animal Husbandry

Hunting wild game was a major part of Egypt's earliest food economy, but even when it was largely replaced by agriculture and the once-extensive wildlife had been greatly reduced, people of all classes still enjoyed the sport. Wall-scenes in the tombs of wealthy officials show the owner, accompanied by many attendants, in pursuit of game. Khary and his sons spent some of their leisure time in this way, riding out into the desert on horseback or in chariots, while the accompanying huntsmen, beaters and dog-handlers gave chase on foot. Khary kept some dogs at home as family pets, but special hounds were also bred on his estate to accompany the hunt.

During the hunt, dogs were used to drive the wild animals into nets; there, the great official and his sons used bows and metal-tipped arrows to shoot the prey, and the carcasses were ultimately retrieved and taken home by his attendants. However, sometimes, especially if the hunting party wished to capture the animal alive, nooses or lassoes were used. In early times, the extensive natural reserves of wild animals included gazelle, ibex, oryx, wild ox, stag, wild sheep, hare and porcupine, but even in the Predynastic Period there was probably some attempt to domesticate the gazelle, oryx and ibex, as well as geese and ducks. In later times, when natural stocks gradually became depleted, some animals were captured and kept in reserved areas of the desert.

The Egyptians also created game parks on the great officials' estates, where animals, including lions, leopards, oryx, ibex, gazelle, baboons and even crocodiles, were bred and tamed for a variety of purposes. The gamekeepers and huntsmen who supervised these areas had to ensure that there was sufficient game for the hunt as well as some delicacies for the great official's table.

However, it was not only the upper classes who hunted these animals. It is recorded that Tuthmosis III, the king whom Khary served, enjoyed pursuing elephants and lions during his military expeditions to Nubia and Syria. At the other end of the social scale, there were more basic reasons for chasing animals than amusement or

Ivory throwsticks from a New Kingdom tomb. Although they replicate the sticks employed for hunting, these delicate pieces, decorated with finely carved jackal heads, were used for playing games. From Thebes. Dynasty 18. Manchester Museum.

acquiring their skins. Some farmers and shepherds set out to destroy marauders such as the hyena because they attacked and ate their domesticated flocks and herds, while other men hunted to provide meat either as an increasingly rare addition to their family diet, or to sell at market. Other expeditions, regarded as essentially commercial exercises, included ostrich hunts that went in search of eggs and feathers that could be sold on to wealthy clients.

Tomb-scenes of the dynastic period continued to depict the hunting and killing of some animals that featured prominently in the predynastic landscape. The hippopotamus and crocodile were simultaneously feared and revered, and pursued not as a food source but because they represented a danger that had to be overcome. The hippopotamus caused damage in the fields at night, and sometimes, Khary's estate workers had to struggle with the creature, chasing it into the river where they trapped it in a noose, and then struck it with a spear. As the animal became increasingly fatigued through frantic attempts to escape, the workers were able to drag it to their boat and then deliver a final blow with a spear.

Farmers also hunted and killed crocodiles. However, in some parts of Egypt where the local population worshipped the crocodile, the animal was treated very differently. Regarded as an earthly manifestation of the crocodile god, special animals were selected and kept in lakes attached to temples dedicated to the crocodile-god; they were adorned with gold earrings, bracelets and necklets, fed on fish, geese and meat, and after death they were mummified and given elaborate burials.

In addition to hunting, the Egyptians also had considerable expertise in animal husbandry. Even before 5000 BCE, they probably bred and reared some indigenous strains of animals such as cattle, pigs, donkeys, dogs and cats, and they may even have attempted to domesticate some wild animals. However, during the Predynastic Period, different animals and plants (which may have come from Western Asia) appeared in Egypt. These more successful strains of winter crops and herd animals (which included sheep, goats, pigs, and perhaps cattle) now became part of the existing economy, with the result that the pattern of food production underwent a profound change.

Pottery bowl from a tomb, decorated with geometric designs and hippopotamus figures around the rim. The hippopotamus was feared as a dangerous animal, but it was also a symbol of fecundity, and is often represented in funerary goods as a symbol of rebirth. From Mahasna. Predynastic Period. Manchester Museum.

By the Old Kingdom, the Egyptians were already successful in their experiments with grain cultivation and animal husbandry. Sheep reared mainly for their wool were first introduced to Egypt in the Middle Kingdom and largely replaced the indigenous strain, while in the New Kingdom, the great estates supported not only agriculture but also game reserves, and had programmes to breed and rear goats, sheep, some pigs, and cattle. New breeds of cattle were introduced in Dynasty 18, and Khary's herds included short-horned, long-horned and hump-back varieties; because these animals sometimes mixed with neighbouring herds, they were branded with their owner's name. Khary's Steward undertook a regular inventory of his master's cattle, counting the animals as they were herded into the estate courtyard. Other staff – oxherds, goatherds, shepherds and swineherds – were employed to work on the estate where they lived in reed huts; they supervised the animals, ensuring that they were placed in the yards and fields to feed or, at the inundation period, removed to the safety of high ground. The estate-workers also undertook sheep-shearing twice a year.

Khary's estate produced the usual variety of food that was found in Egypt in Dynasty 18. Later, in Ptolemaic and Roman times, new cereals and vegetables were introduced, when a more advanced irrigation system was put in place. These additions were probably brought in to meet the different culinary tastes and requirements of the new settlers and colonizers from various Mediterranean countries who came to live in Egypt.

Fowling and Poultry

The earliest inhabitants of Egypt caught and trapped a variety of birds in the thickets and marshlands. This wildlife continued to flourish in dynastic times, since migratory birds such as geese, ducks and ibis still wintered annually on the water and in the marshes. The birds were most abundant at the inundation period, and it was a time-honoured custom for a family or group of friends to take part in fowling expeditions in the Delta marshlands. The upper classes who lived at Thebes in the New Kingdom wanted to continue to enjoy this activity in the afterlife, so although they lived hundreds of miles away from the northern marshlands where fowling had originated, and the environment around Thebes would have offered no opportunity for this pastime, they still had these expeditions symbolically depicted on the walls of their tombs. Khary and his contemporaries believed that this tomb representation could be magically activated so that they could continue to enjoy this activity in the next world.

The scenes show the tomb-owner and his family using a papyrus punt to sail among the reeds, propelling themselves forward with a pole, paddles or a tow-rope. The birds were brought down with throwsticks, and then retrieved either by attendants or possibly by a specially trained cat, which is sometimes shown in the tomb-scenes. As well as amateur sportsmen, there were professional fowlers who pursued partridge, bustard and quail in the desert, and water-fowl in the marshlands. They sometimes used arrows or throwsticks, although more often large clap-nets or traps were employed. These consisted of frames over which networks were stretched; bait was placed in the trap, and when the bird touched it, the flaps of the trap snapped together, capturing the bird in the net.

Although Khary and his family lived many miles from the marshlands, his estate included poultry-yards and ponds where geese, duck, teal and quail were fed for the table. The eggs, collected from the birds reared on the estate as well as from wild birds, were then hatched in special ovens. At markets and in the shops of towns and villages, poulterers sold birds which had either been caught by fowlers or reared and fattened in captivity by farmers (whose stock of birds was supplied by the fowlers). The birds were either sold as fresh poultry, or salted and kept in earthenware jars. In addition to domestic requirements, poultry was also reared to be offered in the tombs and temples, and to provide food for some of the sacred animals kept in temple enclosures.

As elite members of the royal circle, Khary and his family were aware of a new and exciting poultry delicacy – cocks and hens had recently been introduced into Egypt, brought back by the king's military expeditions to Western Asia. This was the subject of excited comment at Court, and these birds soon provided a novel addition to the diet of the upper classes. Generally, Khary was very proud of the standards of animal husbandry and poultry-rearing on his estate, and if any of the domestic animals or captive wild animals became ill, he was punctilious in summoning a veterinary specialist who provided treatment and gave advice to his Steward about the best diet for the livestock.

Fishing

Fish had been part of Egypt's staple diet from earliest times. They continued to be abundant in the Nile and canals during the historic period, and were also kept in pools and ponds on the great estates, where stocks were regularly renewed when the waters rose during the

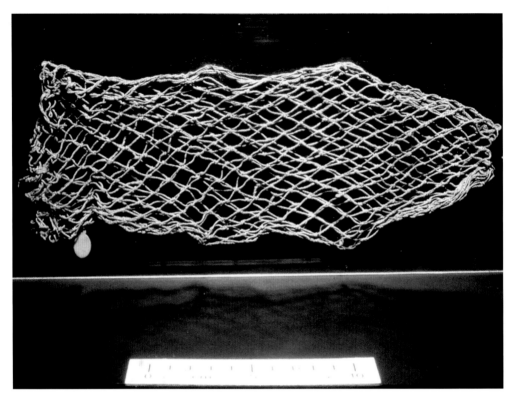

Net bag. Netting was a well-established industry which produced a variety of goods including containers and hunting and fishing equipment. From Kahun. Dynasty 12. Manchester Museum.

inundation period. Khary and his peers greatly enjoyed fishing as a leisure pastime; he and his attendants would sail out in a papyrus skiff, and skilfully spear the fish or catch them in a net let down from the boat.

Another method of catching fish involved two men, who stood on opposite banks of the river, dragging a net across the surface of the water. Some of the catch was sent directly to market but, to provide a reserve source of food, other fish were split open, salted and then dried in the sun. All Egyptians augmented their basic diet with fish; large quantities were consumed and it provided some variety for even the poorest peasants, who often fished with a rod and line. In some parts of Egypt, however, where particular types of fish were regarded as sacred, people were prohibited from catching or eating them;

elsewhere, fish were not only regarded as suitable for human consumption but were also kept in temple lakes and fed to the sacred cult-animals (cats, ibises and crocodiles) at these centres.

Farming Implements

The tombs usually contained everyday items such as high-quality clothing, jewellery and furniture, but more mundane objects of common use were rarely placed with the burial. Therefore, although tomb-scenes frequently show the implements and equipment used in farming and agriculture, the tools themselves have not usually survived. However, archaeologists had the good fortune to discover many of these objects at two town-sites, Gurob and Kahun, which will be discussed in a later chapter.[4] These rare finds are particularly significant because they enable us to understand how communities functioned and performed mundane tasks.

These towns were surrounded by countryside where wheat and barley were grown in the fields, and vegetables, fruit and flowers were cultivated in the gardens. Some of the towns' inhabitants were involved in food production, supplying their own needs and feeding resident officials and craftsmen. Excavation of their houses has revealed examples of most implements used for the various stages of crop production, harvesting, and grinding the corn into flour. These included wooden ploughs and rakes used to clear the ground before ploughing commenced. The rakes, which show evidence of much wear, were made from a single piece of wood with several large teeth cut along one side.

Hoes had been developed in Egypt from c.4000 BCE, but even the much later examples (c.2000 BCE–1400 BCE) found at these sites were simply constructed. The blade (broad and flat in some cases, thick and narrow in others) was inserted into the handle; both the handle and the blade were pierced with holes or grooved to accommodate the twisted rope which bound them together in the middle. Archaeologists also found heavy wooden mallets, cut from single pieces of wood, which were used to break up clods of earth. Similar agricultural tools were employed on Khary's estate. His estate-workers also used ploughs. The earliest type of plough was constructed so that it could be attached to a pair of oxen by fixing a yoke to the

Wooden mattock for hacking up soil prior to sowing seed. Since the original has perished, modern string has been used to bind together the two pieces of the mattock. From Kahun. Dynasty 12. Manchester Museum.

front of the animals' horns. However, by the New Kingdom this was replaced by a shoulder yoke, which was put over the animals' shoulders and required no further harnessing.

The crop was reaped with sickles which simulated the shape of an animal's jawbone. Most of the sickles found at Kahun and Gurob were made of wood, shaped in the form of an animal's jawbone: often two or three pieces were joined together because it was difficult to find a single piece from which the required shape could be carved. A line of short flint blades was set into a groove made along the inside of the handle, and fixed in place with a cement mix of mud and glue. In other cases, an actual animal jawbone was turned into a sickle by setting flints into the teeth sockets. One example found at Kahun was intended for use either by a left-handed person or as a back-handed sickle.

Archaeologists have also found wooden scoops which were used for winnowing, the process of separating the chaff from the wheat, carried out after the grain had been threshed. Finally, a heavy pestle and mortar were employed to reduce the grain to flour, and then the flour was ground even more finely between two stones – a lower millstone and a rounded rubber or pebble. Archaeologists have discovered examples of all these items at Kahun and Gurob.

Situated in the fertile Fayoum oasis, Gurob and Kahun were ideal centres for game-hunting, and implements used by hunters (such as finely polished wooden arrows and throwsticks made of heavy wood which could travel considerable distances) were excavated from the houses. There is also evidence that local industry produced items required for fishing, including fish hooks and different types and sizes of nets. Archaeologists have also found netting needles and clay or stone net sinkers.

A sling, used to drive marauding birds away from crops and vineyards, was discovered at Kahun. This beautifully woven object may be the earliest extant example of a sling from the ancient world: it incorporates a long cord which has a loop at one end to be held on the finger, while the other end is plain. Three small stones found with the sling were probably used as ammunition, and would have been broadcast simultaneously to produce a scatter effect.

Woven sling with long cords, one of which ends in a loop to be retained on the finger; it was found with the three small sling stones (left) which were probably flung from the sling simultaneously, to produce a scatter effect and frighten away birds in gardens and vineyards. This may be the earliest example of a sling ever discovered. In the foreground are two wooden balls and a leather ball (right) which was repaired in antiquity. From Kahun. Dynasty 12. Manchester Museum.

Transport

Khary, his family and his servants would have used various types of transport on the river, and to travel overland from the river's edge to a particular destination.[5] On the estate, the main beast of burden, the donkey, was used for transferring heavy loads, threshing the corn, and riding across the countryside. However, this humble animal would not have been considered a suitable means of conveyance for Khary; an official of his status preferred to ride in a sedan chair, either supported on the backs of two donkeys or carried on the shoulders of a dozen or more attendants. Relaxing on the seat and covered by a canopy, Khary was able to cool himself with water contained in skins carried by servants, who walked beside him, moving the air about with long fans. Another kind of litter which had no canopy was accompanied by a servant who carried a large umbrella. When Khary attended the great festivals in nearby Thebes, he saw that the gods' statues were transported in heavy litters or carrying chairs. In earlier times, these had been used to carry kings and nobles as well as gods, but by the

New Kingdom they were only brought out for religious and ceremonial functions.

The camel, closely associated with Egypt in modern times, does not appear in pharaonic scenes and records: earliest references occur in the Graeco-Roman Period when the animal was first introduced into Egypt. However, Khary could recall his grandfather talking with excitement about the horse and chariot, which had probably been brought to Egypt from Asia Minor during the period of Hyksos rule. Horses were greatly valued, and their ownership was restricted to the royal family and the officials who possessed great estates. In Khary's lifetime, horses were generally used to draw light, two-wheeled chariots that held a driver and a passenger.

Khary's own son, Amenemhet, was a member of the chariotry division in Tuthmosis III's army. The animal's main task was to draw the chariot, but royalty and the upper classes also rode their horses for pleasure, although this activity was never formally depicted in the tomb-scenes. Since Khary and his family were held in high esteem at Court, he had his own stables and staff to attend to the horses on his estate. He ensured that they were adorned with decorative head-plumes, and that the gilded metal parts of the chariots and tackle, as well as the leather covering of the chariot and the harness, were kept in good repair.

In the New Kingdom, a type of carriage that had been introduced from Palestine became popular. It had two wheels made of wood and metal, a carriage which consisted of a floor and wooden front and sides, and a harness by which it could be attached to a pair of horses. Since it was light and durable, Khary used this carriage for travelling overland or for hunting in the desert; sometimes his son was transported into battle in the same type of vehicle.

Despite the availability of several forms of land transport, the river and canals provided the usual and most convenient method for conveying people and cargo.[6] The Egyptians developed many types of boats to meet these different needs, ranging from papyrus skiffs to sea-going vessels designed for warfare or trading expeditions.[7] The earliest boats built in Egypt were rafts made of bundles of reeds bound together, in which two people could travel; larger versions accommodated more passengers and sometimes an animal. The stern stood high out of the river so that it could be easily pushed along or away from the sandbanks, and these boats were propelled through the water by means of poles or short oars with broad blades.

Because they incorporated a good, basic design and cheap building materials, fishermen and hunters who pursued game in the shallow waters of the marshland continued to sail this type of boat thousands of years after they were first invented. These rafts also became the prototype for the transport ships which, since the Old Kingdom, had been the main product of an extensive boat-building industry. Shipyards built wooden craft which were used for a variety of purposes: because of constantly shifting sandbanks, all river vessels had shallow drafts so that they would not become lodged in the sand, and to balance this, the upper part of the boat could not be too high.

Vessels were propelled along by wooden oars; these usually had a narrow pointed blade, and were fastened to the ship and held in oarlocks. There were one or two large steering oars at the helm, fixed into an oarlock and held by a rope. Many boats also had linen sails. When they travelled up the Nile (southwards), the crew used the sails whenever the wind was favourable, but otherwise the oars were employed. If conditions were calm, the sailors walked along the riverbank, using a tow-line to pull the boat. When the boat reached the south, the sail was taken down and laid on top of the cabin, and on the return journey downstream (northwards), it was rowed by oarsmen.

Whenever Khary or his sons walked around the bustling harbour at Thebes and looked out across the river, they saw a variety of vessels. There were large, squat transport ships, incurved at the bow and stern, used for transporting cattle, horses and other commodities; these were accommodated in the space at the ends of the boat, since most of the deck space was occupied with a main and second cabin. A crew of three or four rowers and two steersmen spent their lives in uncomfortable conditions, but they took great pride in their vessel and frequently washed down the decks and the cabins. Sometimes, large vessels were accompanied by smaller boats which carried extra supplies. However, the heaviest vessels could not be rowed, and if the weather conditions prevented them from sailing, they had to be towed

Painted wooden model boats from the Tomb of Two Brothers designed to magically undertake the journey to Abydos. One has oars with narrow pointed blades and a furled sail (to travel downstream) while the other is rigged for sailing upstream (southwards); each has a large steering oar at the helm, a crew of sailors or rowers, two steersmen, and a small deck cabin. From Rifeh. Dynasty 12. Manchester Museum.

either by sailors or special tugboats. Other cargo vessels included the barges which carried grain and stone.

As an important official, Khary sometimes accompanied dignitaries on the special, swift-moving vessels which were built from pine imported from Syria (most other boats were constructed from local woods such as acacia). These long craft differed from other boats in that the prow and stern were not raised high out of the water. There was a cabin on deck, made of plaited matting or linen, where the dignitary or owner could sit; in the finest ships, the cabin walls were hung with tapestries. The owner sat and watched the sailors handling the mast and sails, or rowing the vessel, facing the stern as they pulled the boat through the water. They listened intently to the pilot who, as he measured the depth of the water with a pole, shouted instructions so that the ship would not lodge on a sandbank. When the ship moored, the pilot organized the landing arrangements with great care.

Khary encountered many sailors in the harbour. As well as those engaged in military service on the warships, setting out on expeditions to Western Asia or Nubia, there were men who took part in trading ventures and sailed the merchant vessels at home and abroad. There was always much discussion of the problems they had encountered in bringing the large blocks of granite, intended for temple construction, from Aswan to Thebes. Some of the ships' captains were wealthy and highly regarded, particularly those who sailed the vessels carrying dignitaries, but because of their nautical skills, the steersmen or pilots who guided the river craft enjoyed an almost equal importance.

There were also funerary barques which transported the mummified bodies of the deceased and the mourners from the dwellings on the eastern side of the river to the cemeteries on the west bank. As he moved around, Khary heard the sailors talk of the great seagoing vessels that sailed along the coast of Palestine and Syria to reach Byblos, the port through which timber from the hinterland was exported to Egypt.

The sailors also excitedly discussed the seagoing expeditions which made the hazardous journey along the Red Sea coast to the land of Punt, where they traded for the incense produced by trees in the interior of the country. For these long sea voyages, the Egyptians used sailing vessels which were about sixty-five feet in length; they had sharply pointed bows and were painted with a papyrus design on the stern. Fitted out with oars, each ship accommodated thirty rowers, and also had very large sails. One of these expeditions to Punt was depicted on the walls of the funerary temple of Queen Hatshepsut at Deir el-Bahri. Loyal to his ruler, Tuthmosis III, Khary despised Hatshepsut, the king's stepmother, who had briefly usurped his throne.

Unless they needed to travel abroad to obtain commodities that were not available within Egypt, people generally preferred to stay at home where the Nile was always the lively focus of their world. Egypt was now at the height of its political power, and its prosperity was reflected in the variety of river traffic that Khary surveyed with interest and pleasure. The vibrant scene included fleets of boats which belonged to the king, the temples or private individuals, all moving people and goods to their destinations. The Nile was the country's main artery for trade and communication, but it was also a focus for many religious occasions when, as part of a festival, the god's statue was taken from one temple to another, or people travelled long distances to participate in these celebrations. One of the most important festivals marked the inundation: it was held as the river began to rise, and invoked the blessings associated with this event, in the hope of bringing about a good Nile and a fruitful harvest. People gathered at the capital towns of their districts, and celebrated with music, dancing and singing. For Khary's son, the priest Nakht, this was an annual highlight in the religious calendar.

Chapter 2

Religious Beliefs and Practices

The Nile Festivals

The great Nile festivals of antiquity continued to be celebrated until construction of dams along the river in the twentieth century CE terminated the annual effect of the inundation. Modern celebrations occurred during the summer months, and preserved many of the ancient customs. The 'Night of the Drop' (*Leilat en-Nalqta*) was celebrated on 18 June, when it was believed that a drop from heaven (or, in antiquity, a tear shed by the goddess Isis) fell into the Nile and miraculously caused it to rise. On this occasion, many people spent the night on the riverbanks.

Between 6 and 16 August, the river rose to about twenty feet in one area of Cairo, and then the *Wefa en-Nil* ('Completion or Abundance of the Nile') was proclaimed. When this happened, the government was able to confirm that the water level had reached the sixteenth cubit marked on the Nilometer, and this allowed them to exact land-tax. Then, in the middle of August, the 'Cutting of the Dam' took place. This dam, constructed before or soon after the Nile waters began to increase, was built of earth; it measured about three yards in width and rose about twenty-two feet above the lowest level of the Nile.

About sixty feet away, a round, earthen pillar (called 'the bride') was built in the form of a truncated cone; it had a flat top on which a small amount of maize or millet was grown. The rising Nile waters washed away this pillar about two weeks before the dam was cut, and before the river had reached its full height. According to Arab historians, the first of these pillars was constructed immediately after the Arab conquest of Egypt (670 CE). A legend claims that until then, the Egyptians had followed an annual pharaonic custom when the Nile began to rise: this involved throwing a young virgin into the river in order to celebrate the inundation and to request the god to bestow an adequate flood and grant prosperity to the land and its people. Amr Ibn el-'As, the Arab general who conquered Egypt, abolished this custom. However, when the Nile did not increase for three months after the start of its rise, the population became anxious, and it was decided that a substitute 'bride' should be constructed every year in the form of the earthen pillar; this would then be swallowed by the river as an 'offering'.

The 'Cutting of the Dam' was celebrated in the same way that major events associated with the Nile were the focus of great festivities in antiquity. This scene is described by Edward Lane in his book *An Account of the Manners and Customs of the Modern Egyptians* (1871). On the day before the cutting of the dam, many people hired boats to sail to the area where the ceremony would take place. These included a large, gaudily painted boat, generally believed to represent the fine vessel which, in antiquity, had carried to her fate the virgin destined to become the 'Bride of the Nile'. In Lane's time, it was used to carry passengers to the place of celebration. The occupants of the boats entertained themselves with music and singing, and as night fell they enjoyed an exhibition of fireworks.

Before sunrise, a large gang of workmen began to cut the dam and remove the earth in baskets, completing this work about an hour before dawn. The Governor of Cairo and other dignitaries had already arrived and taken their places inside a tent erected specially for the occasion. Various activities followed: the Governor threw a purse of gold coins to the workmen; then, a boat was driven against the final, narrow ridge of earth and broke through the dam. The remains of the dam were quickly washed away, clearing a way for the boats carrying the Governor and others to pass along the canal. By the early twentieth century CE, the actual cutting of the dam was no longer undertaken, but festivities, including the firework display, still took place in the presence of the Governor.

The Priesthood

Festivals always played an important part in Egyptian religion, and thousands of years before the modern Nile celebrations, Khary's son, the priest Nakht, witnessed the annual cycle of events that were celebrated at Thebes on behalf of the temple gods.

By the New Kingdom, most of the larger temples had full-time, permanent priesthoods, although in smaller establishments many priests acted in a part-time capacity.[1] Indeed, earlier in the Old and Middle Kingdoms, almost all prominent men had acted as part-time priests in their local temple, and at all periods, doctors, lawyers and scribes customarily held priesthoods associated with gods who played a significant role in those professions. These men had a dual function in society, acting as priests and also working for the king and State in a secular capacity; this system ensured that religion and State were totally integrated, and that the temples, although wealthy and powerful in their own right, never achieved total independence.

Nakht worked as a lawyer, and also served in the temple for a period of three months each year. In later times (and this was also probably the case in the New Kingdom), each temple had a rota of four groups of priests who performed the rituals for the god. Each group served three terms of duty every year, with each term lasting for one month. Like other part-time priests, Nakht lived in the temple precinct during his periods of duty, but spent the rest of his time with his wife and family in a house in Thebes.

In many cases, the priesthood was hereditary, and although the king held the right to confirm all such appointments, he was usually only involved in selecting candidates for the most important posts in the major cities of Thebes, Memphis and Heliopolis. At other times, he exercised his right to appoint a particularly deserving candidate to the priesthood, or promote someone who had shown outstanding ability. In some cases, the selection and appointment of priests was carried out by a collegium of priests, or sometimes people could purchase a priestly position. Nakht had inherited his position from his maternal grandfather (if a man had no sons, particular posts could pass to the sons of his daughters), but as a formality this had been approved by the collegium of priests.

Nakht had been initiated into the religious rites of the god's cult during his first term of duty in the temple. Although details of the installation remained secret, he probably received a ritual baptism and purification which allowed him access to certain areas of the temple and the god's possessions. He would also have acquired secret knowledge of the god's cult, and taken vows relating to his own integrity and ritual purity, promising to observe the ethical principles on which Egyptian society was founded and keep the regulations associated with the cult of his god.

Nakht was a minor priest at the great Temple of Amun at Karnak, on the east bank of the river at Thebes. This vast organization employed many thousands of people (perhaps as many as 80,000 in the New Kingdom), and owned over 2,000 square kilometres of land.

At the start of Dynasty 18, Amun, a local god of the air worshipped at Thebes since Dynasty 12 (*c.*1900 BCE), was elevated by the new dynasty whose family originated at Thebes. They decided to unite Amun with Re, the great sun-god whose cult was pre-eminent at Heliopolis, in order to ensure that Re posed no serious threat to Amun.

Stone columns in the Temple of Amun, Karnak. The capitals are represented as closed lotus buds, and the column surfaces are covered with ritual scenes and texts. New Kingdom.

Now known as Amen-Re, the god adopted the mythology and major characteristics of Re, and acquired additional powers associated with the sun-god.

As Egypt gradually established an empire in Asia and Nubia, Amen-Re came to be regarded as a universal creator and ruler of both the Egyptians and those whom they governed. His priesthood at Thebes promoted the belief that the Temple of Karnak, the god's residence, was the original 'Island of Creation' where, according to mythology, the creation of the universe had taken place. Amun was worshipped at Thebes, alongside his wife, Mut (who resided in the nearby Temple of Luxor) and his son, Khonsu, who had his own temple within the Karnak complex.

The Temple of Karnak had been considerably enlarged and enhanced since its foundation in Dynasty 12.[2] During the New Kingdom, the temple was at the centre of Egypt's greatest religious capital, Thebes, a city which, in Dynasty 18, was also the country's political capital, and accommodated the main royal residence and the royal burial sites.

Priests of Amun at Karnak possessed unequalled and unprecedented powers, which they mainly acquired as the result of Egypt's successful military campaigns in Syria/Palestine. Grateful to the god who had helped them establish their dynasty, overthrow their enemies, and create the world's first empire, the kings made lavish donations to Karnak. Large estates were created to support the temple, and booty and prisoners-of-war from Asiatic campaigns were presented to the god to retain his goodwill.

However, the true effects of this policy were revealed as the dynasty wore on. The generosity shown to the god by these kings eventually created an imbalance of power and wealth. As a result, Amen-Re's priesthood began to rival the king's status: in particular, whenever the succession was controversial (if there was more than one claimant), the most senior priests could now influence the selection of the next king by granting or withholding the god's acceptance of a particular candidate. They could exercise this authority because, at this time, each king was considered to be the son of Amun. By the end of Dynasty 18, one pharaoh, Akhenaten (Amenhotep IV), attempted to curtail the powers of the Amun priesthood, and briefly introduced a monotheistic cult dedicated to the Aten, which rivalled and eventually disposed of all the traditional deities.[3]

Nakht worked at the centre of an extensive organization. In addition to its religious functions, the Temple of Amun (and, indeed, even temples of lesser standing) played important economic, educational and social roles in the country. Although they were not entirely independent of the State, temples retained considerable autonomy, and Karnak was so important that it functioned as a department of the royal administration, directly responsible to the king. However, even temples were subject to State scrutiny, and senior government officials paid regular visits to inspect Karnak and its staff.

The temples had two main types of religious personnel. A third category of employees (which included architects, artisans, cleaners, confectioners, bakers, brewers and cooks) were engaged in secular duties. They maintained and repaired the temple building, and prepared the daily offerings for the god. In addition, the temple estates supported livestock, crops, vineyards and gardens; here, the workers produced food for the god, and in addition to their own requirements, for the priests, other temple workers, and the *necropolis* personnel. They also cultivated vast quantities of flowers to supply the floral bouquets offered daily to the god. The cult-statue (the god's image, where his spirit resided whilst in the temple) had to be clothed and adorned with jewellery: textile workers on the temple estates produced these garments, while in the workshops, craftsmen used raw materials from the temple mines to fashion the god's statues, insignia, jewellery and ritual vessels.

In addition to the booty received from the king, the temples were supported by revenue collected in kind from the districts throughout the country. They received, recorded and stored these items in their storehouses, and then redistributed them either as payment to employees, or as taxes that they paid to the State (although royal decrees afforded them certain exemptions and privileges). Temples also received donations of land or services from private individuals; in return, they received a commitment from the priests that mortuary rites would be performed on their behalf after death. Some temple lands were situated close to the sacred precinct, while others were further away; to retain communication with these places, and to collect taxes, some of the larger temples had their own fleets of river vessels.

There were two levels of priests at Karnak. The hierarchy was headed by a permanent, full-time group of men, who wielded considerable religious and political power. All temple personnel were governed by the High-priest of Amun, who held the title 'First Prophet of Amun' and owned a splendid house and great estates. Below him in rank were the 'Fathers of the gods' (the Second, Third and Fourth Prophets of Amun); then came the senior priests (*ḥmw-ntr*: 'Servants of the god') who participated in the daily divine cult and had access to the god's ritual possessions.

The title 'servant' aptly described the main role of these priests; they were primarily temple functionaries who served the god's cultic needs by performing regular and unceasing rituals. Although a priest was expected to understand the liturgy and sometimes to teach his specialization within the temple, he was not regarded as a pastor or preacher and was not expected to give counsel or guidance within the community. A priest was never required to have a vocation, nor was he considered to be a member of an exclusive religious sect. Many were doubtless dedicated men with high ethical standards, but they did not need to express special personal spirituality. The priesthood offered a powerful and prestigious position in society, which also guaranteed a regular source of wealth and income, and for these reasons it attracted competent and ambitious men who usually came from well-established families.

As well as their ritual function, some temples were also places of higher learning. Priests were regarded as the repository of knowledge and wisdom in ancient Egypt, and some of these specialist 'servants' spent part of their time in the House of Life, an institution attached to some major temples. Here, priests and secular scholars preserved the cult's wisdom by composing and copying religious texts. These men, whose knowledge encompassed medicine, geography, the history of Egypt's kings, astronomy, astrology, and the use of plants, probably taught their disciplines to students.

Below the 'Servants of the god' came the category known as '*waab*-priests'. They did not enter the god's sanctuary, but because they handled the ritual and cultic objects which came into contact with the god's statue, they had to reach the same standards of ritual purity that the 'Servants of the god' were expected to maintain. In fact, the term '*waab*-priest' meant 'the purified one'. Nakht belonged to this group: he assisted with the temple rituals, carried the god's barque during the festival processions, and also supervised the men who decorated and renovated the temple.

In order to achieve ritual purity during periods of priestly duty, Nakht had to observe a set of strict requirements before he could enter the temple. He bathed twice daily and twice at night in the Sacred Lake at Karnak (an impressive stretch of water which today retains many of its original features). He also completely shaved his head and body every day, and chewed balls of natron in order to cleanse his mouth. Natron, found in a couple of the dry desert valleys, is a naturally occurring compound of sodium carbonate and bicarbonate, with some deposits of sodium chloride and sulphate.

Then Nakht dressed himself in the linen garments which signified his rank, and slipped on sandals made of woven palm or vegetable fibres. During his temple service, he could not wear woollen or leather garments or leather shoes because they were the products of living animals and would have contaminated the god's sacred resting place. Nakht's simple linen garments had changed little from those worn by priests thousands of years earlier, and his clothes differed only in detail from those of other priestly ranks.

Nakht was not allowed to eat fish and beans during each duty-month, and he also probably abstained from consuming pork, lamb, pigeon or garlic. In other parts of Egypt, additional local restrictions applied regarding the foods the priests could eat; this ensured that they did not consume any meat derived from their cult-animal, or any part of a sacred plant associated with their god.

Like many priests, Nakht had been circumcised when he entered the priesthood. This operation, although not universal, seems to have been widely practised in ancient Egypt. The demands of ritual purity also extended to matters of sexual behaviour; when undertaking priestly duties, Nakht was expected to live within the temple precinct, and to abstain from sexual relations for several days prior to and during his term of duty.

Nakht's role and duties as a priest had their origin in the village worship of predynastic Egypt. The earliest 'priests' were the leaders of neolithic villages who regularly offered food to the statues of local gods to ensure the well-being of their people. This form of worship, based on barter (reciprocal exchange), continued to be the foundation of subsequent temple worship, when the simple reed shrines which housed the earliest divine statues eventually evolved into great stone temples like Karnak. In due course, when the most powerful and politically successful village chieftains became the earliest kings, they continued to act as High-priest for the nation's gods. Despite the fiction that the king was the sole priest of the gods and performed the rituals in every temple throughout Egypt, in practice the rulers eventually delegated these duties and responsibilities to the High-priest of each temple and his assistants, although they may have personally performed some of the temple rituals for the chief god of the dynasty.

Temple Service
The Egyptians started to build stone cultus-temples (buildings designed for the worship of a particular god) during the Middle Kingdom, but most of our knowledge about temple architecture and

The Forecourt at the Temple of Horus at Edfu (the best preserved in Egypt). Unlike the main building (right), this area was unroofed, and lay people were probably allowed to come here to pray and watch festival processions. Graeco-Roman Period.

ritual is derived from the well-preserved buildings of the New Kingdom and Graeco-Roman Period.

The New Kingdom examples, particularly Karnak, developed into splendid, elaborate constructions which retained the main features present in the predynastic reed shrines; although none of these early buildings have survived, depictions have been found on contemporary ivory objects.[4]

Whenever Nakht entered the temple, he felt a sense of awe. The vast building dominated the local landscape, dwarfing all other buildings, even the royal palaces and his father's estate house, which were of inferior and temporary construction. All cultus-temples were built on the same basic plan because they were designed for specific ritual purposes, and had to fulfil universal requirements relating to particular religious beliefs. Another type of building, sometimes referred to as a mortuary temple, also came into existence. Here, rituals were performed for the resident deity and also for the dead, deified king who had built the temple, together with all the legitimate, previous rulers who were known collectively as the 'Royal Ancestors'.

The terms 'cultus-temple' and 'mortuary temple' were invented by Egyptologists in the nineteenth century CE. Current scholarship does not entirely support this categorization, but it is generally agreed that the so-called mortuary temple was built primarily for the cult of a divine king (usually deceased), sometimes accompanied by the worship of a god, whereas each cultus-temple was dedicated specifically to the worship of a god, sometimes accompanied by that of a (usually) living king. These two types of temples shared certain architectural features and spatial provision for rituals, but mortuary temples incorporated additional areas where rites connected with the Royal Ancestors were performed. The cultus-temples on the East Bank at Thebes (including Karnak) were built for the gods' worship, while the mortuary temples situated on the West Bank, near the royal *necropolises*, were associated with the rulers' tombs and their mortuary cults.

Despite some differences, mortuary and cultus-temples were both based on the same mythology. Egyptologists are aware that temple architecture reflected many of the features of the country's prehistoric landscape; however, Egyptians explained these buildings in purely mythological terms. Each temple was built to reflect an underlying mythology which is explained in a set of inscriptions (the 'Building Texts') found on the walls of the Temple of Horus at Edfu. They relate that every temple was regarded as the mythical 'Island of Creation' which emerged from the waters of Nun (the state of non-existence before creation took place). The first deity, a falcon, flew out of the surrounding darkness, and landed on the highest point of the island. Later, reed walls were constructed around this site, and it became the god's sanctuary and place of shelter.

According to mythology, this island was where the 'First Occasion' happened – a time when the gods and mankind came into existence and all the elements of society, such as law, ethics, religion and kingship, were handed down to mankind. As the site of creation, the island was considered to be a place of great magical and religious potency. The Egyptians of later times believed that to harness this spiritual force, they only had to recreate the physical environment of the island in order to gain access to the potent forces which had existed at the original site. Since perfection had been achieved on that 'First Occasion', there was no need to find fresh solutions for their problems: any issues could be resolved by approaching the gods in a building that recreated the sacred environment of the original 'Island'. To achieve this end, the architecture and layout of each temple was designed to reflect the 'Island's' main features. The buildings did not differ markedly from each other, and throughout the millennia there were no major innovations in temple design, since it was unnecessary and undesirable to change the main elements of this 'Island'.

From its basic concept as the 'Island of Creation', the temple also came to represent the god's house – a place of shelter and protection where the deity in the form of his/her cult-statue could receive food and worship. The Egyptian term for the temple was 'Mansion of the God' (ḥwt-ntr), and the temple acted as the deity's residence in the same way that the tomb was regarded as a 'house' for the spirit of its deceased owner. Both tomb and temple recreated the accommodation found in domestic architecture, although the plan of the temple was modified and elongated, to provide a central processional route to accommodate the rituals. The tomb burial chamber and the temple sanctuary fulfilled the same function as the bedroom, while the tomb offering-chapel and the hypostyle hall of a temple mirrored the reception area of a house; all these buildings included rooms for storing the owner's possessions. The Egyptians believed that the living, the dead and the gods all needed food, washing, dressing, rest and recreation: these were provided for the dead through rituals performed in the tombs, while in the temples, they were supplied by the regular divine rituals which the priests carried out.

In later times, the Egyptians also developed various cosmological explanations of the temple, describing it either as a microcosm of the universe, a reflection of the heavens, or a great sarcophagus in which the sun-god was reborn daily. It was believed that the performance of temple rituals – the highest level of State magic – would have a potent effect upon external events and actions throughout the whole universe.

The temple building itself was sacred, and entry was restricted to some members of the royal family and selected groups of temple personnel. One of the priests' most important privileges was to be allowed access to the interior of the building, and to control entry to the temple. The temple precinct incorporated a rectangular stone temple, and a courtyard where the priests' houses, shrines, storage areas and slaughter yards were situated; these were all enclosed within a mudbrick wall. Every temple also had a Sacred Lake; the water was believed to have special purifying properties, and the priests undertook their daily ablutions here before entering the temple, and also washed the utensils and vessels used in the temple rituals. The outer areas of the precinct were accessible to lay personnel who gained entry through a great gateway (*pylon*) pierced in the enclosure wall.

During his term of temple duty, Nakht lived in a mudbrick house located within the temple precinct. With his priestly knowledge of temple mythology, he was aware that the bricks of the wall that encircled the precinct were set in alternate concave and convex sections to represent the waves of the primeval ocean from which the mythical 'Island of Creation' had first appeared. Although the temple and its adjacent buildings were part of the town, they were nevertheless distinct – a religious oasis in the centre of the community; the thick enclosure wall separated and protected the precinct from the continuous bustle of the surrounding neighbourhood.

The temple stood before Nakht as he walked from his house before dawn – a massive stone-built structure which was designed to last for eternity. The temple façade was pierced by a monumental doorway (situated on the main axis of the building), which gave access to an unroofed court where the walls were covered with registers of scenes that showed the king – the gods' son and heir – as a great warrior in battle. This unroofed area had developed from the open enclosure which stood in front of the earliest reed shrines. Nakht and his fellow-priests did not have exclusive use of this court. Because it was less sacred than the innermost areas of the temple, the king allowed wealthy people to set up statues here, so that they could derive some personal benefit from the offerings made to the gods. Even the humblest people could spend time in this court, pouring out libations of water, praying to the gods or, during the great festivals, gathering around in the hope of catching sight of the god's procession.

Nakht moved forward into the sacred, roofed area of the temple that stood behind the court. He and his fellow-priests usually entered this space through a side door, although when they participated in the great processions, they used the central entrance situated on the main axis of the temple. When its huge bronze doors were opened, they could glimpse the dark interior space beyond. Once inside, Nakht blinked to allow his eyes to adjust to the gloom, which contrasted strongly with the vivid blue sky and sunlight in the outer court. He had entered the hypostyle hall, a large area dominated by rows of heavy stone columns that supported elaborate plant-form capitals. Standing here, Nakht was acutely aware that this was the very place where creation had occurred.

The capitals (for which Egyptologists use the terms 'palmiform', 'lotiform', or 'papyriform') symbolized the abundant vegetation of the 'Island of Creation'. Although their primary function was to support the roof, there were more columns than required for this purpose. The columns represented the abundant plant-life on the 'Island of Creation', and were included in the temples in such large numbers so that, through ritual magic, they could be 'brought to life' to recreate this fertile environment. For the same reason, plants were carved on the bases of the walls to represent lush vegetation, and the ceiling was decorated to depict the sky which had existed above the original island.

Stone columns and royal statues in the Temple of Luxor, Thebes. Temples always included more columns than required to support the roof; their other function was to symbolize the abundant plant-life on the 'Island of Creation'. New Kingdom.

The method of illuminating the hall heightened the atmosphere of mystery: roofed and dark, the only light came from flares carried by the priests and the sunlight which filtered through the stone grids inserted between the top of the walls and the ceiling. With great effect, this recreated the illusion of sunlight falling in shafts through densely massed trees, briefly lighting up the painted scenes and inscriptions which covered the columns and the walls.

As a lower-ranking priest, Nakht was not permitted to enter the sanctuary which stood at the rear of the temple. Only the High-priest (acting as the king's delegate) and his attendants could enter this Holy of Holies, to perform the daily ritual for the god. In some temples, the floor level gradually increased as one approached the sanctuary from the temple entrance, and then decreased in the space behind the sanctuary. Again, mythology underpinned this architectural device: the sanctuary was positioned at the highest point to represent the summit of the primeval island where the falcon-god had first alighted.

Matching this increase in floor level, the height of the ceiling was gradually lowered from the temple entrance to the sanctuary, so that a focused sense of awe was created as the priest moved towards the god's presence.

Those priests who did have access to the sanctuary entered this chamber by passing through a pair of massive doors. Inside, the small dark room preserved the shape and dimensions of the predynastic reed shrine. Towards the back of the room, there was a small box-shrine which housed the god's statue – the divine image which provided the focus for the temple's energy and power. Throughout the temple, the walls were decorated with scenes, arranged in two or three horizontal registers. It was intended that lay petitioners visiting the temple would see these scenes in the outer courts; the aim here was to impress these people with the king's power and achievements, and the scenes depicted him as the divine heir, a great warrior, or the father of many children. However, in the most sacred areas of the temple, the wall-scenes either commemorated specific religio-historical events or represented the rituals which were once performed in particular halls and chambers.[5]

Nakht had attended the events that marked the foundation and consecration of the temple. At the Foundation Ceremony, the king formally marked out the temple boundary and consecrated the land before building works commenced. Later on, at the Consecration Ceremony, the completed building was handed over to the resident god, and the priests performed a series of rituals which culminated with the rite known as 'Opening the Mouth'. With an adze (a carpenter's tool), the priest touched the hands, feet and mouths of all the painted and sculpted figures in the temple; this activated the vital energy of the building, renewing the potency of the spiritual forces present on the original 'Island'. The ritual also 'brought to life' all the inanimate representations in the temple so that they would become perpetually effective. This ceremony ensured that the temple could henceforth operate on a cultic level: even if at any time the priests should neglect their ritual duties, activation of the content of the wall-scenes (which depicted the daily rituals) would ensure that State magic would continue to be performed within the building for perpetuity. This would protect the king, the land and its people against all evil.

Scenes of the king's coronation, as well as the foundation and consecration of the temple, were placed on the walls of the hypostyle halls. However, in other areas, the scenes depicted rituals that were once actually performed in those areas. These rites, carried out on a regular basis, dramatized the everyday events of the god's life, and were performed in all traditional temples throughout Egypt.

The most important of these ceremonies was the 'Daily Temple Ritual'. Before sunrise, the king (or his delegate, the High-priest) would wash and dress himself before consecrating the divine offerings. Then, at dawn, he led the procession of priests to the sanctuary, to present the offerings to the god's statue. These formed a link between the gods and mankind: they restored the god's life-force and he in turn granted immortality to the king and prosperity for Egypt. This ritual lay at the heart of the State magic performed in the temples, which essentially ensured that the cosmos did not return to the state of chaos that had prevailed before creation. Because the king was the divine son and heir, only he could present the offerings to the god and so, although his duties were frequently delegated to the High-priest, the wall-scenes always depicted the king making these presentations.

The officiant moved forward to perform the ritual: he drew back the bolts of the great doors and entered the sanctuary, then opened the wooden double doors of the box-shrine, lifted out the statue, and placed it on an altar in front of the box-shrine. The Egyptians believed that the god's divine spirit entered into the statue so that the deity could receive the ritual, but they did not think that the god was confined to this image; he could also be present in other forms and dimensions. The priest removed the clothing (a series of differently coloured cloths) and cosmetics which the god had worn the previous day. He then fumigated the statue with incense, and presented it with natron, a substance which had multiple uses, such as purifying the mouth, laundering clothes and dehydrating the body during mummification procedures.

Next, the priest draped the statue in clean cloths, applied fresh cosmetics to the face, presented the god with jewellery and insignia, and finally offered the morning meal. There were special rooms within the temple where the god's apparel and the sacred utensils used in the rituals were stored; butchering and other activities associated with preparation of the god's food were carried out either in an external courtyard or, more rarely, in a special area of the temple.

Once the meal had been presented, the priest withdrew backwards from the sanctuary, carrying the offerings with him. The same ritual was repeated at midday and in the evening, when the statue was returned to the box-shrine. After the completion of each ritual sequence, the food offerings were either divided up amongst the priests as payment, or sometimes they were presented to the statues of private individuals who had 'bought' this service by making a donation to the temple.

As a priest, Nakht knew that the 'Daily Temple Ritual' was a perpetual reaffirmation of the god's daily rebirth. He was also aware that a secondary daily ceremony, known as the 'Ritual of the Royal Ancestors' and performed at the conclusion of the 'Daily Temple Ritual', was essential to ensure that his king's reign and rulership were universally accepted. There was provision for this ritual in the temples which Egyptologists refer to today either as 'mortuary temples' or 'royal cult complexes'.

This ceremony honoured all the dead, deified kings regarded as legitimate rulers of the country since c.3100 BCE, and sought the gods' approval and acceptance of the living king – essential for the success of his reign. When a king died, it was expected that he would join his ancestors, and so this ritual was designed to confer benefits (in the form of an eternal food supply) both on the ancestors and on the king in his future, anticipated form. During this ceremony, food offerings were removed from the god's altar at the conclusion of the 'Daily Temple Ritual', and then taken to another area of the temple where they were presented to the Royal Ancestors, whose names were usually inscribed in a 'King List' on one of the walls. When these rites were concluded, the food was taken outside the temple and apportioned amongst the priests.

In addition to his daily routine, which involved the performance of minor liturgical tasks relating to the god's ritual, Nakht participated in the divine festivals. These were the other great events of a deity's life but, unlike the daily rituals, the festivals differed from one another: they celebrated major events in each god's mythology, and occurred at different times throughout the year. Some were always held monthly

Columns in the Hypostyle Hall in the Temple of Hathor, Denderah. The capitals represent Hathor as a human-faced, cow-eared deity; the scenes and inscriptions on the ceiling refer to astronomical subjects. Graeco-Roman Period.

or annually, but the dates for others were irregular, determined by local astronomical sightings or calendars.

A festival was usually celebrated at a single temple, but some involved two or more temples. For example, Nakht took part every year in the Festival of Opet at Thebes, which celebrated the divine marriage of Amun and Mut, and the unification of Amun with his son, the king. An important part of this festival was the priestly procession, which transported Amun's statue from his temple at Karnak to the neighbouring Temple of Luxor where his consort, Mut, resided. Nakht also witnessed other festivals, including the New Year celebration, held during the first month of the inundation season, which renewed the consecration of the temple; and also the Festival of Sokar, which took place on the West Bank at Thebes. He had made several pilgrimages to the sacred city of Abydos, to participate in the annual Festival of Khoiakh, which re-enacted sacred events in the life, death and rebirth of the god Osiris.

81

Festivals were times of religious fervour, great pleasure and merriment, and people travelled from many regions to be present at such events. In the capital city, these celebrations were usually led by the king, but elsewhere, the High-priest acted as his delegate. Every festival involved secret, important rites enacted inside the temple, but usually there was also a procession in which the god's statue (a portable version of the cult-statue placed in the temple sanctuary) was carried around outside.

The god's procession included priests, dancers and musicians who danced, burnt incense, and chanted sacred songs as they passed through the town. There was usually little opportunity for ordinary people to have any direct contact with State deities or local gods and their temples, but the processions provided a rare opportunity for them to see the deity from a distance, or even to approach the statue, hidden inside its portable shrine, and ask for divine advice. As a member of the minor clergy at Thebes, Nakht often helped to carry the heavy barque containing the god's shrine and statue; he and his fellow-priests were glad to rest at various stations inside and outside the temple, where they performed special rites.

Personal Religion

There is not a great deal of evidence relating to personal, everyday religious worship before the New Kingdom; however, it is clear that some methods of approaching the gods existed alongside the temples and the cult of the dead.[6]

Whereas official cults (dedicated to State and local gods) were mostly concerned with maintaining the stability of the universe and the status of the gods and king, people engaged in personal religious practices to help themselves deal with feelings of loss, suffering and personal doubts. These practices sometimes overlapped with the 'official' religion or were embedded in the legal and medical systems; they were employed by rich and poor alike, and included oracles and magic, sending letters to the dead, using dreams for divination, and worshipping ancestors and special deities. More evidence of personal religious belief and practice has survived from the New Kingdom than any other period, possibly because increased literacy in the population allowed people to record their thoughts and customs.

An unusual stone offering-stand, probably used to support a dish holding bread and other food presented to the gods in a regular household ritual. The design incorporates two primitive figures of men standing back to back. From a house at Kahun. Dynasty 12. Manchester Museum.

83

Members of Khary's family experienced the usual milestones of existence: childbirth, the onset of puberty, the celebration of marriage, and the sorrow of death. Most of these important stages were marked and celebrated with rituals. Childbirth, regarded as a particularly dangerous time, was the focus of many superstitions and rites; for example, a woman's safe delivery was celebrated with a ceremony fourteen days after birth. The onset of puberty was signified in several ways: youngsters began to wear clothes in public; many boys underwent circumcision (although this was not universal); and the head was now completely shaved, replacing the childhood hairstyle distinguished by a shaven head and a single plait of hair known as the 'Sidelock of Youth'. There is no evidence that marriage, regarded as a secular, legal contract, was ever celebrated with a religious ceremony. However, there is extensive documentation of the many rituals associated with death and burial, considered to be most important rites of passage.

Men and women, who constantly faced dangers associated with illness, sudden or premature death, and natural disasters, needed personal faith to sustain themselves in these times of hardship and tragedy. On such occasions, Khary and his family turned to familiar deities and prayed to special gods who could provide personal comfort. These included Bes, an ugly dwarf-god who protected the young and weak; as a god of love and marriage, he was present at birth and the circumcision ceremony. He employed music, singing and dancing to drive away evil forces, and statuettes often show him holding a drum or other musical instrument.

His consort, Tauert, took the form of an upstanding, pregnant hippopotamus; she was worshipped as a goddess of childbirth and fecundity, and assisted all women to deliver their children. These universally popular deities received worship at Kahun and Deir el-Medina.[7] In houses at these sites, archaeologists also found stone offering-stands that were used to present food to the gods, as well as ancestral busts which probably represented deceased family members. Regarded as the blessed dead, the ancestors were feared and worshipped because they could influence the well-being of the living, and in order to request favours and gain their protection against evil, family members would pray and place offerings for them on small domestic altars.

Amulet of the god Bes with his characteristic feather head-dress, shown playing a drum. He was believed to use music, singing and dancing to drive away evil forces. Unprovenanced. Late Period. Manchester Museum.

Khary and his family used oracles for a variety of reasons, sometimes approaching them as a form of divination or seeking a decision on a legal matter. Occasionally, the family would visit the outer court of the temple to consult an oracle, but they also had access to them elsewhere; for example, the oracle was frequently consulted during festivals. It was customary for the petitioner to stand in front of the god's statue, but he/she could not directly approach the deity. Sometimes, the questions (which could be presented either verbally or in writing) were addressed to the priests who held the god's statue. By moving the deity from side to side or up and down, they could provide an 'answer' to the question posed by the petitioner. Sometimes an intermediary could act for the petitioner, interrupting the god's procession and presenting the deity with two petitions and two responses. The god was then requested to indicate, through the intermediary, which answer he had selected. This provided one way of seeking divine intervention in human lives, and obtaining answers about the future, but the oracle had its limitations, and other methods of divination were also employed.

Seers or 'wise women' were consulted about the future. Also, help and advice was sometimes sought from the gods or the dead through the medium of dreams. Some dreams were believed to be prophetic, providing advance warning of good or evil events, and in these instances special books would be consulted to interpret key signs in the dream. On other occasions, a person could choose to spend the night in a special building attached to a temple renowned as a centre of dream incubation. Here, a dream state was induced (probably by means of hypnosis), so that the petitioner could try to communicate with the gods or deceased relatives in the hope of gaining insight into the future.

Living people could also contact the dead by writing a letter to a deceased person. Sometimes, people who had suffered injustice would do this, asking the dead person to intercede on their behalf. Although relatively few letters have survived, many people may have spoken directly to the dead to ask for their help. The letters were placed near the offering-table in the tomb-chapel so that the deceased's spirit would find them when it came to receive the regular food offerings. The letters varied greatly in their subject matter: some asked for help and support against living or dead enemies, particularly in relation to family disputes; others requested legal assistance to face the divine tribunal on the Day of Judgement; and some pleas were made for special benefits and blessings.

Magic and magicians were an important aspect of State and popular religion, even featuring significantly in the legal and medical systems. Whereas Nakht participated in the State magic performed in the temples, members of his family had regular access to funerary and everyday magic. The Egyptians believed that magic had made creation possible; it allowed the universe to be maintained, and its continued use ultimately ensured that the struggle waged by the gods and the king against evil was always successful.[8]

There was an established belief that the divine creative word and magical energy could turn concepts into reality, and that magic was available to ordinary people as a means of self-defence. Archaeological or literary evidence about practitioners of magic is scanty, but two discoveries dating from the Middle Kingdom give some idea of how magic worked on this level. In the precinct of the Temple of Ramesses II (the Ramesseum) at Thebes, the archaeologist W.M.F. Petrie discovered a tomb which belonged to a lector-priest; these clerics were the principal magical practitioners of ancient Egypt. The burial contained not only the priest's papyri, inscribed with magical and medical texts, but also his collection of magical objects, including

Wooden figurine of a woman wearing a lion-mask and holding a bronze serpent in each hand; it probably represents a female magician impersonating the goddess Beset during the performance of magical rites. Found with a collection of magical and medical texts and magical objects in the tomb of a lector-priest in the Ramesseum precinct, Thebes. Dynasty 12. Manchester Museum.

fertility figurines, a snake-wand, ivory castanets inscribed with fearsome animals, and a wooden statuette of a female magician wearing a lion-mask and holding a bronze serpent in each hand. The magician probably used these items during the course of his rites to invoke various protective spirits.

Petrie discovered another group of magical implements in a house at Kahun. These included a pair of ivory clappers, a canvas face-mask which represented the goddess Beset (Bes' consort), and a figurine of a magician or dancer (probably imitating Beset), wearing a mask and false tail. These items may have belonged to a female magician who perhaps wore the mask to impersonate Beset when she performed rites on behalf of petitioners who consulted her.

Nakht's wife, Merenmut, frequently visited this kind of local practitioner, to seek protection in childbirth and guard her family against a wide range of diseases and ailments. Like everyone else, they

A magician's canvas mask found with a pair of ivory clappers and a wooden figurine. It probably represents Beset, consort of the god Bes, and may have been worn by a female magician to perform magical rites. Holes are made at the eyes and nostrils to allow the wearer to see and breathe, and some of the surface stucco was knocked off during use: the mask has been painted black to cover up this damage. From a house at Kahun. Dynasty 12. Manchester Museum.

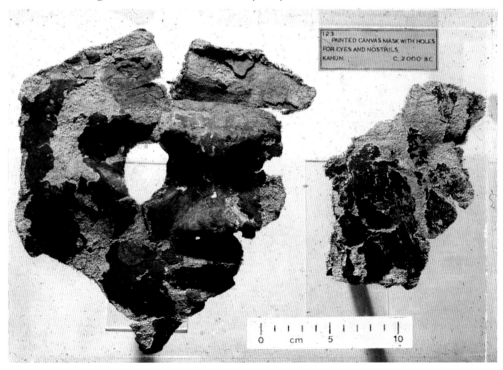

wore amulets to protect themselves against a variety of dangers. Examples of this type of sacred jewellery date back to the fourth millennium BCE, and were worn by both the living and the dead. It was believed that they conferred benefits on the wearer: some amulets, such as the *ankh*-sign, *djed*-column, or 'Sacred Eye of Horus', were regarded as universally beneficial, while others were potent and significant only for the individual owner.

A wide range of amulets was available: some were designed to protect the wearer against a variety of dangers – mysterious hostile forces, terrifying animals, disease, famine, floods and accidents – while others were directed towards a particular weakness in the body, with the aim of bringing about a cure. These amulets often took the shape of a diseased limb: they could heal the condition either by directing magical power towards the limb, or by ensuring that the disease was 'transferred' into the amulet-double, thus enabling the limb to be saved. Amulets often took the shape of, or incorporated in their design, popular magical symbols which were believed to bring health and good luck to the wearer; particular gem-stones also featured in this jewellery because they were thought to possess hidden magical powers.

Chapter 3

Social Customs

Ancient Towns

Much of our knowledge about ancient Egypt is derived from funerary and religious monuments and artifacts, but the towns also provide important evidence about everyday activities.[1] However, for various reasons they are less well preserved than the tombs and temples. Some archaeologists have even claimed that true urban development never existed in Egypt, arguing that because political stability and natural barriers protected the country against most external threats, the Egyptians did not need a network of fortified towns throughout the country. They claim that towns only developed to accommodate the need for a royal capital or centre of district administration, or to facilitate activity along trade routes. It is true that most of the country's resources were directed towards the construction of tombs and temples, perhaps leaving fewer opportunities to promote advanced urbanisation. However, archaeological evidence of urban development is probably relatively scanty not because there was a conscious pattern of non-urbanism, but because towns were built of perishable materials and have consequently disappeared. Indeed, some scholars hold the view that Egypt had an ordinary pattern of town development.

Each dynasty chose the site of its own royal capital or centre of government; there were other royal residences, scattered around the country, which were visited periodically by the reigning monarch. Each *nome* had its own principal urban centre, which included the offices and houses of the administrators and officials. The first capital was established at Memphis in Dynasty 1, but by the Old Kingdom, there were other major towns in Upper Egypt, including Edfu, Abydos and Thebes. Some towns were specially built to house the families of the royal workmen engaged in constructing, decorating and maintaining the king's funerary complex.

All these urban centres accommodated officials, craftsmen, traders, doctors, lawyers, teachers, and some agricultural workers who grew the food for the town's population. There seem to have been two main types of urban development. Some towns evolved from the predynastic villages in a natural and unplanned way, and became important because of their political, religious or commercial significance. Others were planned for specific reasons, such as the construction of a royal tomb; they were often abandoned at the end of the project, and because they were not naturally sited for continued occupation, no effort was made to level them down for resettlement. These towns provide the archaeologist with an excellent opportunity to study the living conditions which prevailed at the time of occupation.

Capitals such as Memphis and Thebes were levelled and resettled many times over thousands of years, but most evidence relating to the various stages of their development is lost or difficult to recover and interpret. Towards the end of Dynasty 18, King Amenhotep IV (Akhenaten) moved his capital from Thebes to a virgin site (known today as Tell el-Amarna or Amarna) where he built a new city as the cult-centre of his patron deity; here, the Aten could be worshipped without the conventions imposed by traditional beliefs. When this brief period of solar monotheism failed, the Court returned to Thebes and Akhenaten's city was abandoned. Today, it provides archaeologists with an excellent opportunity to excavate a site which has only one level of occupation.

Evidence from the royal *necropolis* workmen's towns enables Egyptologists to study the lives of the residents. To date, examples of such habitations have been found at Giza, Kahun, Tell el-Amarna and Deir el-Medina,[2] spanning a period from the Old Kingdom to the end of the New Kingdom. These sites have been extensively excavated and, although constructed at different times, they clearly shared a common function and exhibit many of the same physical and environmental characteristics. Similar sites which must have existed to support the State's extensive building programmes may still await discovery and excavation.

Remains of the town of Deir el-Medina, Thebes, which once housed the families of workmen engaged in building and decorating royal tombs in the Valley of the Kings. The town, originally enclosed inside a thick mudbrick wall, was occupied from Dynasty 18 to Dynasty 20. The houses, arranged in terraces, were small and dark.

These towns, all built to a predetermined plan, were orientated and arranged to conform to certain requirements. Each was situated on the desert edge, close to the worksite but isolated from other habitations. Security appears to have been the major consideration, even more important than proximity to a good water supply; it was essential that the workforce, with its unique knowledge of the location and layout of the royal tomb, should be guarded and isolated at all times.

Although each town was originally enclosed by a thick brick wall, there is evidence at Tell el-Amarna and Deir el-Medina that some houses were eventually built in a random manner outside the wall, to accommodate an overflow population. Homes for the workers were provided in regular rows of terraced houses, while the officials and supervisory personnel had more spacious accommodation. The number of dwellings, the pattern of their development, and their length of occupation varied from one site to another. In each case, archaeologists have discovered different types of evidence. For example, large quantities of written material have been excavated at Deir el-Medina, while many articles of everyday use, apparently abandoned by their owners, have been discovered at Kahun.

Kahun was built to house the workforce and officials engaged in the construction of the pyramid of King Senusret II at Lahun in *c.*1895 BCE. When the site was excavated by Petrie in 1888–90 CE, it provided the first definitive evidence of town-planning in Egypt, although earlier examples have since been found. This excavation was largely funded by a Manchester textile merchant, Jesse Haworth, and according to his wishes, many items from the site were eventually allocated to the Manchester Museum at the University of Manchester

Portrait of Dr Jesse Haworth, patron of Egyptology at the University of Manchester. In return for his continuing support for William Flinders Petrie's excavations in Egypt, the Manchester Museum received artifacts from sites throughout Egypt. As recognition of this generous patronage, and of his position as one of the first patrons of scientific excavation in Egypt, the University conferred on him the honorary degree of Doctor of Laws in 1913. Manchester Museum.

(UK). The other substantial part of the collection was retained by Petrie, and is now housed in the Petrie Museum at University College London.

Altogether, Petrie cleared over 2,000 chambers which, according to his estimate, represented over three-quarters of all the buildings in the town. In most of the houses he found articles of everyday use – cooking utensils, toys, games, cosmetics, jewellery, implements associated with agricultural and various trades and crafts, and objects associated with personal worship. In addition, he uncovered the town's archives of literary, medical and legal documents, which provide insight into the community's social organization and the working conditions of the royal *necropolis* craftsmen. Generally, evidence from Kahun has enabled Egyptologists to study and reconstruct the lifestyle of this community during Dynasty 12, and to observe important technological changes emerging at that period.

At the same time he was excavating Kahun, Petrie also worked (1888–90 CE) at another site known today as Gurob, or Medinet Gurob. In antiquity, this was the location of the town of Mi-wer and its associated cemeteries. Like Kahun, Gurob is situated in the Fayoum, a fertile area south-west of modern Cairo, located some 25 miles west of the Nile on the edge of the desert. The town was probably established as a major centre during the reign of Tuthmosis III (Dynasty 18), and appears to have been continuously occupied until the reign of Merneptah (Dynasty 19).

However, unlike the towns of the *necropolis* workmen, Gurob was not purpose-built to any prearranged plan, but grew up because the environment of the Fayoum offered excellent opportunities for leisure activities such as fishing and fowling. Essentially, Gurob functioned as a royal residence town with a palace which accommodated the king as he travelled around the country. The royal residence had its own staff and administration, which continued to function even when the king was not there, and the town also housed artisans, servants and workmen who maintained the buildings and cultivated the surrounding land to feed the townspeople. The town had different organizational and security needs from the royal *necropolis* workmen's towns, but the archaeological evidence suggests that the inhabitants enjoyed a similar lifestyle.

Again, many articles of daily use were left behind in the houses. It is unclear why Kahun and Gurob were apparently abandoned, although possible reasons include natural disasters, famine, harassment by foreigners, or disease. Evidence from Gurob indicates that weaving was a major industry there and that the women of this subsidiary Royal Court were responsible for training textile workers who performed their tasks either at home or in the workshops. The woven garments and cloth were stored in the royal residence and some were eventually sent to the king for use elsewhere.

Because Jesse Haworth sponsored excavations at Gurob as well as Kahun, artifacts discovered there were divided between Manchester and London. Kahun was functioning earlier than Gurob, but the articles from both sites are very similar. Since Gurob flourished during the period when Khary's imaginary family was living at Thebes, we shall use some examples from this site to demonstrate and describe the various activities on Khary's estate.

Houses

Relatively few examples of houses have survived in Egypt; this is because most were continuously levelled and rebuilt, and constructed of perishable building materials. However, where only one main level of occupation has survived (for example, Tell el-Amarna and the *necropolis* workmen's residences), archaeologists have the opportunity to examine the architecture and construction of the houses. In addition, tomb wall-scenes and tomb-models of houses provide further detailed information.[3]

There were two main types of housing: townhouses and rural dwellings. The townhouse was generally built in long-established cities and *necropolis* workmen's towns where space was at a premium, while country villas for wealthier people were located in areas where there was sufficient land to accommodate a garden. Generally, all houses were constructed to suit the climate, using mudbrick, which is ideal for hot temperatures where there is little rainfall. For this reason, the same material is still used for many village houses in Egypt today. Wealthier homes and even small detached houses were designed so that they would remain cool throughout the summer. They often incorporated a series of passages and a central courtyard from which

95

Pottery soul-houses. These models, which reflect contemporary domestic architecture, were placed in tombs to act as offering-trays for the funerary cult; food was placed on the courtyard area in front of the house. Each of these examples has two storeys, a flat roof, and a shady colonnade. From Rifeh. Dynasty 11. Manchester Museum.

the rooms could be reached, and some included wooden wind-sails fixed over the terrace on the upper storey, positioned to face the prevalent and cooling breezes of the north-west wind, so that this 'air-conditioning' could be conducted to the interior of the house.

It was also essential to exclude the glare of the sunlight, and most houses were quite dark. Windows consisted of small apertures, set high in the walls of the main rooms. These were unglazed, but often had bars, and the light could be totally excluded by closing painted wooden shutters which were fixed and revolved on pins. In the workmen's homes at Deir el-Medina, small holes let into the roof provided some extra light, and lamps and wicks were used everywhere to supply additional illumination. Houses had wooden doors, set into wooden frames; in the wealthier establishments, these were sometimes painted to imitate rare or foreign woods. The excavations at Tell el-Amarna and Kahun give a good indication of the type of villa or house that wealthier people owned. They usually consisted of reception areas, women's quarters, washing and bathing rooms, a kitchen, cellars and granaries. At Tell el-Amarna, some of the residences also included chapels or had kiosks in the gardens which were probably open to the sky but incorporated a partially roofed platform where the family could worship the Aten and the royal family.

Khary's villa was typical of residences owned by wealthy families at Thebes, and was built on two levels plus a basement for storage. On entering the house at ground-floor level, the visitor would be received in a columned reception hall. Here, the master of the house usually entertained his guests, although sometimes he invited specially favoured friends to sit with him on the north-facing terrace on the first floor at the front of the house, where they could enjoy the cooling breezes. Other private areas of the house – the bedrooms, women's quarters, and bathrooms – were located on the same floor. The service areas – which included the silos, stables, kennels, storerooms, servants' quarters and kitchens – were located outside the main house.

At Kahun, the families of officials who administered the pyramid and its associated temple were accommodated in substantial houses. Although there was no space for extensive gardens, such dwellings may have had courtyard gardens, planted with shrubs and flowers. These houses appear to have had a dual function as office and residence, and visitors used different entrances depending on the nature of their business. In the centre of the building, there was a columned hall, and a partly colonnaded open-air reception chamber from which the private family rooms could be accessed. The master's own colonnaded court, situated in this secluded area, incorporated a sunken tank which was used for ablutions and for some aspects of the family's personal religious cults. The women's quarters were reached through a series of rooms and a passageway leading from the main entrance.

In country villas, the courtyard was usually at the centre of the building, providing a private space where the family could relax, away from the heat and dust. Khary's villa incorporated the usual features of a comfortable home: large cool rooms surrounded by colonnades, and a roof supported by fluted or ribbed wooden columns with capitals decorated with plain *abaci* or the palm-leaf motif. The mudbrick walls were stuccoed and painted with designs that incorporated bright colours, and decorative details in the rooms included features which imitated some aspects of temple architecture. The name of the king whom Khary served – Tuthmosis III – was inscribed over the entrance of the house, to bring the family good fortune.

Elsewhere on the estate, Khary's Steward, Pa-neb, lived in a pleasant detached house. The workers and their families were accommodated in simple mudbrick tenements which each had a flat roof made of palm branches laid across a beam taken from a split date tree, covered with mats coated with mud. There was only one door, although some light managed to penetrate through a few small windows that could be closed by using the attached wooden shutters. This single-roomed accommodation provided a storage space for the family's possessions, some degree of privacy, and shelter from the sun. It was very cramped, but fortunately the estate-workers were out-of-doors until sundown, their wives cooked the meals in an open courtyard at the back of the house, and since the weather was warm for most of the year, the family usually slept on the rooftop.

Since Khary was a Court official, he also owned a townhouse in Thebes so that he could readily attend to his duties at the palace. For their townhouses, wealthy owners could choose from a number of designs: some had rooms arranged on three sides of an open court which was often planted with trees, while in others, two rows of rooms flanked a long passageway that led from the street. Khary's house was different again: the rooms were grouped around a central, paved court which contained a fountain and a few trees.

There were three entrances to this house, to admit different types of visitors. A double row of columns, interspersed with statues, supported the porch and formed an impressive main entrance. On either side of this entrance, there was a smaller door that was used by his servants. The house followed the usual pattern for such dwellings, incorporating a court and several corridors which gave access to the rooms. Once inside the main door, Khary's visitors found themselves in this open court, one part of which was closed off to form a columned room where they were entertained. This room was decorated with banners, and the upper part was open to the sky, although an awning was often hung up over this area to protect the occupants from the sun's glare. When he came to meet his guests, Khary used another door on the other side of the court which led from the private apartments.

The rooms in Khary's house were arranged on two levels: the ground floor accommodated the reception area, stores, offices, and a porter's room, while the sleeping quarters were situated on the upper level where there was also a terrace. Covered by an awning, stretched across a light roof supported by columns, the terrace was a cool and pleasant area where the family often sat during the day. Sometimes, in the hot weather, Khary preferred to sleep out on the terrace, and from this vantage point, he could look out over Thebes. Although most houses were single-storey dwellings with just a basement and accommodation at ground level, some 'high-rise' dwellings were also visible. New Kingdom representations of houses show that only a few had three or four storeys, but centuries later, the Classical writer Diodorus Siculus reported that some Theban homes were built with four or even five storeys.

Less wealthy people lived in small houses which formed a continuous terrace. These homes often shared a courtyard, and the rooms opened off a narrow passageway, or directly from the street. They usually only had a basement and ground floor, which incorporated a court and three or four storerooms, and a flight of steps led from the court to a single chamber above. However, in 'high-rise' houses with two or three storeys, where the height of the building exceeded the base area, living conditions were even more cramped because there was not even a court for the occupants' use.

Thebes and other major cities were undoubtedly overcrowded and would have presented a somewhat disorganized and haphazard appearance. However, in the royal workmen's towns, houses were built according to precise official instructions and displayed more uniform characteristics. Arranged in terraced rows, each dwelling, depending on its location, accommodated between four and seven rooms. At Kahun, each worker's mudbrick house had one storey with a flat roof to which a small staircase provided access. The rooms were grouped together and a single door led on to the street. Most roofs were constructed of beams of wood lashed with bundles of reeds or straw, coated on the inner and outer surfaces with mud plaster. The doorways were semi-circular arches of brick, interspersed with limestone chips,

Builders' tools including a wooden mudbrick mould (top) into which alluvial mud mixed with water would have been packed; a wooden mallet (left); and a plasterer's float (front), very similar to modern examples, with some plaster still remaining on the handle. From Kahun. Dynasty 12. Manchester Museum.

while doors, thresholds and door bolts were carved from wood. The roofs of the larger rooms were supported by octagonal wooden columns set in stone bases.

Considerable quantities of wood had to be imported into Egypt; architectural detailing with different types of foreign wood became something of a status symbol, and sometimes poorer people painted native woods such as sycamore to imitate the rarer imported varieties. At Kahun and elsewhere, the scarcity of native timber prompted innovations in construction methods: for example, as a partial substitute for wood, some of the houses were roofed with a barrel vault of brickwork. In poor houses, the floors consisted of beams of date palms, arranged with planks or transverse layers of palm branches and covered with mud-coated mats, whereas in better houses, the floors were made of stone or a composition of lime and other materials.

100

Houses in the workmen's town at Tell el-Amarna had a uniform plan: each consisted of an outer hall, living room, bedroom and a kitchen that gave access to the roof. Two kinds of brick were used in the construction of these houses, leading archaeologists to speculate that the State may have supplied proper mudbricks and an architect to build the enclosure wall and the foundation courses of some of the houses, while the families provided their own additional, inferior bricks and rough stones to complete the buildings. The houses at Deir el-Medina had one storey and a flat roof, although some also incorporated a basement. Each dwelling opened directly off the street, and had four rooms: the entrance hall which incorporated an altar and was probably used for household worship; a main living room; two other rooms probably intended for storage or sleeping space; and a walled kitchen, open to the sky, that contained storage bins, a brick or pottery oven, an open hearth, and an area for grinding grain. A staircase led from one of the rooms to a flat roof, and cellars in the basement provided further storage space.

Palaces

In the course of his official duties as Head of the Royal Household, Khary regularly attended the king's palace at Thebes. Few palaces have survived because, like the houses, they were built of mudbrick; also, most rulers chose to build themselves new residences and so, unlike the temples or tombs, palaces were not maintained over the generations. However, remains of palaces have been uncovered at Abydos, Qantir, Memphis, Malkata, Thebes and Tell el-Amarna, and these indicate that most rulers had a main official residence at the capital, which incorporated private apartments as well as central administration offices.[4] Kings also had several palaces situated in different parts of the country (for example, Gurob), which they visited intermittently.

The palace was called the *per-aa* or 'Great House'. Although he was familiar with his royal master's residence, Khary never ceased to be impressed when he had an audience with the king. The palace was very large, and incorporated two main sections: there were the state rooms which included corridors, courts and porticoes; and the private apartments of the royal family. Above the Antechamber of the state apartments was a wide balcony known as the 'Window of Appearances', decorated with gold, lapis lazuli and malachite; here, on great State occasions, the king and his family presented themselves to the people who gathered in the street below. Sometimes, the king inspected the tribute and prisoners-of-war captured during his successful military campaigns. On other occasions, he handed out honours and collars to courtiers who had excelled in the performance of their duties. Khary had been honoured in this way on more than one occasion, and greatly valued the golden collars he had received as a mark of the king's personal favour and recognition.

Khary also enjoyed privileged access to the King's Room; situated near the Broad Hall, this was where the king held his council meetings and met the chief government officials. Only princes, close friends, and Khary, as Head of the Royal Household, were entertained by Tuthmosis III in the King's Room, and Khary planned to record in his tomb inscriptions that he had often enjoyed the honour of entering the god-king's presence. Although he was a close personal friend of the king and a senior royal servant, Khary was expected to bow and raise his hands in acclamation every time he entered the ruler's presence. However, earlier standards of protocol had now been relaxed, and anyone approaching the king was no longer required to kiss the ground. Nevertheless, Khary addressed his master formally, using the prescribed formula, before they began to discuss palace business.

All the state rooms, with their slender columns, colourful and attractive wall decorations and fine furnishings, were impressive settings for conducting official business, but one area remained the private domain of the king and his family. This was the so-called women's area, sometimes referred to as the 'harem'. The ancient Egyptian 'harem' had none of the connotations or restrictions associated with the use of this term in later times: it was simply a secluded area in palaces and wealthy homes where women pursued their own activities and supervised the family's young children.

Decoration and Furnishings
The Egyptians loved their homes, and decorated and furnished them with care. The interior wall surfaces, floors and ceilings in palaces at Tell el-Amarna and Thebes displayed painted scenes of plants, birds

and animals, while later royal residences were decorated with faience tiles and rosettes inlaid in friezes and borders. The ceilings of wealthy homes were stuccoed, moulded and richly painted, and their rooms incorporated slender, elongated columns which were either free-standing to support the roof, or were painted on to the walls as decorative features.

Interior and exterior walls were painted. At Deir el-Medina, the most affluent occupants plastered and whitewashed the outside of their houses, and painted their doorways red. Interior walls were sometimes painted with a large panel of one colour, often red or yellow; other decoration included a series of coloured horizontal borders, or wall-scenes surrounded by ornamental borders. The subject matter of these scenes was derived from everyday life, and included aspects of the natural world, buildings and domestic goods. One scene on the interior wall of a house at Kahun showed a building with columns, while another depicted a large house with the upper part cut away to reveal a servant attending to the master of the house. Similar murals at Deir el-Medina depict various domestic items with which these homes were once furnished: stools, tables, headrests, chests, boxes, baskets and jars.

Tomb wall-scenes and furniture from the tombs enable us to visualize the home of a great official of this period. Khary's houses were elegantly furnished with beds, couches, chairs, stools, small tables and different-sized chests for storing clothes, jewellery and utensils. Most of the furniture was made of wood, and some pieces were inlaid with ebony and ivory. Although many people sat cross-legged on the ground on mats or carpets, the upper classes always had the choice of using chairs, couches and stools. Reception areas were furnished with single and double chairs, and Khary and his wife often sat together on a double chair to greet their guests. One type of simple wooden seat, used with a cushion, had been popular since earliest times; however, these were uncomfortable because they had a high back and sides, and therefore during the Middle Kingdom the chair back was altered and the sides were lowered.

Other styles introduced in the affluent New Kingdom often incorporated animal feet carved to represent a lion's paws. Most chairs were the same height as those seen in modern Europe; however, some were very low, and Khary's mother-in-law, Nefert, and his older guests found these more comfortable. Folding stools, which had slightly concave seats and folding legs, were also available; they were useful because they could be moved from one area to another. There were also full height stools, often decorated with ebony and ivory, which resembled chairs but did not have backs. Chairs, sometimes used with footstools, had solid or open sides and their seats were covered with leather or interlaced work. To eat their food, Khary's guests did not sit on chairs around a table but used individual round, square or oblong 'occasional' tables made of wood or stone, which each supported a cup or jug, and a flat, woven basket as a plate.

Seats and cushions increased comfort in the home: traditional leather seats – painted with flowers or other motifs, or interlaced with strings or thongs – had always been popular, but Khary's wife preferred to keep up with fashion. Her home was adorned with thick, feathered cushions covered with coloured textiles or material embroidered with threads of gold and silver. Another of the family's treasured possessions was the leopard skin which covered one of their camp-stools; this was carefully taken up when the seat was folded.

When Khary and his family slept at night or rested in the heat of the day, they used couches or beds which had evolved from the designs originally developed for seats. These couches resembled large sofas; they did not have backs, but were nearly the same height as chairs. The lower part of the couch was made of wood, painted with colourful designs, and the feet were carved in the form of a lion's paws. Cushions of leather or richly patterned textiles were piled on top of the couch. The bedrooms were furnished with simple bedsteads consisting of a wooden surround joined together with bronze fittings, and a base woven from palm fibres.

Beds were used in conjunction with headrests made of wood or alabaster, which were placed under the owner's neck so that he could rest without removing his wig. These beds were only slightly more elaborate than those found in poorer homes, which had similar headrests made of pottery or stone. Generally, headrests of wood or stone were considered to be more hygienic than pillows, although an example of a herb pillow has been recovered from one tomb; the aromatic herbs it contained were presumably intended to promote

Basket of woven rushes found in the corner of a house; almost intact, it was used by a workman to transport his tools to the worksite, and contained a copper bowl, chisel and hatchets. From Kahun. Dynasty 12. Manchester Museum.

sleep. Egyptian homes were not furnished with cupboards, but instead clothing, jewellery, cosmetics and domestic items were kept in boxes and baskets, made of wood or woven from plant remains. Khary's wife was able to seal and secure the boxes where she stored her jewellery and cosmetics so that their precious contents remained safe.

The main rooms of Khary's house were decorated with rugs and hangings; although no complete examples have survived from ancient Egypt, there is sufficient pictorial evidence to indicate that thick carpets covered the floors on which people sometimes sat to eat, while brightly coloured woven matting was suspended across the upper parts of the walls. Mats woven from plant fibres were hung over the doors and windows; these acted like roller-blinds since they could be raised on wooden rollers affixed to the top of each door or window. The blinds offered privacy and protection from the sun, while the doors could be left open to let the breezes cool the house interior.

Egyptians were very aware of the need for domestic hygiene, and Khary's family enjoyed the luxury of bathrooms and lavatories. His servants relied on plant recipes (details are preserved in the *Medical Papyri*) to rid the house of vermin and insects, and regularly used ground fleabane mixed with charcoal to dust the rooms and furniture in order to get rid of fleas. Fumigation pellets and burnt scented oils also helped to mask or get rid of household odours.

As darkness fell, the house was lit with candles made of plant fibres dipped in sesame oil, and while a servant served Khary with wine or beer, the household servants began to prepare the evening meal.

An estate of this size and importance employed many servants: amongst others there were cooks, bakers, porters and gardeners; and, like many other New Kingdom establishments, Khary's household included a number of foreign servants from Asia, some of whom held quite important positions.

The management of the household and the grounds of the estate was entrusted to the Head Steward, Pa-neb. He and his staff oversaw arrangements in the house and outside in the granaries, fields, and gardens; he also supervised the livestock, sale of produce, and the estate's accounts. The estate had its own food stores, bakeries and slaughterhouses, and every day, the food required for the family's meals was transferred to the kitchens and cellars, where the servants

Wooden firestick. This implement has four parts: a conical stone drill-cap, wooden firestick, bow-drill, and matrix. By exerting downward pressure on the drill-cap, the user pushed the firestick into a hole in the matrix, and simultaneously pulled the bow-drill to cause sparks to ignite at the matrix. The Egyptians' method of fire-production was unknown until this example was discovered. From Kahun. Dynasty 12. Manchester Museum.

107

stored the wine, oil and grain in large pottery jars, cooled the water in special containers, and cooked the food. Sometimes, Pa-neb had to give orders that one of the workers should be punished for some petty crime or misdemeanour, but generally the estate functioned smoothly and efficiently.

Although their lives were physically demanding, Khary's estate-workers enjoyed a well-ordered existence and, unless there was a famine, they had sufficient food and could afford to pay their taxes. Their houses were small and dark: this provided little incentive to remain indoors, and most of their activities took place out-of-doors. Home furnishings were sparse, and included simple stools, beds, and containers for possessions; sometimes, the wood used for this furniture was painted to imitate their master's household effects.

Gardens

The Egyptians loved plants, flowers and floral decorations. Remnants of plants, wall-scenes in tombs, and tomb-models of villas and houses all suggest that the Egyptians cultivated gardens from at least as early as the Old Kingdom.[5] By representing gardens in their tombs in this way, the owners hoped to be able to enjoy these pleasures in the afterlife.

Khary's townhouse at Thebes was decorated with trees and shrubs, planted in pots and containers and arranged along the façade of the building. However, at his country estate there was space to develop a formal garden. In addition to the 'working areas', which included a park with fish-ponds, an orchard, a kitchen garden, an area for rearing game, yards for hens and geese, and stalls for fattening cattle, gazelles, wild goats and other desert animals, Khary's family also enjoyed a private retreat with shady trees, sweet-smelling flowers, and a cool pond.

The formal garden was enclosed within a mudbrick wall, stuccoed and decorated with panels and grooved lines; this was surmounted by a row of spikes which imitated spearheads. Some of Khary's friends chose to decorate the walls of their own villas differently, with designs that incorporated a cornice or battlements. Khary's name was written in hieroglyphs on the lintel of the single lofty gateway that provided access to the garden. Nearby, there was a lodge which accommodated the porter and some of the gardeners, and also included rooms for receiving visitors.

Inside the impressive portal, the garden was subdivided into 'rooms', arranged on three levels. Each 'room' contained different types of plants and trees including peach, almond, persea, acacia and tamarisk trees, date- and *dom*-palms, and sycamores trained and sculpted into different shapes. Khary was very proud of his exotic trees – imported specimens that he had been able to acquire because of his privileged position at Court. The fig-tree was a particular favourite; it reminded him of a contemporary poem, popular in Court circles, which described how a fig-tree had been brought back from Syria as a love token. Khary especially liked the way in which his garden was planted with formal rows of trees to provide shady walks; full-size trees were interspersed with dwarf trees, and herbs and flowers were grown in earthenware containers.

Khary's family and friends often enjoyed spending time in this secluded garden, sitting in the kiosks and summerhouses which were situated to provide a good view of the trees and plants. The beds and borders were planted with field flowers such as poppies and cornflowers, mixed together with mandrake, iris, lilies, chrysanthemum, and delphinium. The pond – a focal point of the garden – contained fish, two species of blue and white lotuses, and other water plants.

The Egyptians showed initiative and creativity in landscaping and designing their gardens, but all their efforts required a plentiful supply of water, and constant, year-round watering. This level of irrigation was more than the annual flood could deliver; however, the inundation always filled a nearby canal, and with additional resources from large wells and tanks on the estate, the gardeners worked continuously to ensure that the gardens did not dry out. Buckets suspended on yokes were used to carry the water to the trees and flowerbeds, which were planted in small hollow squares on level ground, surrounded by a low ridge of earth which helped to retain the water.

Each area beyond the formal garden – the orchard, kitchen garden and vineyard – was surrounded by a wall, and supplied with water brought from its own dedicated reservoir. These large 'lakes' were situated throughout the estate and connected to the river by canals. As well as their primary practical function, the lakes were ornamental and also offered Khary and his friends some good opportunities for recreational activities such as taking out a boat or spearing fish.

Plants grew profusely all year round in these well-cultivated gardens. They provided foliage and flowers to decorate the house, and small bouquets for the guests who attended Khary's parties and banquets, as well as Perenbast's elaborate floral table decorations which the guests always admired. Enthusiasm for horticulture amongst the upper classes reflected the royal family's own interest, and although no tomb-scenes of palace gardens have survived, there is evidence that kings and queens had a personal interest in garden design. Scenes on an ivory casket found in Tutankhamun's tomb show the young king and his wife relaxing in their palace garden; and the *Great Papyrus Harris* records that Ramesses III established garden cities, planting trees and papyrus plants at Thebes and incorporating vineyards and walks shaded by fruit trees in a new city in the Delta. He also presented nearly two million bouquets to the resident god in the Temple of Amun at Karnak, and ordered that incense trees should be brought back from Punt so that they could be incorporated into temple gardens at Thebes.

Earlier, Queen Hatshepsut had sent envoys to acquire incense trees from Punt, which were subsequently planted in the garden attached to her funerary temple at Deir el-Bahri. Hundreds of years before, in *c.*2000 BCE, King Mentuhotep Nebhepetre built his own temple at Deir el-Bahri, where the discovery of tree pits and tree cuttings found in situ confirms that there was once an associated garden. A plan of this garden, sketched by the landscape artist in charge of the work, can still be seen on a floor slab in the temple. In the tomb of another master gardener (the chief florist of the Temple of Amun), one of the wall-scenes shows the nurseries where plants were cultivated for the gardens around the Temple of Karnak. In the same temple, reliefs on the walls of a small chamber depict the plants that Khary's own king, Tuthmosis III, brought back from his military campaigns in Asia Minor and Syria.

The Egyptians believed that the gods, the dead and the living shared a love of flowers, and that they all derived practical and spiritual benefits from plants and herbs. Temple gardens closely resembled household gardens in design and purpose, providing flowers and herbs for offering to divine statues during the daily rituals. These gardens were planted to please the gods, and to emphasize the importance of the religious and magical symbolism of plants and flowers. Some temples also had physic gardens, established to provide the priests with ingredients for their medicines. Flowers and plants were also an important feature of funerals, and on the day of burial, mourning relatives brought bouquets and garlands to the tomb.

Pets

In addition to working animals on the estate, Khary's household included several pets; there were three dogs, a family of cats, and even some tame geese. The Egyptians interacted with animals on a number of levels.[6] For example, although they never 'worshipped' animals as such, many were venerated because they had close associations with various gods and goddesses. Some temples provided accommodation for specific animals which were regarded in the same way as the god's cult-statue and treated as the locus for the god's spirit.

When these sacred temple animals died, they were often mummified and ritually buried in special precincts; the most famous – the Apis bulls – were interred in the Serapeum at Saqqara. Some temple animals were mummified: the body was injected, probably *per anum*, with resin or turpentine, to remove the viscera; natron was then applied to dehydrate the bodily tissues before the animal was wrapped in linen bandages. Additional adornments included gold-leaf masks, artificial eyes, and in the case of crocodiles, gold jewellery.

Other animals were prepared as votive offerings. This custom became particularly popular during the Late and Graeco-Roman Periods, when pilgrims visiting various cult-centres could purchase animals associated with the temple deity and then present them as gifts to the god. Specially bred at the site, these animals were garrotted and mummified to order and then placed in vast catacombs near the temple. Unlike the sacred temple animals, the votive animals had no intrinsic divinity; they were simply regarded as divine offerings. Popular species included baboons and ibises, dedicated to Thoth at Tuna el-Gebel; dogs and jackals, associated with the gods Khentiamentiu and Wepwawet at Abydos; cats sold to pilgrims visiting

111

Large granite sculpture of a baboon representing the god Thoth. The front of the animal's face has been hacked away and the inlaid eyes are missing. From Koptos. Dynasty 19. Manchester Museum.

the Temple of Bastet at Bubastis; and falcons, hawks and ibises, representing various cults, which were buried in vast numbers in the catacombs at Saqqara.

Family pets (known as 'Beloved Companions') played a significant role in everyday life. Tomb-scenes depict some of these animals accompanying their owners to banquets, and taking part in fishing and fowling expeditions. Cats, domesticated geese and monkeys are often shown as members of the close family circle, sitting under their owners' chairs. From the First Intermediate Period onwards, dogs and cats are increasingly depicted in scenes on *stelae* and tomb walls, but even as early as Dynasty 1, there is evidence that dogs were buried in their own coffins and specially made caskets. One dog – the bodyguard of Cheops, builder of the Great Pyramid – had its own tomb at Giza, and a dog's coffin from Dynasty 11 is even inscribed with the *ḥtp-dí-nsw* formula (see below: the food offerings presented on behalf of deceased humans), so that the animal could enjoy an eternal food supply. Although some dogs accompanied their masters on hunting expeditions or acted as bodyguards, others were simply household

Painted wooden coffin in the shape of a cat. Cats were the sacred animal of the goddess Bast whose cult-centre was at Bubastis. Unprovenanced. Late Period. Manchester Museum.

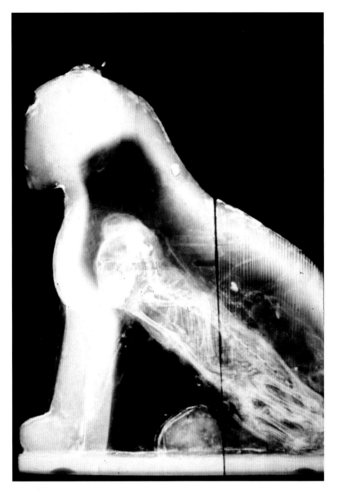

This X-ray reveals the presence of a mummified cat in the above coffin. This animal probably belonged to a wealthy family who could afford to provide an elaborate burial for their beloved pet.

pets. Cats, admired as protectors of the home, were particularly valued for keeping vermin at bay in the houses, and some were buried in special coffins, emphasising the high regard in which they were held.

Diet and Food Preparation
There is ample evidence of the types of food and drink that the Egyptians enjoyed.[7] In order to provide the deceased with an eternal food supply, a ritual menu (the *ḥtp-di-nsw*) was inscribed on the tomb wall; this listed ten different kinds of meat, five types of fowl, sixteen

varieties of bread and cake, four kinds of beer, six different wines, and eleven varieties of fruit. It was customary to supply regular offerings at the tomb to nourish the deceased's spirit, and remnants of these meals have been found in some tombs. This duty, traditionally performed by the deceased's family, was often delegated to a special official (*Ka*-priest). In the event that both the family and official neglected or were no longer able to perform this task, the deceased could obtain nourishment by magically activating the menu inscribed in the tomb.

The staple food of all classes was bread; for the wealthy, it was made from wheat, whereas the poor ate barley bread. Bread-making was an established activity in every household, usually carried out in the domestic kitchen. During the New Kingdom, a wealthy man such as Khary would have employed his own bakers to supply the needs of his family, servants and estate-workers. Scenes on tomb walls show the various stages involved in bread-making. To start with, one or two men crushed the grain by pounding it in large mortars with heavy

Wooden statuettes from the Tomb of Two Brothers: they include two female offering-bearers, and the tomb-owners, inscribed (left to right) with the names of Nekht-Ankh, Nekht-Ankh and Khnum-Nakht. From Rifeh. Dynasty 12. Manchester Museum.

Section of plastered and painted wall-scene from the Tomb of Nefermaat, showing a man scattering seed from a bag suspended around his neck, after the soil had been ploughed and prepared. From Medum. Dynasty 4. Manchester Museum.

pestles; then, this coarse flour was ground to a finer consistency either by means of a large stone or by rubbing the flour between two stones. Women were often employed to carry out this work.

Once the flour was sieved, the dough could be prepared and kneaded. Dough was made of flour and milk, and sometimes other ingredients were added to the mixture. Different types of bread are listed and distinguished in tomb and temple inscriptions. A variety of shapes – oval, round and conical – were produced, and ingredients such as honey, butter, milk and eggs were added to give different flavours. The dough was either kneaded by hand or, for larger quantities produced in the estate bakeries, it was trodden by servants in a large tub. Once it had been moulded into different shapes, the bread was either fried in a large pan or baked in a stove. In earliest times, it was baked on pottery dishes heated in the fire, but by the New Kingdom, conical ovens, about three feet high and open at the top, were in use; these enabled larger quantities to be cooked at one time.

Wealthy households also produced their own pastries. In an area adjacent to the main kitchen, Khary's servants prepared the mixture, sometimes kneading the paste with their feet and mixing it with fruit or other ingredients. The cooks often moulded the cakes into interesting shapes – an ox, crocodile's head, heart or leaf – and sometimes they sprinkled them with cumin and sesame seeds to provide additional flavour before the cakes were carried to the ovens for baking.

The staple diet of the poor was bread, beer and onions, and they tried to eke out their daily food allowance with any extra fruit or vegetables they could grow, or with fish from the canals. Wealthy and poor alike enjoyed beer, but the upper classes had access to different varieties: in addition to the home-brewed type prepared in a dedicated area of the domestic kitchen, they could also obtain imported beer. The first references to beer occur in the early Old Kingdom, but residues have been found even earlier in jars dating to the Predynastic Period. Beer was undoubtedly the Egyptians' favourite drink, enjoyed by the living and also offered to the gods and the dead. Indeed, the Classical writer Diodorus praised Egyptian beer for its smell and sweetness of taste which was 'not much inferior to wine'.

Tomb-scenes and tomb-models illustrate the processes involved in brewing beer, a procedure always closely associated with bread-making. First, well-selected, fine barley was macerated with water, and left out in the air; then, it was moistened again, sieved, and finally ground and kneaded into dough, which was lightly baked to turn it into bread. The bread was then soaked in water (at this stage, dates may have been added to sweeten the mixture), and put in a warm place to aid the process of fermentation. Finally, the mixture was squeezed through a cloth or fine sieve, and the sweet liquid was drained off in a pot. Sometimes, different types of plants were added to flavour the liquid or produce a medicinal treatment for which the beer acted as a vehicle.

Khary served his guests domestically-produced beers and the luxury varieties imported from Asia Minor and Syria. The latter were only available in relatively small quantities, but during the New Kingdom, Egypt's acquisition of an empire and the country's new cosmopolitan political role meant that wealthy Egyptians could obtain 'foreign' food and drink more easily; these were either imported or sometimes produced by immigrant residents. Khary also served his family and guests with a variety of imported and homemade wines. They drank these liquids from elegant vessels, made of alabaster or glazed pottery, which came in a variety of shapes, and included cups without handles, beakers, and shallow bowls. Some examples in glazed pottery (excavated at Gurob and elsewhere) were designed in the shape of lotus flowers or decorated on the inner surface with depictions of fish and lotus flowers. From the New Kingdom onwards, the Egyptians produced a potent drink for special celebrations by mixing various wines together in a large vessel.

While Khary's servants ate simple meals, the estate provided the master and his family with a varied diet. The farm animals produced milk, and the estate's excellent husbandry ensured a ready supply of meat, game, fish and poultry. Fish and poultry were cooked or salted; they were usually served whole on large platters, the feet of the fowl having been removed beforehand. Meat included beef, goat, mutton and pork, as well as gazelle or oryx. For some social and religious groups, pork was forbidden, but the Egyptians certainly kept pigs which were allowed to roam the streets, where they performed a useful duty as disposers of waste food; they were also kept as scavengers in the outer areas of the temples. Together with cats, dogs and fowl, pigs played a significant role in maintaining a primitive sanitation system in towns and villages. Khary kept pigs on his estate and at his Theban townhouse, primarily as a food resource, but also to act as a means of waste disposal.

Animals kept on estates were castrated and force-fed to fatten them for slaughter; this followed a well-established procedure (illustrated in tomb and temple scenes) that was carried out in a courtyard near the estate-house. Beef, the main source of meat, came from oxen; cows were largely kept to produce milk. The ox's legs were tied together, and it was thrown on to the ground; the butcher then cut the animal's throat, often retaining the blood for cooking, and removed the head before he skinned the carcass. Then, the right foreleg or shoulder was cut off, the carcass was butchered, and the joints were carried on wooden trays to the kitchen. The same butchery methods were used for all large animals.

In Khary's large kitchen, the cooks had many attendants who prepared the meat for consumption. The meat had to be used immediately after slaughter, and so even the great households only enjoyed this food on feast days rather than as part of the daily diet. Some joints were boiled, others were roasted. Sometimes, joints of meat, poultry and fish were spit-roasted over live embers (usually

Stone mortar and pestle for grinding food. From Kahun. Dynasty 12. Manchester Museum.

charcoal), but meat was also cooked in large cauldrons which were placed on a stone hearth or propped on two supports or a metal frame over a wood fire. Sometimes, Khary's cooks prepared dishes in large metal pots which combined vegetables, fish, herbs, spices and fragments of meat and poultry.

119

The estate also provided another mainstay of the diet – a rich variety of vegetables and fruit which included figs, persea fruits, dates, pomegranates, grapes, lentils, onions, garlic, leeks, lettuce, radishes, chicory, cucumber and melons. In addition, herbs – coriander, dill and mint – were used to flavour the food. Poor people gathered plants that grew wild along the riverbanks, and animals were trained to collect fruit: tomb-scenes depict tame monkeys assisting gardeners by climbing trees to pick figs.

No Egyptian cookery book has yet been discovered, so we have few details of how the vegetables were prepared or cooked. They were probably eaten raw, roasted, boiled or stewed. Egyptian onions, which have a particularly fine, mild flavour, were doubtless eaten both raw and cooked; lentils – a favourite dish in modern Egypt – would have been equally popular. When archaeologists excavated the contents of

Blue glaze bowls and a vessel decorated with black painted outlines of birds, lotus flowers, other plants and a monkey eating a fruit. Cosmopolitan influences in Egypt at this period are reflected in the foreign 'pilgrim vessel' shape of the flask. From the royal residence town of Gurob. Dynasty 18. Manchester Museum.

120

the tomb of Kha, a senior workman at Deir el-Medina, they found food supplies prepared for the deceased owner's afterlife. Visitors to the Egyptian Museum in Turin, Italy (where the complete tomb-group is now held) can see the variety of food – shredded vegetables, bunches of garlic and onions, bowls of dates, raisins, persea fruits, and spices such as cumin seeds and juniper berries – which even a craftsman could expect to enjoy in the next world.

Family meals were eaten in a well-established order; the courses usually included soup, such as a potage of lentils, followed by a variety of roasted, boiled or salted meat, fish, poultry and vegetables; finally, fruit such as figs, grapes or dates were served fresh or dried, according to season. The servants placed the dishes and bowls on low tables; each table was positioned close to one guest or sometimes to two people who were sharing food dishes. When each course was finished, the servants removed the dishes and brought others. Guests sat on the ground, or on low stools and chairs, and usually ate with their fingers, dipping pieces of bread into the liquids, although when they drank soup or liquids, they often used spoons made of ivory, bone, wood or bronze which had ornamental handles.

Khary's son, the priest Nakht, not only enjoyed the fine fare at his father's home, but he and his family also ate well every day during his term of duty at the Temple of Karnak. At the close of the daily rituals, Nakht and his fellow clergy received a portion of the food and drink that had been offered to the god's statue. The god enjoyed a rich and varied feast, and Nakht particularly liked the bread and cakes sweetened with honey which came to him from the altar. Honey was highly prized for both domestic use and religious rituals; it was collected by temple employees and estate-workers either from wild bees living under stones or in rock clefts, or from hives which consisted of pottery cylinders piled vertically in an arrangement that had the appearance of a 'honeycomb'.

Chapter 4

Artisans, Trades and Crafts

The Artisans

Egypt was able to produce enough food and clothing for its relatively small population, and usually had a surplus of agricultural produce which, together with gold, papyrus, pottery and other manufactured goods, could be traded for imports such as wood, silver, copper and spices. Because the land produced a food excess, it was not necessary for everyone to be engaged in agriculture, horticulture, or animal husbandry, and a section of the population – craftsmen and artisans – was available to manufacture a variety of goods.[1]

The lowest level of workers was usually provided by *corvée*, a system whereby all Egyptians were required to undertake some manual or military duties for the king (although wealthy people opted out by engaging others to work on their behalf). These peasants made bricks and quarried stone to prepare building materials required for the great religious monuments or for domestic architecture. Skilled technicians such as sculptors, goldsmiths, jewellers, carpenters, leather workers, masons, metalsmiths and textile workers held a higher status, and enjoyed a reasonable standard of living. The most important artisans, especially the architects and master goldsmiths, were highly regarded in society, and some of their names and titles have been recorded and preserved. However, most artisans and craftsmen remained anonymous.

Organized in teams, artisans were often employed in State or temple workshops, where several types of production were coordinated by an overseer. This was an early example of mass production, where items were often made by several craftsmen working together, or an object was passed along the line to be crafted, assembled and finished by different men. A master craftsman was probably responsible for designing and planning the more elaborate pieces, giving detailed instructions to the workforce who finished the various sections of an item separately before assembling them. Carpenters and workers on Khary's estate produced textiles, furniture and pottery. The potters were able to turn out two main types of ware in large quantities because the main ingredient – good-quality clay – was readily available. Commonplace pottery, known today as 'coarseware', was made from Nile mud and fashioned into a wide variety of domestic utensils and storage containers, as well as cosmetic vases; recycled potsherds were also employed as a cheap writing material. Artisans used Egyptian faience for finer quality ware; this consisted of a core of body material covered with a vitreous alkaline glaze. Egyptian faience could be produced in a variety of colours and, as well as vases and containers, it was often used for jewellery, *ushabti*-figures and other small funerary items.

Tomb equipment often included large pottery pieces such as canopic jars, soul-houses (model houses with courtyards in front that acted as offering-trays to hold the food presented at the tomb), and even some coffins. Evidence from tomb-scenes and tomb-models illustrates the four main steps involved in producing pottery vessels. First, the potter trampled on the clay to prepare and knead it. Then, straw, chaff and pulverized animal dung were added to reduce its stickiness and produce the required consistency before the clay was shaped into a ball and made into a pot. During the Predynastic Period, and for the production of simple vessels in later times, this process was done by hand, but the potter's wheel was probably introduced in the earliest dynasties; by the New Kingdom, this device consisted of a pivoted turntable that was either moved by foot or turned by an assistant.

The next part of the process was to apply the slip and wash. The most common slip consisted of clay mixed to a fine consistency; this was applied to the pot before it was dried, thus changing the colour of the vessel and forming a smooth surface to which any decoration could be added, often using a metal or wooden instrument. A wash of red ochre was frequently added to red-ware to improve the colour. Then, the pot was placed on a plank to dry and finally put on a tray in the kiln where it was baked to make it hard, durable, and water-resistant. By the New Kingdom, a simple type of pottery kiln had been developed. This resembled a baker's oven; it had separate sections inside and on top where the pots were positioned, while fuel was placed in the furnace area underneath.

Carpenters, joiners, sculptors and shipwrights all needed wood for their work. However, this was a relatively scarce commodity in Egypt, and some timbers had to be imported from Punt, Assyria, Lebanon, and the lands of the Hittites and Mitannians in Western Asia. Tools used for carving, carpentry and joinery first appear in the late Predynastic Period, once Egypt started to import sufficient quantities of copper. Scenes in later tombs and even rare examples of the tools themselves, discovered at sites such as Gurob and Kahun, provide information about working methods.

Many carpenters found employment in the affluent times of the New Kingdom; they produced boxes, chairs, tables, sofas and other fine items to meet a constant demand for high-quality furniture for funerary and domestic use. Their tools included axes, adzes, chisels, saws, awls, borers, knives, rasps, nails, bow drills, mallets and sandstone blocks for polishing the wood. In earliest times, blades were made from copper, but by the New Kingdom bronze was the favourite metal. Leather thongs were used to attach the blades to wooden handles.

Khary observed the carpenters' methods whenever he inspected his estate workshops. They placed each wooden beam upright in a vice which was held between two posts firmly fixed into the ground, and used a handsaw to cut it to the required size. Then, the piece of wood was shaped with an axe and adze, and any small holes that were required were made with a bow drill. The carpenter used a chisel, which he hit with a wooden mallet, to carve the wood or produce a mortise. Once the wood had been carved, it was polished with a piece of fine-grained sandstone. Sometimes, a thin coating of stucco was laid over the prepared wood and colours were applied to the surface. Fine-quality furniture was decorated with veneering (fixing rare wood to more ordinary wood), and ebony or ivory inlays; sometimes coloured stones or pieces of faience or glass were set into the surfaces of wooden boxes.

By the New Kingdom, carpenters had the skills and metal tools required to produce various types of furniture joints. Nails were sometimes used to fix wooden pieces together, or woodwork joints in furniture and coffins were lashed and pegged with hide or leather thongs, linen string, or copper bands. Archaeologists have found examples of dowels, mortise and tenon joints, dovetailing and mitred joints and hinges. Generally, carpenters on wealthy estates would have catered for all everyday needs, as well as producing fine domestic and funerary furniture for the family.

Throughout the New Kingdom, upper class men were attired in linen clothes, which usually consisted of a kilt worn underneath a

Wooden boxes used to contain cosmetics, jewellery and trinkets. One holds powdered haematite and juniper berries for colouring the face, and a bulbous kohl-stick for outlining the eyes. A simple mechanism ensured that the contents could be secured: the lids fitted into the boxes in such a way that the lid could not be raised at one end; at the other end of the lid, there was a knob that could be fastened to a knob on the box by tying them together with string (still visible) which was then sealed. From Kahun. Dynasty 12. Manchester Museum.

wide-sleeved garment that reached to the ankles. The linen was often finely pleated, and sometimes a woollen cloak would be added over these garments. The lower classes wore kilts, aprons or short pants. The kilt was also part of the king's formal dress: additional features included an apron, decorated with rich ornaments made of coloured leather; he wore different crowns, jewellery and insignia which varied according to the role or function he was undertaking. Upper class women such as Khary's relatives dressed in ankle-length linen robes which had tight or full sleeves; sometimes fixed with a coloured girdle at the waist or by straps over the shoulders, they were often worn under a loose, full-sleeved garment of pleated linen which was tied below the breast.

One of Egypt's most important industries, linen production continued from the Predynastic Period through to Roman times.[2] The material was manufactured from the flax plant (*Linum usitatissimum*): various textures were produced for different purposes, and finest-quality linens were highly esteemed at home and abroad. The various stages of production are illustrated in tomb-scenes and tomb-models, and textile tools have been found at Gurob and Kahun. On a typical large estate, an area would be set aside for growing flax for domestic and commercial use. As a first step, the workers gathered the flax by hand, before it was soaked, beaten, and the fibres separated out in preparation for spinning. All yarn was spun by hand, traditionally by women in their own homes; various techniques were employed, including simple hand spinning and three types of spindle spinning.

Weaving was the next stage in the process. Prior to the Hyksos Period, this was undertaken by female home-workers using horizontal, hand-operated ground looms. However, once the vertical loom was introduced into Egypt from Western Asia, production methods changed; most linen was now woven in workshops by employees (usually women) supervised by a male overseer. However, although Khary's estate had its own workshop, some of the textile manufacturing processes were still carried out in the workers' homes. This enabled them to meet their personal needs and contribute to the requirements of Khary's family; also, they could usually provide themselves with a surplus for barter or exchange.

Most linen underwent a simple bleaching process, but some cloth was dyed. This involved the application of mordants to the material

Wooden and stone spindle whorls with remains of original linen thread. It probably took three spinners to keep two weavers and one loom supplied with thread. From Kahun and Gurob. Dynasties 12 and 18. Manchester Museum.

Three wooden heddle-jacks. A pair of heddle-jacks supported the heddle-rod (a key element of the Egyptian loom) which they were roughly shaped to fit. A total of seven heddle-jacks were found at Kahun, providing evidence for the existence of four looms. From Kahun. Dynasty 12. Manchester Museum.

so that it would absorb or take the colour. Then it was dyed with vegetable products such as madder, safflower and indigo. The loom was used to work coloured patterns into some fabrics, and there are surviving examples of tapestry-woven linen and linen embroidered with coloured or gold threads. Cotton was only manufactured in Egypt from the Roman Period onwards; throughout pharaonic times, people undoubtedly had some woollen garments, but because of restrictions on wearing animal products in sacred places, these have never been found in tomb or temple contexts.

The Workshops of Thebes

Many craftsmen and tradesmen manufactured their wares in and around the city of Thebes, and each craft probably had its own quarter in the town. In the search for excellence, it was customary for each craftsman to pursue only one skill, and a son traditionally followed his father's trade. At Kahun, Petrie discovered a caster's shop which contained metal tools and earthenware moulds for casting tools including chisels, knives and a hatchet. From this evidence, he was able to identify the techniques which metalsmiths were employing at that period, and to assess the level of their skills. The metalworking industry which flourished at Thebes during the New Kingdom would have reflected many of the conditions found at Kahun. Generally, metalworking skills were more advanced in some other countries in Western Asia because in Egypt the necessary minerals were not plentiful or easy to obtain, and timber was scarce. Nevertheless, the Egyptians did work the principal metals (copper, gold, iron, lead, silver and tin), and they also produced alloys such as bronze (a mixture of copper and tin) and electrum (a mixture of gold and silver).

Some copper came from Egypt's Eastern Desert and Sinai, but most had to be imported from Western Asia and Cyprus.[3] Silver also came from abroad, but Egypt had considerable quantities of gold which occurred in alluvial sands and gravels, and in veins in quartz rock. The Eastern Desert and Nubia were the most productive sources of gold. The Egyptians had high regard for this metal because of its durability and because its colour reminded them of the sun; it was particularly popular with wealthy clients for their coffins, statuary and jewellery.

The goldsmithing area of Thebes would have had communal workshops where goldsmiths worked alongside lapidaries, bead-makers and stone setters. As a person of considerable importance who had usually been trained both as a scribe and a craftsmen, the master jeweller was responsible for designing items that were then executed by the workforce. First, an official weighed and recorded the gold ingots which were then handed on to the jewellers. The initial stage involved purifying the gold by heating the ingots in a crucible placed over a fire; a workman would use goat-skin bellows to bring the fire to a high temperature, and then he lifted off the crucible with a pair of tongs and poured the molten gold into moulds.

The high-carat gold was soft and easy to work; before it was cold, it was hammered on an anvil to produce the required bars, strips, plates and wires. The goldsmiths were very competent and, although only simple tools were available, they mastered techniques such as

A gold pectoral (chest ornament), set with turquoise, carnelian and lapis lazuli. This fine example of cloisonné work was discovered on a mummy during excavation of a tomb. The archaeologist found the body of an ancient tomb-robber lying across the mummy, in the act of stealing the pectoral. He was killed when the roof partially collapsed. From Riqqeh. Dynasty 12. Manchester Museum.

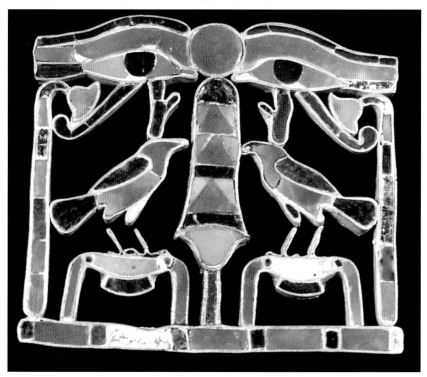

soldering, hammering, beating and moulding, and also employed complicated decorative methods such as chasing, engraving, embossing, inlaying, and cloisonée, repoussé, granular and filigree work. Some pieces of jewellery were set with semi-precious stones (most popular were carnelian, turquoise, or lapis lazuli), or substitutes (calcite and rock crystal backed with coloured cement, faience, or coloured glass). Lapidaries and setters prepared these materials so that they could be incorporated into the jewellery.

Glass manufacture became important in Egypt in Dynasty 18, probably inspired by contact with other centres in the Near East.[4] The earliest glass factory discovered to date was established at Thebes during the reign of Amenhotep III but earlier examples may have existed. Small glass objects such as beads and amulets were produced in earlier times, but decorative perfume jars, other vessels, and inlays for coffins, furniture and jewellery only occur in significant numbers from the middle of Dynasty 18. Blown glass was not introduced into Egypt until the Roman Period, but coloured glass, produced by adding various compounds during the manufacturing process, enjoyed widespread popularity in the New Kingdom.

Shoes and sandals were worn regularly by the middle and upper classes. They were made from interlaced palm-leaves, papyrus stalks, or leather. Tomb-scenes and examples of footwear provide ample evidence of sandal-making and shoe production; at Kahun, the excavators discovered shoemaker's tools as well as a variety of shoes and sandals, and similar workshops would have existed at Thebes.

The leatherworkers' tasks included various procedures. From earliest times, hunters had procured skins and hides from different animals, and some – particularly those from oxen and gazelles – were processed to produce leather. Treatments included drying or curing the skins or hides with smoke, salt or ocherous earths, or softening them with urine, dung or fat; tanning – a process which probably used *Acacia Arabica* pods as a tanning agent – was already known in the Predynastic Period. Tomb-scenes depict the skin being treated in a large jar, either to tan it or in preparation for depilation, cleaning or softening.

Once removed from the jar, the skin was beaten with a stone and stretched over a table or frame so that oil could be worked into it to

Plaited rush sandal, stone grindstone and rubber, fibre brush, wooden grain scoop and wooden door bolt. These objects demonstrate the excellent state of preservation of archaeological material from this site. From Kahun. Dynasty 12. Manchester Museum.

make it supple. Next, the shoemaker placed the prepared leather on a sloping worktable, and with a half-moon knife, cut it into soles and straps before using a piercer to make holes through which thongs could be drawn. Sometimes, the material was dyed (a process in use from earliest times), and red, yellow and green examples have been found. Leather was used not only for shoes and sandals, but was also made into bags, clothes, cushion-covers, ropes, and parts for chariots and tackle, while skins and hides were turned into shield covers, tents and water carriers.

Palm branches and fibres, and the fibres of wild grasses, reeds, rushes and papyrus were gathered and prepared to produce a variety of products, including sandals, shelters, clothing, containers, mats, rope and other domestic items. Some items had more than one use: for example, people carried or stored possessions in baskets but they also functioned as coffins for the poor. Many people on country estates and in towns would have been employed in this industry, which only

131

required knowledge of relatively simple techniques, such as coiling, twining, and wrapping.

Some basketwork is decorated with interwoven dyed and undyed fibres, or ornamental stitching, and mats or matting had various functions: as floor or wall coverings, window hangings, beds, seats, bags or coffins. Some mats were produced by twining, a technique similar to primitive weaving, but others were made on the mat loom – a horizontal frame on which the wefts were threaded by hand.

The production of paper (*papyrus*) was another important industry; papyrus was a convenient, portable writing material which was widely used in Egypt and exported abroad.[5] The early stages of the process involved gathering the plant (*Cyperus papyrus L.*), taking it to the workshops, and stripping and cleaning the stems. These procedures are shown in some tomb-scenes, but no written account of paper manufacture has ever been discovered. However, modern experiments have demonstrated and confirmed how all stages of the process were probably carried out.

Markets and shops undoubtedly existed in the cities and towns, providing a venue where locally-made goods and products could be bought and sold. Shops in Thebes probably consisted of a square room where the goods were displayed on shelves, and an open frontage, which enabled potential buyers to see the stock but which could be closed off with shutters at night. During the daytime, the shopkeeper and his customers would sit out on a bench in front of the shop to discuss the purchases, while additional goods were probably displayed outside the shop, to attract passing trade.

The importance of river transport led to the development of another major industry. Ropes and cords were manufactured from flax, rush and palm fibres; in addition to nautical requirements, they were also made into handles and used to secure heavy containers. String (produced from linen) was used for nets and netting; the finest threads were used for bags and carriers, and the coarser ones for fishing and hunting nets.

Situated near the river, the shipyards at Thebes were centres of intense activity; information about techniques employed in boat-building comes from a variety of sources: inscriptions, tomb-scenes, boat models and rare examples of original ships. The simplest vessels were constructed from reeds, bound together with stalks of papyrus. However, larger boats were built of timber planks fixed together with nails and pins. It is evident that, as early as the Old Kingdom, the Egyptians had mastered sophisticated ship-building skills, as demonstrated by the outstanding royal barque discovered at Giza: over 130 feet in length, it is made of carved pieces of cedarwood bonded with small cords.

By the New Kingdom, permanent dockyards had been established at various locations in Egypt, as well as at Byblos on the Syrian coast where ships were built for Egypt's military campaigns. Some ships were 200 feet in length, and had decks and cabins, two banks of oars, a single oar in the stern to act as rudder, and a trapezoidal sail. Some new features were introduced during the New Kingdom, when specialist warships were built to promote Egypt's imperial ambitions. The so-called 'Byblos-ships' may have been modelled on vessels actually captured by Tuthmosis III during his Syrian campaigns, and then used as a prototype for building Egyptian ships. However, there were few changes in the design of Egyptian vessels after this period, until Greek and Phoenician sailors, brought to Egypt as mercenaries by the kings of Dynasty 26, introduced further innovations.

Building Royal Monuments

As a senior court official, Khary sometimes accompanied the king on inspection visits to the royal tomb which was being prepared in the Valley of the Kings at Thebes. Monumental building was taking place across the whole area of the West Bank: this included the construction of tombs for the royal family and senior officials, as well as magnificent mortuary temples. Stone had to be quarried on a large scale for such enterprises, and the king was expected to exercise his royal prerogative to ensure that the quarries – a State monopoly – were fully exploited.[6] During the Old Kingdom, the best quality limestone was obtained from Tura, near Memphis, while granite was quarried at Aswan. However, most quarries did not work continuously; from the earliest dynasties, it was customary to send expeditions there only when it was necessary to obtain supplies of stone for particular projects. These expeditions were major undertakings, inaugurated by the king and led by his senior officials; they often included artisans,

The method of using individual stone blocks to construct columns in this colonnade at the Temple of Luxor, Thebes, is clearly visible here. The stone was roughly hewn to the required shape and size at the quarry, and then the blocks were transported to the building site where they were finished and decorated with carved scenes and inscriptions. New Kingdom.

caterers and courtiers as well as army personnel to supervise the work. However, during the New Kingdom, building was so extensive at Thebes and elsewhere that quarrying was carried out on a widespread and regular basis.

Working methods can be demonstrated by evidence from monuments, statues and excavated blocks abandoned in the quarries. In limestone and sandstone quarries, trenches were cut around four sides of the required block in order to isolate it. Then, wooden wedges or beams were inserted in these trenches and saturated with water so that they expanded and caused the stone block to split away from the parent rock. Similar techniques were used with hard stones such as granite, basalt and quartzite.

Once the stone blocks had been extracted from the rock, they could be used as building materials, or for statuary and stone vessels. The stonemasons probably roughly dressed the blocks at the quarries before removing them to a building site or sculptors' workshop. Transportation of stone often involved long journeys, and whenever possible, the Egyptians used the Nile for this purpose. Although only simple equipment was available for moving large blocks of stone, obelisks and monumental statuary, the Egyptians' organizational methods and a large workforce usually guaranteed success.

The workforce was able to take advantage of the Nile's cycles. When the inundation came, it was possible to lift the special barges (used in dry docks on the river's edge to load the stone) and employ tugboats to push them along in the water until they reached their destination. Smaller blocks could be sent in boats or on rafts. However, the stone also had to be moved from the quarry to the river, and eventually from the river to the building site. To complete these overland stretches, smaller stones were sometimes piled on to wooden sledges, which had rollers that could be drawn along the roads by oxen, while men used sledges and ropes to pull the larger blocks. In the New Kingdom, this hazardous occupation was largely carried out by prisoners-of-war and convicted criminals. To make the sledge move more easily over the ground, the workmen often prepared and levelled the route, and then lubricated it by pouring milk on the ground in front of the sledge.

Various procedures were used to prepare the stone blocks for different purposes. In his travels around the West Bank, Khary watched some of these activities at the building sites, where men pounded the blocks with balls of dolomite, and rubbed them down with stones and an abrasive powder. Some blocks were sawn with a copper blade and smoothed with an abrasive powder. In the workshops where stone vessels were produced, men used a copper tubular drill (a hollow tube of copper) and abrasive powder to drill holes into a block of stone. The workman rolled the drill between his hands or rotated it by means of a bow. They also used the bow drill: this consisted of a wooden handle and a crescent-shaped flint bit. It was turned by hand, and had heavy stones attached to the handle to provide sufficient weight.

It was the introduction of copper tools that first made it possible to quarry stone for large building projects. These implements were used in most stages of production, from chiselling out the trenches or wedges in the parent rock, to dressing and preparing the stone. Only copper or bronze tools were available throughout most of the pharaonic period, since iron processing was a relatively late introduction to Egypt. The craftsmen's specialized knowledge of how to harden these relatively soft metals – by tempering them and introducing the correct proportions and qualities of alloy – enabled them to produce tools that would cut hard stone.

Whenever the royal tour inspected progress at the king's tomb or mortuary temple, Khary was greatly impressed by the scenes that adorned the walls. On the interior walls of the temples, the figures and inscriptions were usually carved in *bas*-relief (the background was cut away, leaving the figures to stand out from the wall surface), while on the outside walls, the sculptors used *relief en-creux* (where the figures and inscriptions were deeply incised into the wall surface). A layer of plaster (*stucco*) was then applied to the carvings, and finally the colours were added; the *stucco* prevented the colour from being absorbed by the stone.

The parent rock from which Theban tombs are cut is a relatively poor quality stone that would have been difficult for the ancient artisans to sculpt. Therefore, in many royal and non-royal tombs, the scenes were never carved but simply painted directly on to the dry plaster of prepared wall surfaces. Scenes in tombs and temples were primarily religious in purpose; they ensured that, by means of magic, particular rites and activities would continue in perpetuity. They were

Yellow and blue pigments in a granite grinding dish. From Kahun. Dynasty 12.
Manchester Museum.

therefore executed according to a strict set of principles which
remained unchanged over the centuries. Human figures in the scenes
were represented according to an established canon of proportions,
and religious art largely ignored the conventions of perspective and
realism. Colours, believed to possess their own magical qualities and
power, were regarded as an important and integral part of the person
or object represented. Men were traditionally depicted with reddish-
brown skin tones, and women with much lighter complexions, while
deities were sometimes painted with gold or green complexions which
symbolized their life-giving powers.

Today, some of these scenes retain their original vibrant colours,
although in many buildings the plaster and pigments have long since
disappeared. Ancient artists had a limited range of basic colours which
they used in the form of powdery cakes, made from finely ground
minerals or mineral substances. These included black (soot, lampblack
or charcoal), blue (derived from artificial frit or azurite, a mineral
found in Sinai), brown (ochre or iron oxide), green (artificial frit or
powdered malachite – a natural ore of copper), red (red iron oxides
and red ochres), white (whiting, chalk or gypsum), and yellow (yellow

137

Painted wooden panel portrait of a young man, originally placed over the face of his mummy. Unlike the stylized facial representations seen on coffins of the pharaonic period, these portraits from Roman Egypt depict individual people. From Hawara. Roman Period. Manchester Museum.

ochre or orpiment). The artists also used some half-tones: they mixed charcoal and gypsum to produce grey, and red ochre and gypsum for pink, while orange could be made by either mixing red and yellow ochres, or applying red pigment on top of yellow.

Khary watched how the artisans first applied a gypsum plaster to the walls. This was quite coarse, so that any irregular wall surface was covered and evened out. Then they added a second coat of lime plaster to produce a smooth working surface; once this had dried, they could apply the paint. Their simple range of equipment included water pots, palettes made of shells or potsherds, and palm fibre and reed brushes. To bind the pigments to the prepared surface, the artists used a vehicle which combined water with an adhesive such as gelatin, glue, gum, or egg-white. This technique is known today as *tempera* painting. Finally, they sometimes added a transparent varnish to protect the scenes.

The artisans worked as a team, under the direction of a master artist; he was responsible for delivering the overall design of the tomb and its decoration to the tomb-owner. Using detailed plans drawn up on papyrus, he supervised the positioning of the scenes on the walls, and inspected (and where necessary corrected) the painted outlines of figures and other elements included in each scene. Finally, the artisans applied the various colours according to a prescribed order. Working conditions were often difficult; it is uncertain how the tombs were lit: lamps (stone or clay cups filled with oil and a wick), candles or torches were probably used, but they have left no visible smoke marks on the ceilings.

Elsewhere on the West Bank, Khary noticed that many other workers were engaged in brickmaking, producing a cheap and effective building material for public buildings, houses, palaces, fortresses, storage magazines in temple precincts, garden walls, granaries and parts of some tombs. The main ingredient, clay, was widely available, and sun-dried mudbricks were an ideal building material in a country with little rainfall.

Bricks were apparently introduced as a building material for some tombs as early as *c*.3400 BCE. The reason for this innovation remains uncertain, but the introduction of the brick mould, a tool which enabled the builder to produce a required number of bricks with specific dimensions, may have encouraged large-scale brick manufacture. A rare example of such a mould was discovered at Kahun and demonstrates how these wooden tools were made: four sides were fitted and pegged together to create a rectangular mould, with one side projecting beyond the corner to form a handle by which the mould could be lifted.

During the New Kingdom, many activities directly associated with constructing different kinds of religious and domestic buildings

A view of the hypostyle hall in the Temple of Isis on the island of Philae, from a lithograph in David Roberts' Egypt and Nubia *(1846). Almost all the original colour that remained on temple walls, ceilings and columns when he visited Egypt in 1838–39 has now disappeared. Copyright of The University of Manchester.*

were located on the West Bank at Thebes. Brickmakers are depicted in scenes in the Theban tomb of the First Minister Rekhmire (Dynasty 18). Earlier tomb-models, a later temple scene and biblical descriptions also provide information about the various stages of brick manufacture. The basic ingredient of the bricks was Nile alluvium or mud (a mixture of clay and sand). This was broken up with a hoe, and straw or chaff and animal dung were added to act as binders and increase the clay's strength. Water was then poured into this mixture, which was kneaded with the feet to give it the correct consistency before it was taken to the brickmaker who pressed it into a mould.

When the handle of the mould was lifted, the brick was released and fell to the ground; the bricks were then arranged in rows in the sun, and once dried, piled into heaps to be transported to the building site. Bricks could also be hardened by firing them in kilns, but because the dry climate produced such excellent sun-dried bricks, it was not considered necessary to manufacture large numbers of kiln-baked bricks. Apart from a few examples that date to the New Kingdom, they were only introduced for major projects from *c*.600 BCE, and were not widely employed until the Roman Period.

Bricks varied in size according to their date of manufacture and intended use. Some bricks were produced from wooden moulds that were stamped with the name of a ruling king, and these can be used to identify the construction date of a particular building. Brickmaking and construction work were not highly skilled operations; brickmakers did not have a high status, and in the New Kingdom prisoners-of-war and other foreign labourers provided most of the workforce for this industry. Since brick manufacture was organized as a State monopoly, the government was able to supply bricks for all State buildings and monuments; it was also in a position to provide temples and private individuals with a moderately-priced building material.

Section 2

Planting

The Season of Planting

The winter season, known as *Peret*, was the time when the water levels dropped, the fields re-emerged, and crops and plants could be sown and planted. It started at the end of November and lasted through to the end of March. During this time, although the weather was cooler than in the summer and autumn months, the days were generally warm and sunny, although northern Egypt experienced occasional rainfall. Once the sun had set, the temperature fell sharply and it was necessary to sleep indoors and wear additional clothing. Even on Khary's estate, situated in the south of Egypt, there was a noticeable difference between day and night. During the daytime, the sun shone constantly in a clear blue sky, and the cooler temperatures enabled people to go about their work more easily.

The winter season was a time of activity on the land. Over the previous months, the Nile flood had gradually subsided, but the mud embankments retained water in the fields as long as possible. The soil continued to absorb the water, ensuring that the ground reached its maximum level of fertility for planting crops. Eventually, the falling riverhead, natural drainage, and the evaporation caused by the sun and north-west winds, cleared the water away from the land. The flood-waters had deposited silt on the riverbeds, and the irrigation process had spread it across an extensive area; it now acted as a rich fertilizer for the soil, and was so effective that additional manure was not needed.

Khary's workers now prepared the land for sowing. They used pigs to clear the ground of roots and weeds that had flourished as a result of the inundation, and broke up the heavy clods of earth with wooden rakes, hoes and mattocks. Next, the farmer worked the fields with a plough and oxen. The plough – brought into use at an early date in Egypt – had a significant influence on the development of agriculture: it facilitated weeding, and allowed the farmer (who held a long stick to guide the oxen so that they ploughed straight furrows) to sow the seed consistently and evenly in narrow shallow furrows, thus greatly improving the crop yield. Then, the seed, which the sower carried in a basket on his back, was scattered loosely over the surface of the ground. Finally, to ensure that the seed was firmly established in the soil, animals including cattle, donkeys, pigs, sheep and goats were driven into the fields to trample on the furrows and tread in the grain. The seeds, firmly embedded in the thick black silt, were left to grow and produce ample crops that would be harvested several months later. Crops matured at different times, depending on the date when sowing took place, and the condition of the soil.

Information about planting and sowing is provided not only by tomb-scenes and agricultural implements, but also by special sets of figurines (*ushabtis*), traditionally placed in tombs to undertake agricultural duties for the tomb-owner in the next world. The Egyptians believed that these figurines, activated by magical spells, would work in the 'Fields of Reeds', a paradise where there was eternal springtime, unfailing harvests, and no illness or pain. The word *ushabti* is probably derived from the Egyptian verb meaning 'to answer', and indicates that the figurine was expected to respond to the owner's daily requests.

Each set of *ushabtis* included several hundred figurines (possibly one to work for each day of the year) and several 'overseer' figures to supervise their labours. *Ushabtis* are represented as mummiform figures, moulded or carved from a variety of materials including baked clay, wax, stone, wood, metal or faience. They hold hoes, mattocks, and baskets which have been carved or painted on to their bodies. Also, there is often a painted or carved text inscription which provides the owner's name and a magical formula stipulating the *ushabti*'s agricultural duties.

Chapter 5

The Medical Profession

The winter months brought winds from the desert that were cold and dry. In March and April, the south wind, known in modern times as the *Khamsin*, blew in from the surrounding deserts. This wind continued for a couple of days at a time, carrying with it sand and dust which sometimes caused a thick yellow fog that covered the sun. Climatic conditions at this time of year exacerbated breathlessness and coughing fits, from which many elderly people suffered. In our imaginary family, Perenbast's mother, Nefert, often became ill during these months and had to consult a doctor. Her granddaughter, Meryamun, was married to a renowned physician, Amenmose, and he offered advice and suggested treatments to alleviate Nefert's symptoms.

The Doctors
Amenmose was a priest-doctor, a medical practitioner of the highest status; he undertook duties in the temple on a part-time basis, and followed his medical profession in Thebes for the remainder of the year. Doctors of his rank were known as *wabau*, a title which indicated that they regularly underwent ritual purification to allow them to enter the presence of the god's statue. These doctors often specialized in particular areas of medicine, and were known as priests of the lioness deity Sekhmet.[1]

In predynastic times, tribal and village chieftains performed magical acts and rituals to heal members of their communities. Eventually, the most powerful chieftain became king; he was believed to possess special healing powers which, in turn, he delegated to

Sacred Lake, Temple of Hathor, Denderah. Each temple had a lake where priests washed and purified themselves before entering the temple. This lake, now dry, was once fed by an underground source which still provides sufficient water to support a group of palm trees. Graeco-Roman Period.

special categories of priests. Originally, these men probably acted as religious functionaries; they mediated between the goddess Sekhmet and their patients and tried to persuade the deity to remove all illnesses and afflictions. However, over the generations, through a process of trial and error, the priests gradually acquired practical skills and medical knowledge: they observed their patients, learnt to diagnose their symptoms, and were able to offer help and prescribe treatments.

The medical profession was evidently well organized even in the Old Kingdom; however, the first king of Egypt (who ruled long before that date) was credited as the author of a treatise on anatomy and dissection. At the start of the Old Kingdom, Imhotep (First Minister of King Djoser and architect of the Step Pyramid at Saqqara) was renowned as a great healer; later, the Egyptians worshipped Imhotep as the founder of medical science, and eventually the Greeks identified him with their own god of medicine, Asklepios.

145

No records survive to provide information about medical training. Some temples acquired special reputations for healing, and patients were taken there to undergo particular forms of treatment. Amenmose and his colleagues may have studied in the 'House of Life' associated with these temples, where the *wabau* perhaps spent some periods of their temple duty in teaching students and attending to patients. It remains unclear how medical training was organized; for example, we do not know if it involved formal examinations as well as practical instruction.

The *wabau* headed the medical hierarchy; doctors in a lower grade, known as *swnw*, were State employees who treated patients suffering from a wide variety of illnesses; they worked especially at building sites, burial grounds, the Royal Court, and with the army. Other health care workers included magicians (*sau*) who played an important role in towns and villages; specialist midwives responsible for delivering babies; and nurses, masseurs and bandagers who assisted the doctors.

The practice of mummification familiarized the Egyptians with the idea of autopsying a corpse and ensured that there was no taboo on human dissection. In later times, many Greeks chose to undergo their medical training in Alexandria in Egypt, where they could perform autopsies prohibited in their own country. Mummification and bandaging the body also gave the Egyptians a detailed knowledge of human anatomy and the techniques required to bind dislocated and broken limbs.

Medical Concepts

Nefert's medical practitioner visited her at home, and prescribed several treatments for her various ailments. Both irrational (magical) and rational methods were employed to heal the sick, and they were considered to be equally valid and efficacious. If the cause of the problem was outward and visible (for example, an accident), then the practitioner usually recommended objective and scientific measures, based on his observation of the patient, knowledge of anatomy, and general experience of disease and illness. However, sometimes the cause was inward and hidden (for example, a virus or bacterium which resulted in an infectious disease), and then the healer might use magic. The Egyptians were not aware of the true nature of such diseases, and

Gilded stucco head-piece from a mummy. When immigrants from other parts of the Hellenistic world and Roman Empire settled in Egypt, many adopted Egyptian funerary customs, particularly mummification. This example shows some of the developments in style and decoration that were introduced for these new, wealthy clients. From Hawara. Graeco-Roman Period. Manchester Museum.

Pharmaceutical treatments were frequently recommended for many illnesses. The patient took some medicines orally, applied ointments externally, or was treated with fumigation. The medicines incorporated a wide variety of ingredients, which included pulverized minerals and precious stones; herbs, plants and plant extracts; the fat, blood, horns, hides, hooves and bones of various animals; and excrement, urine and aromatic oils. Some treatments used fragrant oils and pleasant substances to attract good deities to help the patient, while in other cases, disagreeable substances were included in the expectation that they would drive out evil. Honey was sometimes given to the patient to 'sweeten the pill', and it was recommended that unpleasant ingredients should be swallowed with liquid vehicles such as water, wine, milk and beer.

Other types of remedy were used to 'transfer' pain or sickness away from the patient; in one example, a migraine headache was treated by rubbing the patient's head with a fish-head in the hope that the pain would move into the fish. However, when no physical treatments were available, the physician might resort to a magical spell. In the case of the common cold, for example, the spell was designed to drive the cold out of the patient:

> 'Flow forth, fetid nose! Flow forth, son of fetid nose! Flow forth, you who break the bones, destroy the skull, and make ill the seven holes in the head.' [*Papyrus Ebers* 763. Author's translation]

Nefert had endured her symptoms – a severe cough, breathlessness when she exerted herself, and pains in her chest – for many years, but they gradually worsened as she grew older. The *Medical Papyri* provide various remedies to 'drive out cough' – either suppressants which included sweet liquids made from honey, carob and dates, or expectorants (woodworm was the main ingredient of one medicine), which made the cough productive.

Nefert's symptoms were caused by a disease known today as sand pneumoconiosis.[2] This is characterized by severe inflammation and scarring of lung tissue, caused by breathing in fine dust and sand from the atmosphere. The disease is similar to silicosis, a condition observed

Painted wooden anthropoid coffin belonging to Nekht-Ankh. Studies on his mummy showed that he had suffered from several diseases, including sand pneumoconiosis and parasitic infestations. From the Tomb of Two Brothers, Rifeh. Dynasty 12. Manchester Museum.

151

Painted wooden anthropoid coffin of Khnum-Nakht. Studies on his mummy showed evidence of growth arrest in his lower limbs resulting from a period of temporary generalized illness in his youth. From the Tomb of Two Brothers, Rifeh. Dynasty 12. Manchester Museum.

152

today in miners and stonemasons, which results from damage to their lungs caused by a lifetime of inhaling coal and stone particles. A major factor in sand pneumoconiosis is exposure to blown sand and sandstorms. These conditions existed in antiquity but are also prevalent in some areas today, with the result that modern populations living in the Sahara and Negev desert suffer a high incidence of sand pneumoconiosis.

For some years, scientists have been able to use Analytical Electron Microscopy (AEM) to identify silica particles in mummified lung tissue, thus confirming the presence of sand pneumoconiosis in antiquity. Indeed, it is likely that many adults living in ancient Egypt developed this condition as a result of continuing exposure to dust and sand, and consequently suffered serious ill-health from its debilitating symptoms.

Parasitic diseases were another major problem for the ancient Egyptians, and most people, regardless of class or status, would have experienced a variety of chronic and debilitating symptoms from parasitic infestations. Many of these afflictions are described in the *Medical Papyri*, but although the symptoms associated with these diseases are listed, the texts do not confirm that a specific parasite was responsible for causing a particular infestation. Today, scientists use radiological, histological and immunological techniques to examine the mummies, and can sometimes positively identify the genus of a particular parasite.[3]

In addition to problems caused by the deterioration of her lungs, Nefert was also afflicted with several parasitic diseases. Unable to identify the specific cause of her problems, the doctors simply tried to treat the symptoms of these conditions. Modern scientific tests would today demonstrate that one infection was caused by the parasite *Strongyloides*; this worm would have entered Nefert's body through the skin of her feet when she came into contact with soil that was contaminated with larval forms of the worm. Her symptoms included stomach-ache, diarrhoea, and some blood in the faeces; eventually, when the worms reached her lungs and matured into adult forms, they caused inflammation which led to coughing and wheezing.

Nefert suffered from another parasitic infestation, schistosomiasis or bilharzia, which was caused by a flatworm (a *schistosome*).[4] Three

Painted wooden coffin of Asru. She was a Chantress in the Temple of Amun at Karnak. The horizontal scene on the front of the coffin shows the scene of 'Weighing the Heart'. Probably from Thebes. Late Period. Manchester Museum.

Mummy of Asru. Scientific studies show that she suffered from a range of diseases including an infection caused by the parasite Strongyloides. However, her estimated age at death, between fifty and sixty, exceeded the normal lifespan of forty years. Probably from Thebes. Late Period. Manchester Museum.

elements are required in order for this parasite to complete its complex lifecycle: two hosts (a human, and a freshwater pulmonate snail), and stretches of stagnant water (lakes, ponds or canals) in which these snails can live. Throughout her life, Nefert had bathed in lakes and ponds on her family's country estate, and in her youth she had been infected by larval forms of a type of worm, *Schistosoma haematobium*, which inhabits the veins of the bladder area. These parasites eventually matured into adult worms inside her body, and the male and female worms paired. The female then laid eggs, and some became trapped and were retained inside Nefert's body, causing frequent urination, tenderness of the bladder, and blood in the urine. This disease can vary in its intensity, depending on the number of retained eggs and the reaction of the body to their presence. Nefert's infection was relatively light, but she still experienced a degree of chronic ill health and debility throughout her life.

None of the medicines that Nefert's doctors prescribed had much effect on the course or outcome of her afflictions, and like so many Egyptians she suffered a substandard level of health for most of her life. The medicinal ingredients in these remedies included herbs, plants, fruit, berries, various minerals such as salt, natron and malachite, and animal products (ox and goose fat, oil and honey).

Nefert and other adult members of the family also suffered from dental problems. Caries [tooth decay] was not widespread in Egypt before the Graeco-Roman Period; in pharaonic times, the main dental problems were the result of severe wear [attrition] on the grinding and biting surfaces of the teeth.[5]

This condition frequently led to deterioration of the teeth and gums. Attrition was mainly caused by the bread which the Egyptians ate in large quantities. Samples placed in the tombs for the owner to consume in the afterlife have been scientifically analyzed and subjected to radiological and microscopic studies, and these have revealed the presence of high levels of mineral particles. Small fragments of sand and stone contaminated the bread at different stages of its production: these included windblown sand, debris that entered from the soil, and material that infiltrated during the grinding process or when the grain was stored.

Even in childhood, the bread caused some damage to the teeth, but the problem became exacerbated throughout adolescence and adulthood. The diet of gritty bread wore down the cusps of the teeth, and if secondary dentine was not deposited in the pulp chamber faster than the wear occurred, the body of the tooth could become affected, resulting in an apical abscess. This led to a pocket of infection which

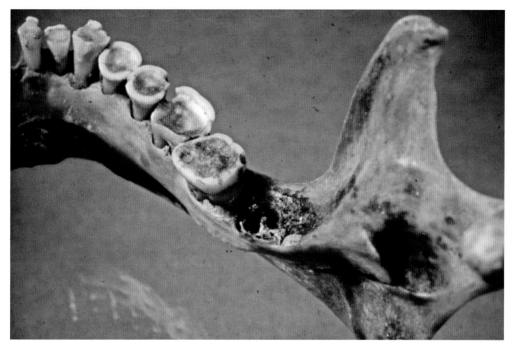

Mandible of Khnum-Nakht, showing attrition (severe wear) on the biting surfaces of the teeth. This was caused by sand and grit in the bread. From the Tomb of Two Brothers, Rifeh. Dynasty 12. Manchester Museum.

caused general debility and lowered resistance to disease, in some cases even resulting in death. However, despite widespread dental problems, there is no convincing evidence that specialist dentists existed.

Dental techniques were probably no more advanced than extracting teeth; modern examination of skulls and dentitions has demonstrated a high incidence of abscesses and other dental problems which seem to indicate that professional help was probably not available, and that many people suffered painful and distressing conditions.

Temples as Medical Centres

Famous centres of medical science and healing existed in Greek temples at Epidauros and on the island of Kos, where Hippocrates, the 'father of medicine', was born in *c*.460 BCE. He established a purely

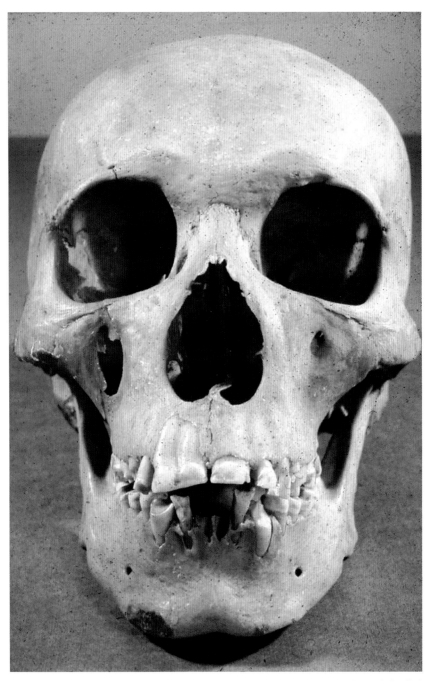

Skull of Khnum-Nakht, showing a rare developmental abnormality of the left upper-central tooth and a supernumerary tooth; this condition is known as double gemination or 'fusion of the teeth'. From the Tomb of Two Brothers, Rifeh. Dynasty 12. Manchester Museum.

scientific basis for medical theory and practice, replacing the ideas of earlier Greek physicians who had relied largely on traditional methods and faith-healing, which functioned around the cult of the god Asklepios. It is also known that during the Graeco-Roman Period, Egyptian temples at Memphis, Denderah and Deir el-Bahri were renowned as centres of medical healing. One Classical writer, Diodorus Siculus, attributed the idea of healing dreams to the Egyptian goddess Isis, and it appears that the Egyptian temples had a long tradition of healing.

Although no archaeological evidence of this earlier tradition has yet been found, texts dating back to the Middle Kingdom (c.1900 BCE) refer to Sais and Heliopolis as famous religious healing centres. Inscriptions also state that the Persian king, Darius, who ruled Egypt in c.500 BCE, ordered the reorganization of the medical school at Sais. We can therefore assume that medical knowledge and the treatment of patients were important functions of several temples during the pharaonic period, and that the Egyptian physicians were the first to care for patients within an institutionalized, religious context.

There is ample evidence during the Graeco-Roman Period that temple healers used isolation and therapy as forms of treatment, and that they were credited with miraculous cures. The temples at Deir el-Bahri and Denderah are of particular interest. Two ancient Egyptian sages became patrons of healing at Deir el-Bahri: these were Imhotep, credited as the founder of medical science, and Amenhotep, son of Hapu, a wise and learned man who lived at Thebes in the New Kingdom. Deir el-Bahri became a centre of healing where many visitors came to seek cures; some painted or scratched their names on the walls of a colonnaded upper terrace where patients sat out in the open air. Sometimes these describe how healing occurred: for example, a Macedonian 'hired hand' named Andromachos records that the god cured him as soon as he arrived at the temple. The physician Zoilos visited the temple in the second century CE, perhaps to observe how the priests treated their patients so successfully.

At Denderah, archaeologists have discovered a very interesting mudbrick building which stands adjacent to the Temple of Hathor.

When first excavated, one Egyptologist tentatively identified it as the temple's 'House of Life', but it is now considered to be a medical centre or 'sanatorium'. It was arranged around a colonnaded court which gave access to other rooms; although probably of Graeco-Roman date, it may incorporate earlier structures.

Sacred water was an essential element in conveying the life-force of the god Osiris to temple patients, and played an important part in various medical treatments such as bathing patients' bodies, feet, or limbs, and in the use of healing statues. Part of an inscription dedicated to Osiris, identifying him as the water of life, was found in the sanatorium; such texts usually appear on the bases of healing statues which were probably once an important feature of the original building at Denderah. Statues played a significant role in treating the sick: water was directed over the statue base so that it could absorb the magical, curative properties of the text, and was then channelled into the treatment cubicles where patients received its life-giving benefits.

The 'Sanatorium' (foreground) at the Temple of Hathor, Denderah. This mudbrick building incorporates a series of cubicles where the patients were bathed with sacred water. Late Period/Graeco-Roman Period.

The sanatorium at Denderah specialized in treating patients suffering from mental illness, preparing them for temple incubation (the 'Therapeutic Dream'). Although most evidence for this procedure dates to the Graeco-Roman Period, the system had existed in Egypt from at least the Middle Kingdom (c.1900 BCE). Isolated in a silent, darkened room lit by lamps and perfumed with the aroma of burnt wood, the patient was induced into a dreamlike state which transported his soul to 'Nun', the great primaeval ocean from which life had emerged and where the dead lived.

This state of deep sleep lasted a couple of nights, and allowed the patient to use spells to make contact with the gods. He could ask about his future and any dangers or evils that awaited him, and could petition the deities to cure his illness. Singing was regarded as a particularly effective method of driving away mental illness: the earliest known reference occurs in the *Papyrus of Merikare* (c.2200 BCE), where the goddess healed the patient directly through song. Hundreds of years later, it was claimed that Isis-Hathor, the resident goddess of Denderah, would sometimes intervene, appearing to the patient and holding him; as divine inventor of the most efficacious healing formulae, she was able to drive away the patient's affliction with her sacred songs. Isis had this ability because she had personally attained immortality, and could even restore to full health those who had given up any hope of a cure. In other cases, divine treatment would be handed down to the patient indirectly through the words and interpretation of a priest. The Egyptians firmly believed that this trance-like state gave the patient a unique opportunity to receive divine healing and unravel and resolve their personal problems.

Gods of Healing

No one specific deity presided over medicine and healing; instead, various gods held responsibility for different areas of medicine. Sekhmet, patron of the most senior priest-doctors, and her consort, Seth, were both regarded as destroyers who brought epidemics, and were worshipped and petitioned in the hope of averting these plagues. Ibis-headed Thoth, god of scribes and learning, was honoured as the inventor of healing formulae and divine author of medical texts. Isis-

Hathor was another important healer; according to mythology, she had reassembled the scattered limbs of her husband Osiris and, through her knowledge of magic, had brought about his resurrection: this enabled her to take on the role of patroness of magicians. Horus and Amun possessed special powers to cure eye diseases, and Tauert, represented as an upstanding, pregnant hippopotamus, with influence over all aspects of fecundity and childbirth, received the special prayers offered up by women in their homes. Wise men such as Imhotep and Amenhotep, son of Hapu, were also credited with special curative powers, and Imhotep was widely worshipped as a god of medicine.

Medical Sources
No single description of medical science in ancient Egypt has ever been found. Information comes from several sources: scenes and statuary showing people with various afflictions; tombstones (*stelae*) of physicians which list their titles and provide some idea of specialization and career progression; surgical instruments (although the only examples found to date are from the Graeco-Roman Period); and a wall-scene from the Temple of Kom Ombo which may depict a set of surgical instruments. Also, scientific techniques can be used to detect evidence of disease and disease patterns, thus providing a clearer picture of the Egyptians' state of health and living conditions.

The ten major *Medical Papyri* that have been identified to date are perhaps the most important source of evidence about disease and treatment in ancient Egypt.[6] These carry the names of their modern owners (Edwin Smith, Chester Beatty, Carlsberg and Hearst); the towns where they are kept in museum collections (London, Leyden and Berlin); or the ancient sites where they were discovered (Kahun and the Ramesseum). The *Ebers Papyrus* is called after its modern editor. Most of these papyri date from *c.*1550 BCE, but they are all probably copies of earlier works, and the total must represent only a minute proportion of the medical texts that once existed in ancient Egypt. Each document contains a wide range of subject matter, and it is evident that the contents were not brought together to form any consistent or coherent group of material.

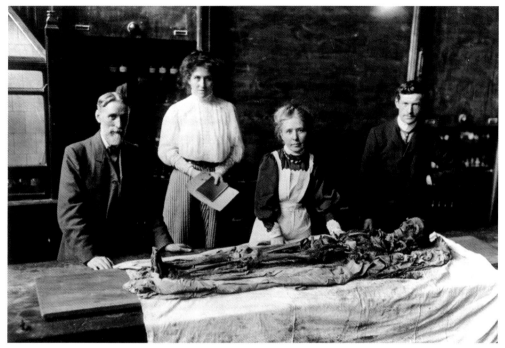

Dr Margaret Murray (second right) and members of her team unwrap and autopsy the mummy of Khnum-Nakht at the University of Manchester on 7 May 1908. Manchester Museum.

Drs Rosalie David (right) and Edmund Tapp unwrap and autopsy Mummy 1770 from the Manchester Museum collection, in June 1975. Copyright of The University of Manchester.

Chapter 6

The Legal Profession

The Legal System

Khary's son, the lawyer Nakht, was an official of the judiciary and also held a priesthood of Ma'at. She was the goddess who personified law and symbolized truth, justice and righteousness, as well as maintaining the correct balance and order of the universe and its inhabitants. The Egyptians believed that the concept of law, along with all other principles of their civilization, had been handed down to mankind by the gods at the time of creation. Law and religion were closely interwoven, and the gods were accredited with establishing and upholding the legal system.

In theory, because the ruler was a god-king, he acted as Egypt's sole legislator, holding power of life and death over his subjects. However, although he was nominally chief official of the judiciary system and High-priest of Ma'at, in reality the king had only limited freedom of choice in legal matters, since outcomes were largely determined by legal precedent. The king was himself subject to the law, and in practical terms, most of his duties were delegated to the First Minister who functioned as High-priest of Ma'at and head of the courts of justice.[1]

Sources for Legal Practice

Some form of legal system was probably first developed during the Predynastic Period so that people could regularize sales, inheritance, and crime and punishment issues in their own towns and villages. The earliest references to legal arrangements are found on texts inscribed on Old Kingdom papyri (Dynasty 6), and tomb walls and *stelae*

(Dynasty 3). These demonstrate that a formal legal system was already in place by this date, probably as the culmination of a long period of experimentation and development.

Egyptian and Sumerian law (which developed early in Mesopotamia, a region now occupied by Iraq) represent the oldest surviving legal systems. They differed from each other in that the Sumerians had a formalized law code, whereas the Egyptians did not; instead, their legal system was based on custom, with decisions handed down that largely relied on precedent. Nevertheless, Egyptian law was sophisticated and complex, and can be compared with ancient Greek or medieval legal systems.

Archaeology provides some details of legal undertakings: for example, Old Kingdom tomb and *stelae* inscriptions preserve transactions relating to funerary property, while wall-scenes in the New Kingdom tomb of Rekhmire at Thebes depict his many duties as First Minister, and show him supervising the High Court at Thebes. Rekhmire held high office and was head of the legal system during the reigns of Tuthmosis III and his son, Amenhotep II.

However, most information about Egyptian law is derived from documentary evidence, and this often demonstrates that, although in theory the king had absolute control over the life, death, labour and property of all his subjects, private law existed as an important part of the system, and property could be the subject of private transactions. The earliest extant examples of certain types of legal documents have been identified in papyri fragments discovered at Kahun and Gurob. At Kahun, archaeologists discovered deeds (*amt-pr*) which record the transfer of property from one individual to another, and in some cases, acted as wills or marriage settlements. Legal documents from Deir el-Medina throw light on the social and domestic law of a *necropolis* workmen's community,[2] and include accounts of strikes and industrial unrest amongst a workforce engaged in building the royal tomb of Ramesses III (Dynasty 20).[3]

A papyrus from the same period, perhaps originally housed in the temple library at Medinet Habu, gives a detailed description of the so-called 'Harem Conspiracy'. It relates how a number of people, including the women and officials of one of the royal harems, conspired to kill the king, possibly in order to place a rival on the throne. Another document tells how the conspirators attempted to achieve this by writing spells and making wax images which they then tried to smuggle into the harem. The plot appears to have been unsuccessful, and the culprits were severely punished.[4]

In the later Ramesside Period, a series of well-preserved papyri provides information about a number of other trials which continued over a period of many years. The documents describe legal action taken by the kings against those who plundered the royal tombs at Thebes. Although there had always been instances of tomb robbery, the poverty and wretched social conditions that existed towards the end of Dynasty 20 brought about such an increase in crime that the kings were forced to take action and bring the perpetrators to trial.[5]

Some Legal Transactions

There is a significant increase in information about legal transactions from the New Kingdom onwards, making it possible to outline some of the cases that lawyers such as the imaginary Nakht would have encountered. Some of these transactions focused on private ownership and the transfer of property between individuals. Possession of a legal document usually confirmed that a particular person had acquired ownership of a house or other valuable object. Drawn up by the original owner, this document set out the transfer of ownership and the original owner's agreement to this transaction, and was witnessed by three named persons. The document was then rolled up, sealed by an official, and given to the new owner. Wills as such did not exist in pharaonic Egypt, although they were known from Roman and later times. However, the Egyptians achieved the same end by using a transfer of ownership transaction: a document could be drawn up with instructions that, after the owner's death, a house or other valuable item was to be passed on to a chosen heir.

The ancient Egyptians enjoyed life: since they needed few clothes because of the warm climate, and the countryside supplied them with an abundance of food, it was unnecessary to borrow in order to survive at subsistence level. However, Egypt was a consumer-driven society: people amassed luxurious goods (readily available and always in great demand) to enhance their homes and personal appearance, and to prepare their tombs for eternity. Therefore, it is not surprising that some people fell into debt.

A debt was essentially a loan that had to be fulfilled at some time in the future, and a debtor would initially confirm this commitment by taking an oath in which he invoked the king or a god. The rate of interest payable on the debt was fixed to ensure that the value of the original sum could not be doubled. Payments had to be made in kind (coinage was not introduced to Egypt until *c*.500 BCE), and consisted of objects that were acceptable to the creditor; all were valued according to a general standard. In earlier times, the creditor could only take possession of the debtor's goods; he could not make the debtor work for him in lieu of payment because every individual was owned by the State and had to be available for *corvée* duty or conscription into the army. However, from *c*.700 BCE, it became possible to sell oneself into servitude to repay a loan, or to sell oneself to become a 'son'. This involved certain duties towards the 'father', the most important being the obligation to ensure that the 'father's' burial was carried out in an appropriate manner. A childless couple would sometimes adopt an adult 'son' so that he would ensure that they received the correct burial rites.

Customs and property associated with funerary beliefs were among the most important aspects of ancient Egyptian existence. Many legal transactions deal with these funerary matters: for example, the tomb had to be provisioned in perpetuity and special arrangements were set in place to ensure that this was not neglected. Along with all tomb-owners, Khary expected his family and heirs to perform his burial rites (under the law of succession, the person who acted in this capacity would inherit his property and possessions); the family would also continue to bring food and drink to his tomb-chapel after his death, so that his *Ka* (soul) would have perpetual sustenance in the afterlife.

However, even if these rites were performed regularly in the years immediately after Khary's death, he knew that they would probably be neglected after a few generations when he had been forgotten. With the passing of each generation, the family would have an increasing number of tombs to care for and some families had no surviving descendants. Therefore, it became the custom to set up a legal arrangement whereby the tomb-owner would establish an 'eternal property' or 'Ka-settlement'. This was a profit-bearing part of the owner's estate which he settled on a special priest known as a 'Ka-servant'. According to this arrangement, the priest received an income from the settlement in exchange for providing offerings at the tomb. When the priest died, his own heirs would inherit the income and the obligation of the 'Ka-settlement'.

However, this system depended on the reliability of the Ka-servant and his descendants, and the duty was often neglected. So, from early times, tomb-owners provided themselves with an additional 'insurance policy'; in the tomb, they included models illustrating food production, and wall-scenes depicting food offerings, which were also listed in a menu inscribed on one of the walls. The Egyptians believed that magic rites performed at the time of burial would activate this food, providing the owner's soul with an eternal supply of nourishment.

Family Law

Men and women of all classes enjoyed equal status under Egyptian law, and although the laws were made and executed by men, the system sought to protect and perpetuate the family, and safeguard the economic status of women and children.[6] Property was vested in women who passed it on to the next generation. The Greek historian Diodorus Siculus claimed that Egyptian women held a superior position to men regarding the possession and inheritance of property. Although this may have exaggerated the situation, women certainly enjoyed a privileged status which was not found elsewhere in the ancient world.

People expected to get married when they were young. Members of Khary's imaginary family had married in their early teens; marriages were arranged for members of the royal family, but commoners were free to choose their own partners, although they doubtless took advice from their parents. Marriage does not seem to have been marked with a religious ceremony, but a legal contract was drawn up, and the families of the new couple undoubtedly celebrated with a fine banquet to which friends and relatives were invited. In pharaonic times, there were some marriages between close relatives, but apart from the royal family, these included very few unions between brothers and sisters.

Wooden tomb-model of a man and woman in discussion. Women's privileged legal status regarding the family's domestic and funerary property was not found in other contemporary societies. Unprovenanced. Probably Dynasty 12. Manchester Museum.

When Perenbast married Khary, she retained all the property she had inherited from her own family and the possessions she had brought with her to the marital home. Sometimes, a husband even transferred to his wife the whole of his existing estate and pledged her any future property he might acquire; his wife would hold these assets and pass them on to her children. In practice, however, the husband probably possessed the rights of administration and use of his own property, and even those of his wife, throughout their marriage. It was possible to end a marriage by divorce; this was easier for the man, although he had to pay his wife compensation and she kept all the property that she had brought to the family unit.

Like most commoners, Khary had only one wife; he did not follow the custom, found in some families, of taking serf-concubines.

usually the preferred option; this was based on the belief that disgrace could be worse than death, and that whereas an executed criminal would never be a useful member of society again, a living person might repent or perform a courageous deed which would re-establish them in the community.

Various death penalties existed. Some criminals were thrown to the crocodiles – a dreadful death since it meant that even their bodies were destroyed, condemning them to eternal oblivion. Occasionally, because of a criminal's former high status or as a mark of special favour, he would be allowed to commit suicide and his body would be returned to the family for a proper burial. Those who intentionally murdered Egyptians or even slaves always received the death penalty, although the king could commute a capital sentence and send the offender to work on State building projects.

Other important features of the penal system were imprisonment or forced labour in the mines and quarries. The latter was designed to ensure that prisoners earned a living and did not become an economic burden on the State. Convicted criminals were held in prisons, usually attached to the law courts, until they could be sent to the mines or quarries. If they were caught while running away, their ears and noses were amputated, and they were returned to their allocated workplaces. Amputation was used as a severe punishment for other crimes. When dishonest officials falsified weights and measures, forged seals and signatures, or made alterations to documents without authorization, both their hands were amputated, while the tongues of those who disclosed military secrets were cut out. Even quite minor misdemeanours (some thefts, taking bribes, petty fraud, keeping false accounts, and other breaches of trust) were punished with a hundred strokes.

In these cases, a male culprit was placed prostrate on the ground and held down by his hands and feet while he was beaten with a stick; women were restrained in a seat and beaten on their backs.

Punishment for theft and burglary was allocated according to the severity of the crime. Some offences carried the death penalty, but usually the authorities acknowledged that theft and burglary could not be stopped or prevented. Instead of punishment, they adopted a pragmatic approach: the thief was required to register his name with the Chief of Robbers, and provide details of everything he had taken.

The original owner of the stolen property then gave the Chief some details of his missing items and a payment equivalent to a quarter of the property's value, which was then handed back to him. The Chief's payment was probably a compound sum which included a share of the goods, a subvention from the thieves, and an income from the government. Although this arrangement meant that a compromise had to be reached with the thieves, it at least ensured that that the rightful owner could reclaim his property.

The Law Courts
The law courts were pivotal to the legal system, although settlements could sometimes be reached out of court. The High Court sat at Thebes during the New Kingdom, and was presided over by the First Minister, as depicted in scenes in Rekhmire's tomb. All capital offences had to be decided at the High Court and, by the New Kingdom, much of the administration was also centralized here: for example, all documents dealing with the ownership and transfer of houses were brought to be sealed in the First Minister's office. Each sizeable town or city also had its own law court (*kenbet*), presided over by an assembly of local dignitaries under the chairmanship of an official. The *kenbet* functioned on a local basis, and members of this court, who were paid by the State, acted as judges for less serious cases.

It was their duty to assess all kinds of evidence, and it was considered a great crime to give false information. The complainant presented his case in writing to the court, describing how the alleged offence had been committed, and estimating the damage and extent of his personal injury. The defendant set out a written response which either denied the charge or attempted to show that only a minor offence had taken place. Even if the defendant admitted guilt, he took care to emphasize the excessive nature of the estimated damages. The complainant then replied in writing, and the judges weighed up the evidence.

Judges made every effort to remain impartial: they looked at documentary sources, including tax rolls for disputed ownership cases, and they had powers to ruthlessly interrogate the accused, who was regarded as guilty until proven innocent. He could be beaten until he 'confessed' to his crime, and even independent witnesses could be roughly treated until they adjusted their 'evidence' to fit in with the decision that the judges had reached. Once the judges had decided on the final outcome, this was ratified and announced by the chairman of the court, but the case was not concluded until the defeated party declared his submission and accepted the verdict.

When assessing a case, it was customary for judges to receive most reports in writing; this sought to ensure that they were not unduly swayed by orations and verbal pleas presented in court. Nakht and his fellow lawyers amassed and organized the written evidence, but did not argue a client's case in court. Men and women of all classes were accorded equal status under the law (an important advantage of this system), and were expected to present their own petitions in court.

The general aim of the courts was to judge each case on its legal merits rather than reach a decision based on the personalities of the accuser and defendant. However, from Dynasty 19 onwards, law court procedures became more complex and less convincing because a change was introduced which provided greater opportunity for corruption and abuse. This involved the use of an oracle which could be consulted to obtain a verdict: the god's decision was ascertained by performing various ceremonies in front of a divine statue which was brought into court to act as judge. The petitioner stood in front of the statue, and read out a list of suspects: the god's statue was expected to move in a particular direction or give a sign when the name of the perpetrator of the crime was announced. However, law-court officials who held and carried the statue had the opportunity to manipulate its responses, and there was obviously a much greater chance that a biased verdict would be returned, based on their personal wishes rather than any judicial assessment of the evidence.

The legal system to which Nakht and his colleagues contributed played an important role in society. It was designed to help ordinary people by protecting the role of women and the family, and emphasizing that all petitioners had equal rights, regardless of gender or status. The severity of punitive methods and some procedural aspects of the law courts were less appealing, but nevertheless the system served the country well enough for over 3,000 years, and provided the necessary checks and balances for what was by nature a law-abiding society.

Chapter 7

Entertainment and Personal Appearance

Social Entertainment

According to New Kingdom tomb-scenes at Thebes, hosting and attending parties and banquets were important and pleasurable activities of the wealthy which they hoped to continue to enjoy in the afterlife. Male and female guests are shown sitting together or separately, and hospitality included a meal followed by entertainment provided by musicians, singers and dancers.

As a man of senior status at Thebes, the imaginary Khary regularly entertained his friends and colleagues at such events. When their guests arrived, Khary and Perenbast met and greeted them. The guests then prepared themselves for the meal, washing their hands and feet with water poured from ewers brought to them by the servants, and cleansing their hands with an absorbent substance (soap was unknown at that time). Then, taking ointments from cool alabaster containers, the servants anointed each guest's head, sometimes placing scented wax cones on top of their wigs; these would melt during the course of the party and the guests would be surrounded with a pleasant perfume. The atmosphere in the room was scented with myrrh and frankincense, enhanced by the heady aroma of flowers and garlands used as decoration. In addition, each guest was presented with a floral necklet and head circlet, and an individual lotus flower which was worn on the forehead.

When the guests were comfortably seated on high chairs, the servants brought wine: men were often served with a one-handed goblet made of bronze, gold, silver, glass or faience, while women drank from a special cup into which a servant poured wine from a small vessel. The guests continued to be served wine throughout the meal, and tomb-scenes provide ample evidence of drunkenness at these parties. Usually they depict servants and entertainers in an inebriated state, but there is little doubt that sometimes the tomb-owner and his guests also indulged themselves to excess.

The meal consisted of selected meats, vegetables, bread, cakes, and fruit as well as wine and beer, and included imported beverages and foreign delicacies from Syria and Western Asia. Since the Egyptians ate with their fingers, they washed their hands frequently with water that servants poured from a ewer into a basin positioned on a stand in the dining room. Some of the household pets were present at these banquets, tethered to the legs of their owners' chairs. Khary's guests conversed with each other, discussing the major events of the day, admiring each other's clothes and jewellery, and commenting on their host's fine house with its elegant furnishings, and the excellence of his food and drink.

Before and after the meal, Khary's visitors were entertained by professional musicians and dancers.[1] The Egyptians loved music, and it featured in many aspects of their lives. In the temple, musicians accompanied Perenbast and her fellow chantresses in their regular performance of liturgical hymns and chants that were part of the daily rituals and festivals. These performers were members of the temple staff, closely associated with the priesthood, and received special instruction and training in music and singing.

Although no buildings have been found that can be identified as theatres in the modern sense (the theatre seems to have been a Greek innovation), it is known that the Egyptians performed sacred dramas at some of their temples.[2] Musicians and singers played a prominent role in these enactments of major events in the gods' lives. Singing also featured at the burial ceremony, and was employed as therapy for the sick in the temples. Apart from a formal role in religious functions, singing and music were also a popular and integral part of everyday life. People working in the fields, at building sites, or on the river had their own special songs, handed down from one generation to the next, which lifted their spirits and provided rhythm for their communal activities.

Copper mirror, razor (bottom left), two pairs of tweezers, and selection of alabaster, anhydrite and faience containers for ointment and kohl. Unprovenanced, or from Kahun and Amarna. Middle and New Kingdoms. Manchester Museum.

As members of the upper classes, Khary's family and their guests did not play musical instruments or dance at home themselves; instead, they employed non-religious musicians and female dancers to provide entertainment. Some tomb-scenes show the owner, alone with his wife, listening to a harpist, while others depict troupes of musicians and dancers entertaining guests at parties. Individual musicians and troupes of entertainers who performed in private houses all came from the lower classes, and acquired their skills in order to earn a living.

The musicians, singers and dancers took their places in front of Khary's seated guests. We have no details of how Egyptian music was played or sounded, but tomb-scenes and the relatively few musical instruments that have survived provide some information about the range of their music. Some instruments were probably used to give a solo performance, but musicians also accompanied singers. Men and women participating in religious and secular ceremonies played the harp, lyre, lute, double pipe, flutes made of wood, bone or ivory, and the reed pipe or double pipe. Trumpets and drums were employed to marshal army troops and supply the rhythmic and musical background for military marches; on other occasions, male and female musicians used drums, ivory or wooden clappers, circular or square tambourines and hand-clapping to mark rhythm and provide a lively beat.

Stringed instruments included lutes, lyres, and harps, which varied considerably in terms of shape, size and number of strings. Some instruments were large but others were hand-held; many were made of wood covered in leather, and had strings of catgut. The earliest examples of harps are depicted in scenes in Old Kingdom tombs at Giza; however, the lyre (which had five, seven, ten or eighteen strings), and the lute (which resembles a modern guitar) were imported to Egypt from Western Asia during the Hyksos Period (*c*.1550 BCE). Other musical instruments included large bead collars and metal or faience *sistra* which were shaken as rattles. The *sistrum* was an important instrument in temple ritual, and art depictions show it being carried by queens, noblewomen and temple chantresses.

A new type of literature appeared in Egypt during the New Kingdom which Egyptologists call 'love-songs' or 'love poems'.[3] Men and women express their deepest emotions in these sophisticated compositions which frequently describe human love in terms of the physical beauty of the landscape – the trees, flowers, gardens and stretches of water. Many of these songs were probably presented as unaccompanied pieces, perhaps followed by an instrumental performance. They may have contributed to entertainments held at the king's Court or in the houses of wealthy courtiers and officials. Sentiments expressed in these poems delighted Khary's family and his guests:

My heart quickens,
When I think of my love for you,
It does not let me act sensibly,
It leaps out of its place.
It does not let me get dressed,
Nor wrap my scarf around myself;
I do not paint my eyes,
I am not even anointed.'
(*Love Song*. Author's translation)

Musicians and singers performing at Khary's parties were often accompanied by dancers and acrobats. They wore scanty clothing, and performed sinuous and rhythmic actions with great elegance and style. Away from these indoor venues, the residents of Thebes and other large cities doubtless enjoyed the noisy songs and dances of street entertainers.

Dancing played an important role in religious as well as secular activities. Magicians danced to imitate gods and take possession of their powers, and dancing was included in temple rituals, festivals and funerals when dancers often wore special costumes and masks to impersonate particular deities.

Personal Adornment

Personal appearance was very important to the ancient Egyptians, and Khary's family and guests spent a great deal of time and effort preparing themselves for parties and other social occasions. As previously mentioned, clothes worn by men and women of the upper classes were usually made of fine, white linen, although sometimes fabrics were coloured with natural dyes to produce yellow, red or blue cloth. Garments worn during the New Kingdom were elaborate: often, the linen was finely pleated, and clothing was layered, with one almost transparent tunic placed over another.[4] Sandals were made from rush, papyrus or leather.

Many children of all classes went without clothes or shoes until they reached puberty, and in the New Kingdom they were quite often dressed in scaled-down versions of their parents' garments and footwear. Mothers and nursemaids carried their babies in shawls which they wrapped around themselves. Female servants attending guests at Khary's parties were often scantily dressed in a loincloth, although some wore dresses made of geometric-patterned, multicoloured textiles. Men working as agricultural labourers in the fields of the estate had linen loincloths, while their wives were wore simple linen dresses.

Evidence survives in tomb-scenes, inscriptions, statues, wigs and hair ornaments to indicate that the Egyptians paid great attention to their hairstyles. In order to ensure cleanliness, many men and women shaved their heads with copper or bronze razors, but others retained their natural hair, sometimes dyeing it with henna. Prescriptions preserved in the *Medical Papyri* show that they tried to prevent baldness and obliterate any grey hairs. Tomb-scenes show that members of the upper and middle classes whose hair was shaved or cut short often wore wigs outside the home, particularly for social occasions. Wigs were made of natural hair or hair mixed with vegetable fibres, and provided the wearer with some protection against the heat of the sun.

Natural hair and wigs were dressed in many different styles, often incorporating plaits, curls and fringes which were fixed with ivory or metal pins. By the New Kingdom, hair was usually worn long, descending well below the shoulders; Khary and the adult members of his family had fashionable, elaborate styles in which flowers, ribbons and ornaments were attached to their plaited and curled tresses. These hairstyles, whether adopted for natural hair or wigs, required constant attention. Like all wealthy people, each member of Khary's family owned several wigs, and even planned to take a set of boxed wigs into the tomb for use in the next world. In contrast, Ipy (Khary's son who had not yet reached puberty) had a simple hairstyle: a shaven head, and a single strand of hair known as a 'Sidelock of Youth'.

The Egyptians possessed a wide range of toilette equipment;[5] this included wooden combs, which were usually double-sided with coarse and fine sets of teeth. There were also mirrors made of metals, especially copper, set in wooden, stone or metal handles, carved or moulded in the form of a woman, flower, bird, column, or head of Hathor (the goddess of love and beauty). These mirrors were highly polished to give good reflective images. Wealthy women such as Perenbast and her daughters used fine toilette boxes to store their cosmetic containers: pots and vases made of different kinds of stone (alabaster was highly desirable), glass, ivory, bone and shell; copper and bronze tweezers; and alabaster ointment spoons to pour oils over the body.

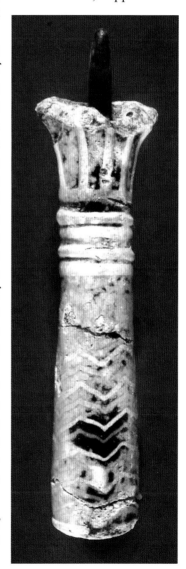

The shape of the eyes was outlined with kohl, a black powder containing a mixture of antimony and other substances; this was applied to the eye with a kohl stick which was bulbous at one end. Other eye pigments such as malachite (green ore of copper) and galena (dark grey ore of lead), ground into powders and then mixed with ointment, were also applied to the eyes. All these eye-liners and paints were kept in small jars or tubes; made of stone, faience or wood, these usually have a simple, cylindrical shape, but others are more elaborate: some take the form of a lotus column or are carved to represent the figure of an ape or other animal holding a jar. Some containers even have up to five separate compartments, each intended to hold a different coloured powder.

Cosmetics and beauty care were firmly established features of everyday life. Eye make-up and associated equipment have been discovered in tombs dating from the Predynastic Period when they were already considered to be essential requirements for the

Glass kohl tube (in the form of a lotus flower) and kohl-stick, used for applying eye make-up. From Gerzeh. Dynasty 18. Manchester Museum.

183

Amethyst amulet in the form of a scarab (dung-beetle). The scarab was especially popular because it was believed to symbolize renewal and rebirth. From Tell el-Yahudiyah. Middle Kingdom. Manchester Museum.

of jewellery and the intrinsic magical power of the materials from which it was made would protect the owner against a range of afflictions and disasters. Jewellery often incorporated sacred symbols such as the dung beetle, 'Eye of Horus', or the *ankh*-sign which represented life; it was believed that these amulets could combat disease, accidents, floods, famine, or attacks by wild animals. When worn in life, jewellery provided potent protection for its owner, and it acted in the same way after death when placed between the bandages of the mummy. To avail themselves of these benefits, wealthy people purchased jewellery to wear in life, and also prepared a collection of items for the tomb which were usually heavier and more traditional in style than those worn every day.

As well as providing magical protection, jewellery also displayed a person's wealth and status. Some honours were presented by the king to reward individual bravery, and Khary and his son, the soldier Amenemhet, were proud possessors of the 'Order of the Golden

Collar' and the 'Order of the Golden Fly'. Gifts of jewellery also marked special royal occasions: a king would bestow personal ornaments on his bride on the occasion of their marriage, and Khary joined other courtiers in presenting valuable pieces to the king and queen when they celebrated a jubilee festival.

By the New Kingdom, a wide range of materials was employed in jewellery-making; these included metals, gem-stones, glass, shells, seeds, bone and flowers. Copper was used extensively, but gold was the most popular metal, acquired by all who could afford it; however, silver – which the Egyptians regarded as 'white gold' – was especially rare and desirable because it had to be imported from Western Asia. These precious metals were often set with semi-precious gem-stones which were chosen for their depth of colour rather than refraction of light. The most popular were carnelian, turquoise and lapis lazuli; others included garnets, jasper, green feldspar, amethyst, rock crystal, obsidian and calcite. Jewellery was also set with glass, and artificial substitutes which were produced by backing calcite and rock crystal with coloured cements and faience. Jewellers used other natural materials – pebbles, shells, seeds, teeth and bone – which they pierced with bow-drills, polished, and then threaded to make necklaces and bracelets. They also produced large quantities of beads – especially those made of Egyptian faience.

The resplendent guests attending Khary's party wore their finest pieces of jewellery to excite admiration and arouse their friends' envy. Men and women adorned themselves with necklaces made of gold, natural materials and artificial substances; some pieces were simple

Faience pectoral (chest ornament) to place on a mummy. The images show the Djed-pillar (symbol of rebirth) in the centre, flanked by two representations of the sign (s3w) meaning protection. The pectoral was supposed to provide these benefits for the deceased owner in the next world. From Sedment. Dynasty 19. Manchester Museum.

Mummy of a woman with a gilded stucco head/chest piece; the inlaid eyes are made of obsidian and calcite, and the moulded jewellery is set with glass 'stones'. Tombs were almost invariably robbed, and so by this period, jewellery was usually no longer placed with the burial but simply represented in this way on the head/chest cover. From Hawara. Roman Period. Manchester Museum.

gold chains or collars, whereas others incorporated representations of fish, frogs, lions, birds, gods, reptiles, shells or flies. The guests also wore gold anklets, bracelets, and armlets which, in many cases, were inlaid with semi-precious stones. Some of their gold rings incorporated an inscribed seal or scarab which could be used as a signet to mark possessions or authorize a letter or written instruction. Two or three rings were sometimes worn on the same finger, although it was also fashionable to place rings on the third finger of the left hand or even on the thumb. Earrings had been introduced to Egypt from Syria and Western Asia during the New Kingdom, and Khary's visitors – keen to follow the latest trends – wore large, round, single hoops of gold which dangled from their earlobes.

Games and Entertainment

Egyptians enjoyed a variety of indoor and outdoor games.[7] The kings prided themselves on their physical fitness and prowess: for example, temple scenes and inscriptions proclaim that Amenhotep II was a good athlete, a trainer of horses, skilled charioteer, powerful archer and outstanding horseman. The kings and the upper classes participated in target practice, and enjoyed hunting in the deserts, and fishing and fowling in the marshes. They were also spectators at wrestling and javelin-throwing contests. Scenes in Middle Kingdom tombs at Beni Hasan show the various wrestling holds and modes of attack which were practised; it was apparently permissible to take hold of any part of the head, body, neck or legs, and to continue to fight an opponent even after he had been thrown to the ground. Training for army recruits included wrestling and mock fights, but they do not appear to have engaged in boxing. Mock fights involved two sets of contenders: one group had to defend a temporary fort, which the others attacked with a battering-ram. Audiences also enjoyed weight-lifting contests and gymnastic displays.

Indoors, people entertained themselves with board games, and the names of some of these – 'serpent', 'dog and jackal' and *senet* – have survived. *Senet* is a particularly interesting game: although the rules remain unclear, the introduction to Chapter 17 in the *Book of the Dead* states that *senet* continued to be played in the afterlife. Vignettes (small illustrations set into the text) show the owner, often accompanied by his wife, sitting at a *senet* board; no opponent is present – presumably it was believed that the couple were playing against evil forces that were trying to prevent them from attaining eternal life.

Archaeologists have discovered a number of *senet* boards. Four were found in Tutankhamun's tomb; these range from a miniature set to a fine, full-size example crafted in ebony and ivory. This forms part of a double-sided box which has a *senet* board marked on one surface, and a board for another game on the reverse. There is a small drawer at one end of the box for storing gaming pieces. Two other *senet* boards discovered at Kahun were used when their owners were alive. One board is marked out on the inside of a wooden chest lid; three horizontal rows, each containing ten squares, are painted in red on a white background. In the bottom row, the seventh square from the left is marked with an indistinct trace of Hieratic writing. However, the gaming pieces which once presumably accompanied this board were not discovered. The second board, made from a slab of limestone, is incomplete, although it is clear that it was marked out in three horizontal rows, each containing ten squares. The lines are lightly incised on the stone, and in the top row, in the first square on the left, the hieroglyph *nfr* (meaning 'good') is inscribed in black ink. A cross is marked in black ink in the square immediately below this in the middle row.

Although it is difficult to reconstruct exactly how the game was played, it is evident that a standard board had three rows, each containing ten squares, and that five of these might be inscribed with hieroglyphs. Each player was allocated five or seven pieces, usually made of faience and often conical in shape; the ultimate aim was to be the first to place a piece on the square inscribed with three signs (*nfr*) each meaning 'good' or 'happy', at the angle of the L-shaped section. The hieroglyph in the square before this, which represented water, may have indicated a 'hazard'. In order to move the pieces forward, players threw knucklebones or casting sticks which determined the number of squares they could pass over. Although *senet* was a game of chance, and the players had little influence over the eventual outcome, it was universally popular in life and was also believed to have religious significance in the next world.

Archaeological evidence demonstrates that children enjoyed playing a wide range of games. Tomb scenes and objects from Kahun and Gurob show that older boys and girls juggled with balls, performed acrobatic dances, played with hoops, threw and caught balls, practised target-shooting, walked a tightrope, wrestled, and participated in a jumping game similar to leapfrog. They also played with dice, and were entertained with conjuring tricks: one involved the conjuror asking his opponent to identify the location of a ball which he had placed under one of four cups.

Wooden and leather balls were also uncovered at Kahun. Two of these were roughly shaped from wood; another ball, stuffed with dried grass, was made from six gores of leather which were sewn together, but one of the gores had evidently cracked and been restitched in antiquity. In another example, the stuffing had long since fallen out through the broken leather casing. There were a large number of whip tops – circular pieces of wood, flattened at one end and worked to an obtuse point at the other. Excavation also revealed tipcats: these wooden sticks, pointed at each end, were used to play a game in which the stick or 'cat' was hit into the air with a bat or stick, and then struck again before it landed on the ground. The aim of the contest was to hit the 'cat' as far as possible, and thus become the winner.

Children also played with simple toys; examples found in tombs and at Kahun show how youngsters on Khary's imaginary estate would

Wooden whip-tops and tipcats (bottom row); tipcats – wooden sticks pointed at both ends – are known in other parts of the world. From Kahun. Dynasty 12. Manchester Museum.

Two painted wooden 'paddle dolls' (centre and right). Unprovenanced. Middle Kingdom. Wooden figurine (left). From the Ramesseum Tomb Group, Ramesseum, Thebes. Dynasty 12. Manchester Museum. These 'dolls' were very different from the genuine toys found at Kahun. 'Paddle dolls' were probably placed in tombs as concubine figures to enhance fertility and rebirth and also perhaps to entertain the owner in the afterlife. The Ramesseum figurine was included in the funerary assemblage of a lector-priest who may have been a magician.

have entertained themselves. Some of the toys are made of painted limestone: figures from Kahun include a boy nursing a pet monkey, and two boys wrestling. There are also examples of quite sophisticated playthings: a collection of commercially-produced dolls came to light in a house at Kahun which probably belonged to the local toy-maker, who presumably manufactured the dolls for sale to the town's residents. Made of painted wood, they have jointed limbs which move on pins and can be made to assume various postures. Pellets of hair piled up in one room were clearly intended for insertion into holes punched in the dolls' heads. At other sites, archaeologists have found dolls in cradles; animal toys which include a crocodile with moveable

192

jaws; puppets exemplified by a set of dancing dwarfs; and a model of a man washing or kneading dough which can be worked by pulling a string. Rattles and miniature weapons have also been discovered.

These toys have survived against all the odds: they have endured frequent use, and many (for example, the rag dolls) are made of fragile materials. One set of clay figurines discovered at Kahun is especially remarkable because the pieces may have been modelled by the children themselves. Representing a man, a small boat, and animals – a crocodile, hippopotamus, and an ape with blue beads inserted for eyes – they reflect the everyday world and limited horizons of these children. These simple toys – very different from the games placed in the tomb of Tutankhamun to entertain the king in his afterlife – offer a unique opportunity to see how the children of royal craftsmen amused themselves over 4,000 years ago.

Clay figurines, all made from Nile mud, which the children may have modelled as toys. This group includes (left to right) a crocodile (bottom left), an ape with beads inserted to represent eyes, a pig, an unidentified animal, and a model boat with two seats (one of which is pierced with a hole to take a mast) and the remains of a rudder. From Kahun. Dynasty 12. Manchester Musuem.

Section 3

Harvesting

The Harvest Season

The third season, known as *Shemu*, lasted from the end of March until the end of July. These months witnessed a change in the climate when cooler weather was replaced by the heat of summer. Far to the south of Egypt, in Ethiopia, the whole cycle started again with the arrival of monsoons in May; these gave rise to the Nile inundation, the effects of which were first experienced in Egypt at Elephantine (modern Aswan).

This was the season when crops were harvested in Egypt. Communities worked closely together during this particularly busy time of year, with the men spending long hours in the fields, cutting the corn with short sickles, and gathering in the harvest. Most New Kingdom estates were located at a single site, and this enabled the owner to supervise the different stages of harvesting (depicted in many tomb-scenes) in one place. The initial steps were carried out in the fields, where the men worked laboriously, pausing every so often to chat to each other, or drink from a communal jug of beer. Once the corn had been cut, it was bound in sheaves, packed into baskets, and taken by donkeys to the threshing floor; women used hand baskets to collect any ears of corn dropped along the way. Once the sheaves arrived at the threshing floor – a flat area in the midst of the corn-stack – the corn was spread out over the floor so that animals could be driven over it to tread out the grain. Donkeys were usually employed for this task in the Old Kingdom, but by the New Kingdom they were largely replaced by oxen. Once the threshing was finished, workers used large wooden forks to assemble the corn and chaff together in a large heap.

The next task involved removing any impurities from the corn: it was passed through a large sieve to extract some of the debris, but most chaff and dirt were taken out by winnowing. This process was usually carried out by women; wooden shovels or scoops were used to throw the corn up in the air to separate the grain from the chaff, and the grain fell to the ground as the chaff was blown forwards. Afterwards, the grain was scooped off the threshing floor, weighed by two estate officials, and then stored in sacks which each contained a fixed quantity of grain. Details of the contents of these sacks were recorded by officials before they were removed by road or river to the granary, a building surrounded by its own wall which stood apart from the main estate-villa. All the main elements of the estate – the family home, granary, stables, sheds for chariots and carts, cattle pens, the yard for daytime animal feeding, and the granary – were themselves enclosed within a boundary wall. The workers climbed up steps to deposit the grain through a small window positioned high up in the wall of the conical-roofed granary, and when supplies were needed, the grain could be removed through another small window lower down in the building. The final stage in preparing this vital food ingredient for the Egyptian diet was to grind the grain into flour.

The Egyptians used the straw, a by-product of cultivating barley and wheat, to make bricks, while the long stubble left behind in the fields was collected and prepared as food for cattle and horses. They also grew a wide variety of plants and vegetables in gardens near their houses and on the mud dykes. Although irrigation occurred only once a year, orchards and gardens which lay near large basins fed by a regular intake of water from the river were productive throughout the year.

Chapter 8

Education

Khary's youngest child, Ipy, was a fourteen-year-old schoolboy. As the son of a senior official, he was expected to enter the civil service or become a doctor or lawyer. In keeping with his family's status, Ipy received a higher academic education, attending the palace school with the sons of other senior officials. The royal tutors taught these boys alongside the king's own sons. Some other children intended for senior positions went to government schools where they were trained to take up posts as officials in specialist departments: they all studied reading, writing and literature, but instruction in foreign languages prepared some for the Diplomatic Service, while others pursued mathematics so that they could become architects and engineers in the Home Civil Service.

The Educational System
We have no single surviving account of how the education system worked in Egypt; however, some texts are informative about educational aims and practices, and give us a rare insight into the moral and ethical values held dear by the ancient Egyptians. The *Instructions in Wisdom* (known today as the *Wisdom Texts*) provided a set of rules for conducting personal relationships, and laid down the standards of behaviour taught to young people as the basis for an acceptable way for life.[1] First written down in the Old Kingdom (*c*.2400 BCE) as a set of useful and popular teaching tools, the texts were subsequently copied by successive generations of schoolboys who used them as models of good conduct and behaviour, as well as examples of fine literary style and expression.

Mummy of an ibis. This bird was associated with the cult of Thoth, the god of writing, knowledge, and learning, usually depicted with an ibis head and human body. The bird inside these elaborate, diagonal, linen bandages was a votive offering, purchased by a pilgrim visiting Thoth's shrine, and then dedicated to the god. Many thousands of animal votive offerings have been found in catacombs at Saqqara. From Saqqara. Graeco-Roman Period. Manchester Museum.

The earliest *Instructions* usually took the form of an address by a wise man, such as the king or First Minister, to his son or pupils, so that they could advance their position in society. In the Old and Middle Kingdoms, they were composed as addresses to the sons of upper-class families; the intention was to hand down a code of behaviour which would prepare these youngsters for a future role as 'ideal' courtiers or officials. The underlying principles of the *Instructions* emphasized the fact that personal attainment would bring contentment; they praised the qualities of kindness, moderation, and the ability to exercise good judgement and wield power with clemency and righteousness.

Early *Wisdom Texts* are usually only preserved in later copies produced as schoolboy exercises, but new examples were also composed in the New Kingdom and later periods. However, by the New Kingdom, the *Instructions* were no longer regarded as manuals written exclusively for the sons of upper-class officials. They were now also directed at middle-class schoolboys, and new texts incorporated ideas which addressed middle-class aspirations. Although the tradition of an older man giving advice to a young boy was retained, the advisor was now represented as a minor official addressing his own son, rather than a king or First Minister. Also, a successful life was differently defined: although material wealth and personal recognition were still regarded as the main aspirations of a righteous life, it was no longer necessary for the 'ideal' man to hold a position of power. Instead, he was expected to be honest, humble in his dealings with gods and men, to have the inner qualities of endurance, self-control and kindness, and never to express anger. Most importantly, the new order recognized that because only the gods were perfect, no individual human could hope to achieve personal perfection.

Egyptian literary works are usually anonymous. It is therefore unusual that many *Wisdom Texts* (all believed to have been authorized by the gods) were actually attributed to named human authors. Prince Hardedef, a well-known sage of the Old Kingdom, is acknowledged as author of the earliest known *Instruction*. The famous *Instruction of Ptah-hotep* carries the name of a First Minister of King Isesi of Dynasty 5; such a person is known to have lived at this time and owned a famous tomb at Saqqara.[2] The original of another *Instruction*, addressed to Kagemni, a son of King Huni of Dynasty 3, was probably composed during the Old Kingdom. However, it is unlikely that these men actually wrote any of the texts in their existing form: such attributions to famous people were probably made simply to enhance the value and reliability of the works.

One particularly interesting text, probably composed in the period between the Old and Middle Kingdoms, is known by various titles: the 'Satire on Trades', the 'Instruction of Duauf', or the 'Instruction of Khety'.[2] Authorship was attributed to Duauf, the son of Khety, a man who, despite his humble background, set out to give advice to his own son, Pepy. Unlike his father, Pepy enjoyed the good fortune of attending the 'School of Books', where he was taught with the magistrates' children. Duauf was anxious that his son should devote himself to books and his schoolwork so that he could become a scribe ('a learned man'); only in this way could Pepy escape the relentless toil and hardships associated with the various trades and occupations listed in this text. Duauf emphasized this point by describing some of their most unpleasant aspects, and comparing them unfavourably with the status and excellence of the scribe's profession. Duauf keenly urged his son to follow his advice:

'I have seen him who is beaten, him who is beaten. You must set your heart on books. I have seen him that is set free from forced labour [i.e. the scribe]. Behold, there is nothing greater than books.' (*Satire on Trades*. Author's translation)

Other important texts composed in later times include the *Instruction* attributed to Any, a minor palace official, who gives advice to his son, and the text accredited to Amenemope where the style and content have been compared to sections in the biblical *Book of Proverbs*.

The so-called *Schoolboy Exercises* are another important source of information about the educational system.[3] They were written down on numerous papyri and *ostraca* (inscribed potsherds and limestone flakes) dating from the Ramesside Period (*c.*1250 BCE). The education of the upper and middle classes, expanded and developed in the New Kingdom, now had a more structured approach.

Schoolboys were required to copy out various highly-regarded texts which they took down from the teacher's dictation. This type of instruction enabled them to acquire reading and writing skills and an understanding of grammar, vocabulary and composition. Some texts, especially the *Instructions in Wisdom*, were also selected because of their moral and ethical content which, it was hoped, would help to form the boys' characters.

Various documents used for dictation and instruction include not only early *Wisdom Texts*, but also business and legal documents. However, there were also new compositions, apparently written by teachers and their pupils, which were copied as models and eventually handed on to later generations. These texts were highly regarded because they emphasized the benefits of education and the teacher/pupil relationship. They are often presented as letters written by a teacher to his pupil: letter-writing style, correct grammar, and accuracy in depicting hieroglyphs were all very important, but these compositions also emphasized the moral content.[4] The letters provided a channel through which the teacher could give good advice to his pupil, encouraging hard work and advocating the avoidance of excessive pleasure and foolishness. The texts also praised the scribal profession, emphasizing its superiority over all other careers, and they provided an opportunity for the student to praise his teacher and offer good wishes for his health and happiness.

These model compositions are preserved on papyri, wooden writing boards or tablets, and cheaper materials including *ostraca*. *Papyrus Lansing* is one of the most famous educational tools: it comprises a set of passages, selected and compiled by a scribe with the intention of providing a 'book' of model compositions for the student to copy. The theme of this 'book' is 'Be a Scribe': it deals with aspects of the teacher/pupil relationship, praising the scribal profession and emphasizing the disadvantages of other careers, particularly those endured by soldiers. The texts include not only the student's praise for his teacher, but also encouragement for the pupil to persevere with his studies.

This group of writings preserves unique material which has not survived elsewhere; it provides invaluable information about education, religion and everyday life during the late New Kingdom.

However, the texts present modern translators with many difficulties because the boys did not always fully understand what they were copying and made many mistakes. The masters corrected these exercises, but they were mainly concerned with their pupils' ability to draw hieroglyphs correctly rather than their accuracy in copying down the texts. Pupils also experienced difficulties with the foreign names and words that now occur more frequently in the texts, reflecting Egypt's cosmopolitanism, which resulted from possessing a large empire in the New Kingdom.

Other educational texts include examples from the town archive at Kahun, and possibly some of the *Medical Papyri* such as the *Edwin Smith Papyrus*,[5] an important medical document once owned by a practising physician. This document is the world's earliest known surgical treatise, notable because its facts are organized in a structured and scientific manner. Its owner may have used it as an instruction manual when he was studying medicine, and then as a reference book throughout his career; it may also have been interred in his tomb so that he could continue to consult it in the next world.

Most information about schools and education is derived from literary sources; little is added by contemporary archaeological evidence, although the remains of a school have been discovered in the precinct of the Ramesseum, Ramesses II's Theban mortuary temple. Here, excavation has revealed large numbers of inscribed sherds which pupils discarded once they had finished their writing exercises. The inscribed texts indicate that certain passages were copied out many times, perhaps suggesting that the teachers gave their pupils specific examples to learn and study.

The Schools and their Curriculum

Ipy's earliest years were spent at home in the women's quarters of the house. Here, he played with his toys and received training and simple lessons from his mother, to whom he was expected to show great respect. When he reached the age of four, his father took charge of his upbringing and education. It was customary for boys to follow the trades and professions of their fathers, and many were able to pursue education up to a certain level. The sons of some of Khary's estate-workers attended the local school, but their education finished when they reached their early teens; then they followed their fathers, some joining the workforce in the fields while others were apprenticed to particular crafts in the estate workshops. However, examples such as Duauf's son Pepy in the 'Satire on Trades' (see above) indicate that sometimes children from humble backgrounds could enter schools where it was possible to pursue an academic career.

Girls generally received minimal education, although the daughters of kings or nobles were probably given some formal instruction. Khary's daughter Meryamun had taken lessons in reading and writing at the Royal School, but her sister Merenmut had followed the usual pattern for girls, passing her time at home where she helped her mother with domestic duties and acquired the necessary skills for marriage and motherhood. Some women did work outside the home: on Khary's estate, those in the lower social groups were engaged in food production and the textile workshops, while others provided some of the musical entertainment at his parties. Women were also employed as professional mourners at funerals. Some received specialist training for particular careers: these included midwives, and the relatively few females who became teachers or doctors. The temples also provided instruction for upper-class women like Perenbast who were employed as chantresses to perform the musical accompaniments to the divine rituals.

Ipy and his schoolmates undertook a variety of lessons when they started to attend school. They learnt reading, writing and mathematics.[6] Writing was regarded as a character-forming exercise because it was difficult to master the complexities of the grammar and to learn how to draw hieroglyphs.[7] Sometimes, children copied out their exercises on papyrus, but potsherds and limestone flakes were used more widely as cheaper writing materials. Ipy also owned a wooden writing case in which he carried his reed pens, a palette which consisted of a red and black cake of paint, and flask of water for mixing the paints.

The school curriculum also included sports: Ipy particularly enjoyed swimming and boating, but boys also engaged in wrestling, ball games and shooting with bows and arrows. The Egyptian educational system – which, in later times, was highly regarded by the Greeks – attempted to provide not only scientific and scholarly knowledge, but also to make the youngsters physically strong and agile. Perhaps most importantly, it tried to ensure that pupils had self-

The trilingual inscription on the Rosetta Stone – in Greek, Egyptian Hieroglyphs and Demotic – provided scholars with a new opportunity to decipher the Egyptian scripts. This table in Champollion's Précis du Système Hiéroglyphique (1824) *compares Greek letters (left column) with Demotic (centre) and Hieroglyphs (right). Copyright of The University of Manchester.*

control, and good manners and morals, so that ultimately they would fit well into society.[8] Corporal punishment was regarded as a desirable means of correcting laziness and disobedience. However, the *Wisdom Texts* always remained the basic method of training in ethical and moral standards, and at some point in their education, Ipy and his classmates were taught these concepts. They were advised to be cautious in speech and prudent in choosing their friends:

'If you look for friendship, do not question him, but draw near and be alone with him ... Test his heart by conversation. If he betrays anything that he has seen, or does anything that does not please you, then be careful, especially with your replies...' (*Instruction of Ptah-hotep*. Author's translation)

203

The boys were also asked to show good manners when they visited another person's home, and were advised on how they should behave towards their social superiors, equals, or inferiors:

'If you are sitting with a greedy person, only eat when he has finished his meal; if you are sitting with a drunken man, only take (drink) when his desire is satisfied...' (*Instruction for Kagemni*. Author's translation)

'If you are one who receives requests, be kind when you listen to the petitioner's speech. Do not deal with him sharply, until he has unburdened himself and spoken about what he wants to say. A petitioner will be very pleased if you nod while he speaks, until he finishes what he has come to say...' (*Instruction of Ptah-hotep*. Author's translation)

The texts indicated that a man should take a wife while he was still young, so that she would provide him with a son, and warned against criticizing and trying to control a good woman, recommending instead that she should be praised for her home-making skills. The boys were instructed not to envy other people's happiness and possessions, and advised against unsuitable relationships with women in other households. Generally, young men were expected to be discreet in speech, restrained over food and drink, and to behave well when visiting other people's homes.

From the age of fourteen, boys destined to pursue professional careers as scribes, doctors or lawyers continued their education at specialist centres. No stage of the educational process was provided free of charge: each family was expected to pay in kind (in some instances, this took the form of agricultural produce), which meant that only the wealthier classes could support their sons through higher education. Some types of further education may have been undertaken in the 'House of Life' where priests specialized in religious liturgy, astronomy, astrology, the interpretation of dreams, geography, music, history and geometry.

Advanced education for schoolboys like Ipy probably included a foundation course which taught the pupils how to write and the basics of literary appreciation. They were then allocated to a centre of administration or instruction where, as junior scribes, each boy received personal tuition from a senior official. He was expected to copy out long model compositions which his tutor would correct in the margins of the page. However, generally little is known of professional training methods: for example, were medical students expected to undertake both theoretical and practical training, and did this involve the cooperation of patients brought to the temple for healing? Also, were students required to take examinations?

Ipy was regarded as a serious and well-behaved student, but some of his friends presented the teachers with discipline problems. This was probably not an uncommon feature of the schools, and ancient texts preserve the teachers' warnings against strong drink and girls:

'I am told that you neglect your studies and instead pursue pleasure! You wander around from street to street, smelling of beer! Beer robs you of all men's respect, it affects your mind. Here you are like a broken rudder that moves from side to side. You are like a shrine without its god, and like a house without its bread. You have been found climbing a wall!' (*A Schoolboy Exercise*, preserved in *Papyrus Sallier* and *Papyrus Anastasi*. Author's translation)

The Teachers

From at least the Old Kingdom, scribes were regarded as a separate and privileged group in society, whose mastery of reading and writing made them superior to the masses,[9] and as bureaucracy increased, the king needed their assistance to rule and govern the country.

Scribes had a wide range of duties, which included the imposition and collection of taxes, keeping accounts, keeping army records and controlling the law courts. Particularly important tasks included composing and copying religious and other texts in the temple *scriptoria*, and educating the young. No other profession or trade could equal their position in society. The ability to write gave the scribe access to the highest posts in the bureaucracy, and this enabled him to direct and control everyone else. Some of the special advantages they enjoyed included exemption from the payment of certain taxes, and from heavy labour and agricultural duties; also, most of them did not have to answer to a supervisor.

They enjoyed good food, wore fine clothes, and were treated with respect.

Scribes worked at various levels within society, ranging from minor officials on the lowest rungs of the bureaucratic system, to the highest positions held by the king's own sons. However, they all enjoyed a relatively privileged status, and were expected to demonstrate qualities well beyond a basic ability to write and record facts. The scribe was required to set and maintain the highest standards of excellence for the whole society, and to uphold the morals and ethics that were regarded as an essential part of everyday life.

The concept of the 'ideal' scribe was established during the Old Kingdom, but it continued through to the New Kingdom and beyond. He was expected to be educated and cultured, to have the ability to express himself well in writing and speech, and to be able to resolve difficult problems. He was also required to show impartiality in protecting the humble against the powerful, and to achieve his goals without fuss and boasting. Access to books and education was expected to produce a thoughtful, discerning man who loved learning and wisdom. By using the *Wisdom Instructions*, school compositions, hymns and prayers, scribes were required to achieve society's essential aim of handing on this code of behaviour to the next generation.[10]

It was the scribe's ability to write that not only provided him with employment as a teacher, but also gave him his special rank and power in society. Those who instructed the young were all expected to be learned, trustworthy, and able to impart their knowledge and wisdom to their pupils. However, they came from a variety of backgrounds: some had started their careers as scribes in the Royal Treasury or pharaoh's workshop, and one had even previously supervised the royal stables.

The Egyptians created an elite ruling class by segregating a particular group of children from the rest of society at an early age, and then developing their skills through higher education. The educational system was not equal or universal, but it did provide a proportion of the population with some access to knowledge, and attempted to build character as well as impart information. Over thousands of years, their educational system produced people who had the talents and ability to organize and administer a fairly complex society. It also established the expectation that high standards of character and conduct were required for all government officials.

Chapter 9

Military Campaigns

In our imaginary family, Khary's second son, Amenemhet, was a soldier who fought in the campaigns of Tuthmosis III. After they expelled the foreign rulers (the Hyksos) from Egypt, the kings of Dynasty 18 became aware of a need for a national army. Prior to this, there had been no standing army: whenever the king decided to fight or launch campaigns, his district governors simply conscripted peasants from the local population. However, the kings now recognized the need to maintain a standing army so that they could foil any future attempted invasions. The earliest rulers of Dynasty 18 therefore set out to organize an army on a national basis, manned by officers who were professional soldiers.[1]

This standing army was probably started by King Amosis I. He and his immediate predecessors had successfully driven the Hyksos from Egypt, and he completed the task by pushing them back into southern Palestine where he finally subdued them so that they could not regroup and return to Egypt. He also dealt with an insurrection in Nubia. With Egypt's northern and southern borders secured, Amosis I's successors were now ready to conquer foreign lands and establish an Egyptian empire.

Some evidence about military expeditions and campaigns comes from scenes and inscriptions on tomb and temple walls. The most significant account of the expulsion of the Hyksos is preserved in an autobiographical account inscribed on the walls of the tomb of Ahmose, son of Ebana, at El Kab. The text relates events in the life and career of Ahmose, a professional soldier who fought against the Hyksos and was rewarded by the king. Following this, he accompanied the king to Sharuhen in Palestine, where again the army was successful:

'Then Sharuhen was besieged for three years. His Majesty despoiled it and I brought booty away from it: two women and a hand [i.e., the hand of a slaughtered captive]. Then the gold of favour [i.e., a royal reward] was awarded to me, and my captives were given to me as slaves.' (*The Autobiography of Ahmose, Son of Ebana*. Author's translation)

This inscription also provides information about Ahmose's illustrious career: at first, he served on board a ship, but when King Amosis became aware of his ability, he had him transferred to take part in military action against the Hyksos:

'Now when I had established a household [that is, he had married], I was taken to the ship 'Northern' on account of my bravery. I followed the ruler on foot when he rode around in his chariot. When the town of Avaris was besieged, I fought bravely on foot in His Majesty's presence.' (*The Autobiography of Ahmose, Son of Ebana*. Author's translation)

Once the Hyksos problem had been resolved, Ahmose accompanied the king to Nubia on a campaign to put down a local insurrection. He continued his career under the kings who succeeded Amosis I – Amenhotep I and Tuthmosis I – and took part in these rulers' Nubian campaigns to subdue local rebellions. Finally, he accompanied Tuthmosis I's campaign to the River Euphrates in northern Syria, a military action which was part of Egypt's new strategy to establish an empire.

Ahmose was rewarded with promotion to the rank of 'Commander of the Crew', and received a royal gift of land in his hometown of El Kab. His career was typical of the new professional soldier: promoted from the ranks, he spent his whole life in the armed forces, serving a succession of rulers. Ultimately, the king rewarded his loyalty and ability with a high-level position and considerable wealth, which he was able to pass on to his family. His grandson,

Paheri, eventually built the best tomb at El Kab, and became mayor of two towns.

In the early part of Dynasty 18, Egyptian rulers were primarily concerned with establishing their power in Syria/Palestine.[2] At the beginning of this dynasty, ethnic movements in the Near East had created a power vacuum, and a new kingdom – Mitanni – had established itself in the land of Naharin, situated between the rivers Tigris and Euphrates. The population of Mitanni consisted of a ruling aristocracy of Indo-Aryan origin, and the Hurrians – people who had branched out in *c*.2300 BCE from their original homeland situated south of the Caspian Sea.

The Mitannians were one of the most powerful enemies that Egypt faced in Dynasty 18, although eventually the two countries became allies. The Egyptians wanted to set their own northern boundary at the Euphrates, so when Mitanni first began to push southwards, this led to direct conflict. Northern Syria became the main focus of Egypt's campaigns and the most significant arena of warfare. However, the princedoms and city-states which occupied Palestine and the rest of Syria at this time were also drawn into the conflict; although they presented no cohesive threat to Egypt or Mitanni, both sides tried to coerce them into becoming vassal states.

Amenhotep I left no record of his military activities in this area, although he may have taken preliminary actions which laid the foundations for Tuthmosis I's new, aggressive policy. Tuthmosis I, the first Egyptian king to launch a major offensive in Syria, led an expedition across the Euphrates into Naharin, where he set up a commemorative *stela*. His army killed many of the enemy and took others as prisoners before it returned home through Syria, where the king celebrated his success by organizing an elephant hunt at Niy. Wall inscriptions in tombs at El Kab belonging to Ahmose, and a relative, Ahmose Pennekheb, provide details of the roles these men played in the campaign.

Tuthmosis I also fought in Nubia, extending Egypt's power as far as the region of the Fourth Cataract, where he built new fortresses.[3] He established control over an area that stretched from this part of Nubia to the Euphrates in the north – the ultimate limits of Egypt's empire. His policies were continued by his son, Tuthmosis II, who campaigned in Palestine and overthrew a rebellion in Nubia, but it was his grandson, Tuthmosis III, who ensured that Egypt became the greatest military power in the region.

Since Tuthmosis III acceded to the throne as a minor, his step-mother Hatshepsut had the opportunity to seize power and, for a time, she ruled in his stead. During Hatshepsut's reign, some city-states in Syria/Palestine had formed alliances with the Mitannians, while others declared themselves independent of Egypt's influence. However, once Tuthmosis III established himself on the throne, he wasted no time in reasserting Egypt's supremacy. In Year 23 (the first year of his independent reign), he mounted a campaign against Mitanni and a coalition of city-states led by the Prince of Kadesh, a city on the River Orontes. The Egyptian armies were able to capture the city of Megiddo, a victory which formed the basis for future expansion in Syria/Palestine.[4]

Tuthmosis III sent a further sixteen campaigns to Syria over the next twenty years, which successfully sacked the city of Kadesh twice,[5] and crossed the Euphrates to penetrate deep into Naharin. In the eighth campaign, which took place in Year 33, the Egyptians resoundingly defeated the Mitannians, but despite some significant successes there was no outright winner in this contest and, ultimately, the two powers were forced to recognize that neither would ever win a conclusive victory. Therefore, towards the end of Dynasty 18, they changed their policies and became allies. Tuthmosis III also reasserted Egypt's control of Nubia, leading campaigns as far south as the Fourth Cataract. His excellent strategies and well-executed campaigns ensured that he is now appropriately recognized as Egypt's greatest military ruler.

Wall inscriptions in some temples preserve historical accounts of military exploits undertaken by kings of the New Kingdom.[6] However, these often provide propagandist versions of events, their main aim being to record the pharaoh's glory and battle prowess.[7,8] The campaigns of Tuthmosis III are described in wall-scenes and inscriptions found in the Temple of Karnak,[9] and on two *stelae*: one comes from Armant, and the other was set up in the king's temple at Napata (Gebel Barkal), near the Fourth Cataract. Taken together, these literary sources provide sufficient information for Egyptologists to reconstruct some events in Tuthmosis III's campaigns.

One of the Karnak records, carved on the walls of two halls situated behind the Sixth *Pylon* in the temple, is known as *The Annals*. These provided a factual account of Tuthmosis III's annual campaigns; they give most information about the first one, and the others are recounted more briefly. Another inscriptional source, the so-called *Poetical Stela of Tuthmosis III*, was placed in a court in the same temple. This hymn of triumph, written in terms of a speech given by the god Amen-Re, also recounts the king's victories.

According to these sources, the king's campaigns were all successful. *The Annals* relate how his first campaign was undertaken in the fourth month of winter; he set out through Palestine, and by the first month of summer had reached Gaza. He took this city and then marched to Megiddo where a group of princes, led by the ruler of the city of Kadesh, awaited him. Through his own great personal valour and clever tactics, the king achieved victory and the enemy was routed, but this was followed by a seven-month siege of Megiddo. *The Annals* go on to describe the preparations his army took before attacking the city.

An important feature of Tuthmosis III's military strategy was subjugation and provisioning of harbours along the Palestine/Syria coast; this was undertaken in order to support his campaigns in the hinterland.[8] The inscriptions relate that, in the sixth campaign, some of the Egyptian forces were transported by ship to the Palestine/Syria coastal area. In the seventh campaign, Tuthmosis III sailed along the coastal cities, proceeding from one harbour to the next; he subdued and equipped them with provisions which would support his army's actions in the hinterland. Inspecting and supplying the harbours became a regular feature of Egyptian warfare.

Tuthmosis III's eighth campaign, which he undertook in Year 33, made use of boats to cross the River Euphrates and defeat the Mitannians. According to the *Gebel Barkal Stela*, these vessels were built every year at Byblos. They formed part of the annual tribute that Byblos, a vassal-city, paid to Egypt. These measures ensured that Egypt, although deficient in its native wood supplies, was still able to build up an adequate fleet. However, on the eighth campaign, the boats were not sent by sea from Byblos to Egypt; instead, they were transported overland to the Euphrates on wheeled wagons drawn by oxen.

Wooden Royal Boat. Dismantled into many pieces, this boat was discovered in a pit south of the Great Pyramid, and was then painstakingly reassembled over a period of forty years. It may have been used once at the king's funeral, or was possibly a symbolic boat in which the deceased ruler could sail around the heavens. From Giza, now displayed there in the Solar Boat Museum. Dynasty 4.

The Egyptians became the greatest military power in the region during the New Kingdom. Their empire was the first to be established there, although it was much smaller than the later Assyrian and Persian empires. The Egyptians had always pursued a policy of colonization in Nubia, and by the New Kingdom, this region was effectively ruled as part of Egypt. However, circumstances in areas to the north of Egypt were different, and although the Egyptians had conquered many of the city-states there, they decided to leave local governors in control of their own cities, provided that they gave allegiance to Egypt. This arrangement made it unnecessary for the Egyptians to establish any centralized system of administration to control the region.

Egypt became a wealthy, powerful and cosmopolitan state during the New Kingdom. Gifts from other great nations, tribute from vassal states, and booty and prisoners-of-war brought back from the military campaigns all added to the country's status. The *Poetical Stela of Tuthmosis III* emphasizes the crucial role played by Amen-Re in ensuring Egyptian victories and, to demonstrate their gratitude, the kings donated booty and prisoners-of-war to the god's temple at Karnak.

Organization of the Army

Amenemhet was trained from youth in a military school to prepare him for a career as a professional soldier and member of the chariotry. Training included exercises such as wrestling movements and holds depicted in tomb-scenes at Beni Hasan; he also learnt horsemanship.

The field army was split into divisions; each division, which consisted of infantry and chariotry and numbered about 5,000 men, carried the name of a major god and was commanded by the pharaoh or one of the princes. The king was commander-in-chief of the army and led the troops in major campaigns, but minor expeditions were usually headed by princes or officials. In addition to all his other duties, the First Minister was also Minister of War; he and the king regularly consulted the Army Council (which included senior officials and advisors) about military strategy and tactics.

Major sources of information about the army and warfare include reliefs and inscriptions placed on buildings in the capital city of Tell el-Amarna and on the walls of temples at Abydos, Beit el-Wali, the

Ramesseum, Karnak and Abu Simbel. These refer to great campaigns undertaken in Dynasties 18 and 19. Other evidence comes from surviving weapons, scenes in the Theban tombs of Kenamun and Hapu, reliefs on the chariot of Tuthmosis IV, paintings on the lid of a wooden chest belonging to Tutankhamun, and chariots found in the Theban tombs of Userhet, Yuya and Tuthmosis IV. In addition, the *Edict of Horemheb* provides information about reorganization of the army that took place at the end of Dynasty 18. According to this *Edict*, when the army was in Egypt it was divided into two corps – one based in Upper Egypt, the other in Lower Egypt. Each was led by a lieutenant-commander, responsible to the general; duties included garrisoning the frontier forts, escorting royal processions and public celebrations, dealing with riots, and supplying the unskilled labour for public building projects.

The chariotry[10] was probably introduced during the Hyksos Period. It was divided into squadrons which each had twenty-five chariots. The 'Charioteer of the Residence' was commander of the chariotry, which was probably divided into two sections – light and heavy troops – who were both armed with bows. The main duty of the light troops was to shoot missiles into the enemy ranks, while the heavy fighters were expected to break into the enemy's massed infantry.

The Hyksos probably introduced the chariot to Egypt from Palestine. Chariots from both these regions were of a similar design, and Egyptian words for 'horse', 'chariot', and associated trappings were probably adopted from Indo-Aryan terms. The chariots had frames of pliable wood which were covered in leather decorated with metal and leather binding. The back of the chariot was open, and the sides were largely cut away. The earliest examples had two four-spoke wheels but, by the reign of Tuthmosis IV, these were replaced by six-spoke or, more rarely, eight-spoke wheels. All chariots seem to have been drawn by a maximum of two horses: no representations have been found of chariots being pulled by a greater number of animals.

Each vehicle held two men – a driver and a fighting soldier who carried bows and arrows, a javelin, shield and sword. In the temple scenes, the king is often shown alone in his chariot, although in reality, he was probably usually driven by a courtier of very high status known as the 'First Charioteer of His Majesty'. This man was also periodically sent on foreign missions, perhaps to acquire stud horses. A royal stable-master supervised the stables where the horses were trained to take the chariots; other stable masters of lower rank were employed to feed and exercise the animals.

Although wealthy people who owned horses probably rode them on their own estates, there are no art representations from the New Kingdom showing the cavalry (soldiers riding horses into battle), perhaps because the horses were not large or strong enough for this purpose. However, it is recorded that Tuthmosis III captured horses during his campaigns in Syria/Palestine and these were probably transported to Egypt to increase and improve the bloodstock.

The infantry was Egypt's original fighting force. During the Middle Kingdom, this consisted of two main divisions – older foot soldiers, and the younger, less experienced men. By the New Kingdom, this had increased to three groups – recruits, trained men, and specialized troops. The infantry, divided into regiments according to the arms that they carried, included bowmen, spearmen, swordsmen, clubmen, and slingers. Bowmen provided a major force of the army, fighting in both the chariotry and the infantry. Each division of an infantry regiment had its own standard, which became a rallying point during battle.

From the titles held by the soldiers, we can assume that the lowest commander was known as the 'Greatest of 50'. The next in line – the 'Standard-bearer' – was in charge of 200 men, while a higher-ranking officer supervised 250 soldiers. Next, there was the 'Captain of the Troop', and then came the 'Commander of the Troop', whose duties may have included heading a brigade or several regiments, or commanding a fortress. His superior, the 'Overseer of Garrison Troops', was responsible to one of two 'Overseers of Fortresses'; they supervised the Nubian border and the Mediterranean coast. Next in rank came the 'Lieutenant-Commander', who combined the duties of a senior officer, general administrator, and military commander. He was responsible to the General ('Overseer of the Army'), who answered to the king. In many instances, the rank of general was held by a prince, who commanded a wing or division in battle.

The army also appears to have had some specialized troops. An elite fighting force known as the 'Braves of the King' was trained to take charge of attacks. The *'w'yt* were garrison troops who served at home or abroad; one of their duties was to protect the king and the royal household. The 'Retainers' may have started out as the Royal Bodyguard, but in later times their role was to issue rations to troops and act as letter-carriers.

An extensive support system assembled and administered the army's supplies at home and on foreign campaigns. This was supervised by military scribes: when the army was campaigning abroad, they acquired any necessary supplies *en route* from local governors, and also listed booty taken in battle. In addition, they organized the army's transport system of pack-asses and ox-drawn wagons; these animals accompanied the army and were sometimes used alongside each other.

When a professional army was first established in the New Kingdom, some men from wealthy families chose to become professional fighters, but most soldiers were still conscripted from the peasants. However, the Egyptians were not a naturally warlike people; they preferred to remain at home with their families, and did not wish to die in a foreign country where the correct burial procedures would not be followed, thus jeopardizing their chances of eternal life. Therefore, the State had to provide incentives for men to join and remain in the army: they had the opportunity to seize booty on campaigns, and royal land gifted to professional soldiers could only be inherited by their sons if they also joined the army.

However, even these measures were insufficient to establish an army that was strong enough to build and retain an empire, and so the kings had to employ other methods. By Ramesses III's reign in Dynasty 20, one in ten males amongst the native population was conscripted for military service. Also, nations or groups of people whom the Egyptians had conquered or made their allies began to provide mercenary troops for the army. For example, in Dynasty 18, some soldiers were recruited from Nubia, and Amenhotep III also started to enlist prisoners-of-war as soldiers, a practice which continued until the Ramesside Period. In later times, foreign recruits formed a substantial and significant part of the Egyptian army. They fought alongside Egyptian soldiers on campaigns to invade other lands and suppress rebellions, and sometimes undertook garrison duty in

Egypt when native troops were absent on expeditions. Mercenaries were allowed to retain their own battledress and weapons, but do not appear to have received gifts of land in exchange for their services: they were simply paid as hired soldiers.

Weapons and Warfare

Weapons have survived in some tombs, and are also depicted in wall-scenes in tombs and temples. Soldiers' equipment included both offensive and defensive weapons. There were wooden bows, strung with catgut, and the composite bow, introduced to Egypt from Palestine during the Hyksos Period, which is depicted in reliefs on the chariot of Tuthmosis IV, where it is shown in the hands of both the king and his enemies. Arrows made of wood or reeds and tipped with metal or stone were carried in a large quiver.

Other offensive weapons included metal and wooden maces, curved sticks, spears which consisted of a metal shaft inserted into a wooden handle, and javelins which had a two-edged metal head. There were also leather or string slings, daggers and knives, and short, straight swords which often had a double edge tapering to a sharp point. Both officers and soldiers in the heavy and light troops were equipped with the *khepresh* (sickle-sword). This weapon, which had a bronze blade, was probably introduced to Egypt from Palestine during the Hyksos Period; by the New Kingdom, it was more widely used in the Egyptian army than the conventional sword.

Soldiers also carried a fixed-blade pole-axe, and a small axe with a single blade which resembled the tool that carpenters employed to cut up timbers. This axe, which was wielded in close-combat fighting and to attack the gates of fortified towns, exemplifies the Egyptians' conservative approach to weaponry. They generally favoured traditional weapons of proven ability: for example, while contemporary armies had already introduced the socket-type axe, the Egyptians continued to use the tang-type axe, although the design was gradually changed so that the blade became shorter and had a narrower edge. This type of weapon appears in the hands of infantrymen depicted on the lid of a wooden chest found in the tomb of Tutankhamun; also, a wall-relief at Karnak shows that it was used later by Ramesses II's soldiers.

The Egyptians' defensive equipment included thick, heavily padded helmets, coats-of-armour, and large shields. The coats-of-armour, probably introduced during the Hyksos Period, were made entirely of metal bands or were quilted and had metal bands attached. Even by the middle of Dynasty 18, these coats were rare, expensive items, although they were more widely used in later times. Shields, made of wood, covered with leather, and sometimes strengthened with metal rims, offered another form of protection.

The Navy

Essentially an extension of the army, the main role of the Egyptian navy was to transport troops and supplies over long distances, although it occasionally became engaged in active warfare.[11] In effect, sailors were 'soldiers at sea' rather than a separate force, and it was even possible for a man to be transferred or promoted from one Service to another. Naval recruits ($w'w$) were often drawn from military families, and usually served on warships, being assigned first to training-crews of rowers supervised by a Standard-bearer, before they joined the crew of a ship. Once part of a crew, recruits were directed by a 'Commander of Rowers'; he answered to a 'Standard-bearer' who was responsible to the 'Commander of Troops', which was perhaps a land position rather than an active naval role. At the highest levels, the Admirals took their orders from the 'Commander-in-Chief' (a prince) who reported to the king. Ships' navigation appears to have been organized under a separate chain of command, remaining the responsibility of the Captain and the Captain's mates. In the navy, it was possible to be promoted either to a higher rank or to a larger ship, or to be transferred to an army regiment. Indeed, in some inscriptions it is unclear whether a title refers to a ship or a regiment.

During Dynasty 18, the navy played an important role as a support service for the military campaigns to Syria, but in the reign of Ramesses III, it apparently became an active fighting force, helping to repel the raiders who attacked the Egyptian Delta.[12, 13]

In peacetime, the navy helped to develop trading links: in the New Kingdom, Egyptians not only developed naval dockyards along the Syria/Palestine coast, but also established an important naval base, Perw-nefer, probably located in the vicinity of Memphis. Perw-nefer became the country's chief port in the reigns of Tuthmosis III and his

Temple at Medinet Habu, Thebes. This shows a typical temple, with two open courts (left) leading into the hypostyle hall (once roofed). Temple wall-scenes at Medinet Habu show sea-battles fought by the Egyptians against the Libyans and the 'Sea-peoples'. New Kingdom.

son, Amenhotep II, and the naval base from which ships set sail during their Syrian campaigns.

The ships which the ancient Egyptians used for long distance travel have been the subject of much discussion.[14,15] During the New Kingdom, it is known that the navy possessed so-called 'Byblos ships' and 'Keftiu ships'; however, scholars are uncertain whether Byblos ships were given this name because they were specially built to travel to Byblos, or because they were constructed in the harbours of Byblos and other Syrian coastal towns. There is one suggestion that, after they captured enemy ships during Tuthmosis III's Syrian campaigns, the Egyptians used these vessels as prototypes for building their own fleet. However, they had been sending naval expeditions to Punt long before this date, and, as experienced seafarers, already possessed and knew how to sail large, impressive ships. Therefore, it is more likely that the term 'Byblos ship' applies to the vessel's destination port rather than to the place where it was built.

Amenemhet's Campaigns

As a professional soldier, Amenemhet regularly participated in Tuthmosis III's campaigns. Troops conscripted from all the provinces came together at the start of each campaign to slaughter animals and offer them as sacrifices to the gods. Then, as orders were given for the march to start, the troops were summoned with the sound of trumpets.

As a member of the chariotry, Amenemhet played an important role in the army and had experienced many different types of warfare during his long career. Battlefield tactics required that the chariots, led by the king who rode at their centre, were preceded and followed by the infantry. Once the trumpets had signalled the troops to start an attack, the archers sent their arrows into the enemy ranks; then, the chariotry charged forward to flank the infantry who, protected by their own heavy shields, pressed ahead into the centre of the enemy's forces. Throughout this onslaught, the archers continued to discharge their weapons, causing havoc amongst the enemy. After a successful engagement, the hands and sometimes the penises of the slain were cut off and counted in front of the King or General, so that the number of dead enemies could be calculated. All members of the enemy who begged for mercy and laid down their arms were taken prisoner. Eventually, supervised at the rear of the army, these prisoners would be escorted back to Egypt where they would be allocated to work on building sites or as domestic servants.

In the meantime, enemy possessions were divided up amongst the Egyptian soldiers as their battlefield share of the spoils. This booty, which included arms, horses and chariots, was sometimes laid out in an open area surrounded by a temporarily-constructed wall.

Amenemhet had also taken part in sieges, when the army attacked towns which were often fortified with thick mudbrick walls interspersed by square towers. The main objective of this type of warfare was to keep the attacker as far away as possible from the main wall, and this was sometimes achieved by building an outer circuit wall. The attackers would have to breach this wall first, and when they were in this vulnerable position, it was easier for the besieged townspeople to bombard them with missiles.

Nevertheless, the Egyptians were frequently victorious in these situations, advancing under the protection of their bowmen's arrows,

Wall-relief in the Great Temple of Ramesses II at Abu Simbel showing bound prisoners taken captive by the Egyptian army. Prisoners from different geographical areas are distinguished by their facial features and headdresses. Dynasty 19.

and then using scaling ladders to climb over the walls or force entry through the gates.

Egyptian troops were accommodated in field encampments during their campaigns. The encampment was arranged in a square formation with the main entrance located in one side; Amenemhet and other senior officers, including the General, had tents at the centre of this area while the space towards the outer part of the enclosure was used for feeding the horses and pack-animals, and storing chariots and baggage.

Occasionally, the stresses of campaigning gave rise to insubordination, and some soldiers even deserted. These were not regarded as capital offences: the soldier was simply rebuked by his peers, and was expected to show renewed valour and bravery so that he could be reinstated. However, there was severe punishment for those who revealed military secrets to the enemy, and their tongues were cut out.

When Amenmehet and his comrades returned from the Syrian campaigns, they were greeted along the way by people living in towns that owed allegiance to Egypt: men and women ran from their homes, calling out greetings to the king and his troops. Upon reaching the Egyptian capital, the soldiers received further rewards, and attended a thanksgiving ceremony in the Temple of Karnak where, for many weeks, the priests had been making preparations for these great celebrations. Ceremonies performed in this resplendent setting included the presentation of offerings and prisoners-of-war to the god, Amen-Re, to honour him as the divine author of Egypt's victories.

As a reward for his services as a professional soldier, Amenemhet had already received land from the king, where he had established a fine country estate. This property was free from any charges, and he planned to hand it on to his descendants. Amenemhet was a man of good character who was careful not to incur expenses he could not afford, but as a soldier, he enjoyed the additional reassurance that he could not be thrown into prison for debt. Indeed, military service had given him rapid wealth and promotion, and there was always the possibility, once his best fighting years were over, that the king would appoint him to a senior position at the Royal Court where he would enjoy many privileges. Kings sometimes made these promotions from the ranks of senior army officers (for example, the post of 'Tutor of the Royal Children' had been filled in this way). They hoped that this personal honour would ensure the men's loyalty at Court, and offset the lack of support they sometimes faced from members of the nobility.

Chapter 10

Funerary Customs

Nefert, Khary's mother-in-law in our imaginary family, had not survived the year. She became increasingly debilitated with her chronic illnesses and afflictions, and suffered particularly from pain and breathlessness, the results of sand pneumoconiosis. Much weakened, she eventually succumbed to a bout of pneumonia, and passed away in her sixtieth year, during the fourth month of *Shemu*. By ancient Egyptian standards of life expectancy (the average age was about forty), Nefert had enjoyed a long life, but nevertheless, her death came unexpectedly, and the family were thrown into a state of deep mourning.

Urgent preparations had to be made for elaborate funerary and burial arrangements, which would ensure that Nefert had every chance of surviving death and attaining immortality.[1] From the Middle Kingdom onwards, the Egyptians believed that every person, whether rich or poor, could aspire to an individual eternity which they hoped would be spent in the kingdom of Osiris, god of the dead.[2]

This realm was envisaged as a land of eternal springtime which mirrored Egypt itself, but was free from illness and suffering. The Egyptians believed that this place, known as the 'Fields of Reeds', was situated somewhere beyond the western horizon. Poverty was no bar to entering this kingdom; the requirements were personal piety, performance of the correct burial procedures, and a successful outcome before the tribunal of forty-two divine judges at the Day of Judgement.[3]

On this occasion, the deceased was required to attend an interrogation and recite the 'Negative Confession' – forty-two

Wooden statuette of the god Osiris, showing him as a mummiform figure holding the symbols of kingship – the crook and the flail. Traces of paint remain, as well as the copper inlays for the uraeus (snake) on the front of the headdress, eyebrows and outlines of the eyes. From Saqqara. Dynasty 26. Manchester Museum.

statements which denied any personal guilt of various sins, crimes and misdemeanours. Scenes on coffins and papyri which depict this event show the confession taking place in front of a balance: one pan holds the person's heart, while the other contains the 'Feather of Truth'. If the person lied, then his heart would weigh against him, but if he was innocent, then his heart and the feather would achieve an equal balance, and he would be declared 'true of voice'.

If the deceased successfully convinced the divine judges that he was innocent of all sin, then his body would be reunited with his soul, and he would pass into Osiris' kingdom.[4] However, if his heart weighed against him, then his body (or, in some instances, his heart) would be thrown to a fearsome creature known as the 'Devourer', whose body combined parts of several different animals. This creature would then consume the deceased's body, thus destroying his chance of attaining eternity.

Funerary Customs
The Tomb
According to custom, Nefert's husband had started to prepare a tomb for himself and his wife as soon as they married and established a home. Known as the 'House of the *Ka*', the tomb was regarded as a

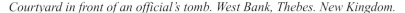

Courtyard in front of an official's tomb. West Bank, Thebes. New Kingdom.

View of the Valley of the Kings, Thebes, with the mountain behind. The pyramid shape of the mountain (known as 'the Peak'), as well as the site's isolated location, may have persuaded the kings to select this area for their tombs when pyramid-building was discontinued. New Kingdom.

home for the spirit (*Ka*) of the deceased. The *Ka* could return to the tomb at any time, in order to gain sustenance from the food offerings placed in the adjoining chapel or from the menu inscribed on the tomb walls.[5]

Kings of the New Kingdom were no longer buried in pyramids, choosing instead to be interred in rock-cut tombs in the Valley of the Kings on the West Bank at Thebes.[6] Here, one day, the body of Tuthmosis III, the king whom Khary served, would be laid to rest. Unlike non-royal tombs, the royal burial place did not represent the king's house. The royal tomb provided the king with a gateway to his eternal kingdom. It represented a sacred space (the interior walls were decorated with appropriate scenes and inscriptions from various funerary texts) where he faced and triumphed over various dangers, and was ultimately transformed from a living into a dead ruler.

During the New Kingdom, officials and their families who lived at Thebes were buried in tombs scattered across the West Bank *necropolises*. Nefert's tomb was typical of a non-royal burial place for a wealthy family of Dynasty 18. In front of the tomb was an open rectangular courtyard which gave access to a rock-cut, inverted T-shaped offering-chapel. In the centre of the back wall of this wide, shallow chamber an entrance led off into a long, narrow room where statues of Nefert and her husband were placed in a niche cut into the wall at the far end. A concealed shaft at the rear of this narrow room gave access to two subterranean chambers which held the burials and tomb goods. This shaft was sealed and covered over after each burial, but relatives and funerary priests could continue to visit the offering-chapel, where they prayed and presented funerary offerings.

Many family burial places were built and decorated well in advance of death, but if preparations were not already in place, some tombs – probably owned by embalmers (wealthy men who mummified the dead) as a commercial investment – were available for sale at short notice. Less affluent people could either choose to share a rock-tomb, or to be buried in rock-cut recesses or pits that had no upper chambers. The poorest men and women were buried in mass graves.

Ostracon (limestone sherd) decorated with a unique sketch of a funeral at a rock-cut tomb. At the top of the tomb-shaft, a priest (left) holds a burning censer and pours out a libation, while four women raise their arms to lament the deceased tomb-owner. A man descends the shaft to enter the burial area where, in the left chamber, two kneeling mourners await the arrival of the mummy, preceded by a priest wearing the jackal-headed mask of Anubis, god of cemeteries and mummification. Two mummies from earlier burials can be seen in the right-hand chamber. Steps lead down to another room where the owner's funerary possessions were stored. From Qurneh, Thebes. Dynasty 18. Manchester Museum.

Nefert's deceased husband had made good provision for their burial, and their tomb was kept in good order. It was approached through a small, flower-filled courtyard garden, regularly tended by a paid employee, which emphasized the tomb's role as the home of the deceased. The upper and middle classes believed that they would spend eternity in the kingdom of Osiris, but they also expected to pass time in the tomb. Here, the walls were decorated with horizontal registers of scenes depicting many everyday activities. At the funeral service, special rites were performed to magically activate these scenes, as well as the relevant funerary models and tomb goods. In this way, the deceased owner hoped to be able to derive pleasure and benefits from these activities and situations even after death. For example, scenes and models of food production ensured that he would have an eternal food supply; he was portrayed as well-regarded and successful in his career so that he would continue to hold high office in the next world; and pastimes that he and his family enjoyed were represented in the tomb so that they could continue to experience them after death.

Tomb Goods

The dead were believed to have the same needs as the living, and therefore it was customary to place food, clothing, jewellery, cosmetics, tools, weapons and domestic equipment in the tombs.[7] Manufacturing tomb equipment played a key role in the Egyptian economy, and many workshops were engaged in the production of a variety of goods for the dead as well as the living.

Reed and pottery coffins had been used from earliest times to protect the dead, but from c.3400 BCE, a rectangular wooden coffin was introduced for the upper classes; this was probably intended to represent a 'house' for the deceased. Democratization of religious beliefs and funerary customs, which started in the Middle Kingdom, encouraged everyone to provide themselves with tomb equipment, according to their means.

Increasingly, the middle classes furnished their tombs with a range of burial goods which included a 'nest' of at least two coffins. The outer coffin, usually made of wood, was rectangular in shape; the inner coffin was anthropoid (body-shaped) and represented the deceased as a wrapped mummy. In the New Kingdom, this arrangement was replaced by a nest of two or even three anthropoid coffins. Coffin-makers, often employed in workshops run by embalmers, were members of a separate and distinctive craft who combined the skills of carpenter and painter. In addition to coffins, these men made wooden models and figurines, and other items for the tomb.

The external surface of a typical anthropoid coffin was painted with representations that imitated real items found inside the mummy: a bead collar, girdle, bandaging and jewellery. During the New Kingdom, coffin decoration also included scenes of gods, the Day of Judgement and the deceased's resurrection, as well as inscriptions from funerary 'books'.[8] These contained spells to help the deceased enter and survive in the kingdom of Osiris; however, by this period, the spells were also inscribed in a more complete form on a roll of papyrus (the so-called *Book of the Dead*) which was either placed inside the bandages of the mummy or elsewhere in the tomb.[9]

Coffins and papyri were generally mass-produced, but most were also inscribed with the names and titles of the purchaser, in order to

Two canopic jars from a set of four, with human-headed lids. The name of the owner, Nekht-Ankh, is inscribed on the front of each jar. These containers were used to store the owner's mummified viscera. From the Tomb of Two Brothers, Rifeh. Dynasty 12. Manchester Musuem.

identify ownership. The coffin fulfilled a dual purpose: it protected the body and also provided a *locus* to which the deceased's spirit could return at will. Facial features were represented in a stylized manner on anthropoid coffins: no attempt was made to depict the features of an individual owner. The eyes were painted or carved, and often inlaid with obsidian and alabaster to make them look lifelike. A separately-made wooden false beard was pegged into the chin; this beard indicated that the deceased had become an 'Osiris' – someone who had successfully faced the Day of Judgement had thus become a manifestation of the god.

Many tombs also contained a set of canopic jars. These were used to store the viscera removed from the deceased's body during mummification. The viscera were cut out from the chest and abdominal cavities, and then natron was used to dehydrate them. Finally, they were either returned as packages to the bodily cavities or placed in containers known today as canopic jars.

Each set included four jars; they were dedicated to a group of gods known as the 'Four Sons of Horus' who protected the viscera and prevented the owner from experiencing hunger. When the jars were first introduced in the Middle Kingdom, their stoppers were often carved to represent four human heads. However, by Dynasty 18, the stoppers portrayed the 'Four Sons': Imset (human-headed) who protected the stomach and large intestine; Hapy (ape-headed) who guarded the small intestine; Duamutef (jackal-headed) who cared for the lungs; and Qebehsennuef (hawk-headed) who was responsible for the liver and gall-bladder. The 'Four Sons' were themselves protected by the goddesses Isis, Nephthys, Neith and Selket.

A funerary priest performed a special ritual at the burial service: known as the 'Ceremony of Opening the Mouth', this 'brought to life' all the tomb-scenes, statues, models, and the owner's mummy.[10] It was believed that this ritual charged them with a magical force so that they could be used by the deceased owner. When performed on the mummy, the rites allowed the owner's spirit to enter the body, and restored his original life-force and physical capabilities so that he could function again in the afterlife.

Statues and figurines placed in the tomb represented the owner and sometimes other members of his family. Most of these images were not lifesize, but the Egyptians believed that the 'Ceremony of Opening the Mouth' would restore their original size and functional abilities. Most of these figurines do not show the exact facial features of an individual person, but items were given the owner's identity by adding his name at the time of purchase.

A tomb assemblage usually included models of servants as well as statues of the owner and his family. Carved in wood, with painted details sometimes added to produce a realistic and lifelike appearance, these models often duplicated or resembled the content of the wall-scenes. Both were designed to provide for the needs of the owner in the next world. Some models represent a group activity; the most common examples show figurines working in granaries, breweries, slaughterhouses, kitchens or weaving workshops to produce food or textiles for the deceased. There are also models of the owner's whole estate, complete with its villa, fields and herds, while other examples represent a single agricultural activity, such as men and oxen ploughing the fields. A special group of servant models known as *ushabtis* were included so that they could undertake agricultural work in the next world on behalf of the deceased (see above, p143).

From the Middle Kingdom onwards, tombs often included a model boat, or set of boats, so that the deceased owner could travel on the river.[11] Again, the 'Ceremony of Opening the Mouth' was expected to restore these miniature versions to the full size and capacity of the originals. The model boats were made of wood, and have oars, deck cabins, crew, and linen sails; carefully carved or painted details were added. Wealthy people often included a variety of craft in their tombs for different purposes. For example, there are vessels to transport the body of the deceased across the river for burial in the *necropolis* on the West Bank; to take part in fishing expeditions to augment the owner's food supply; and, most importantly, to enable him to make the journey to Abydos, the supposed burial place of Osiris, so that he could increase his chances of resurrection and eternal life.

Amulets – sacred jewellery inserted between the mummy bandages – provided additional protection for the deceased (see above, p186). A particularly important amulet, the heart scarab, was placed amongst the bandages over the heart of the mummy. This essential item of funerary equipment often carried an inscription which invoked the

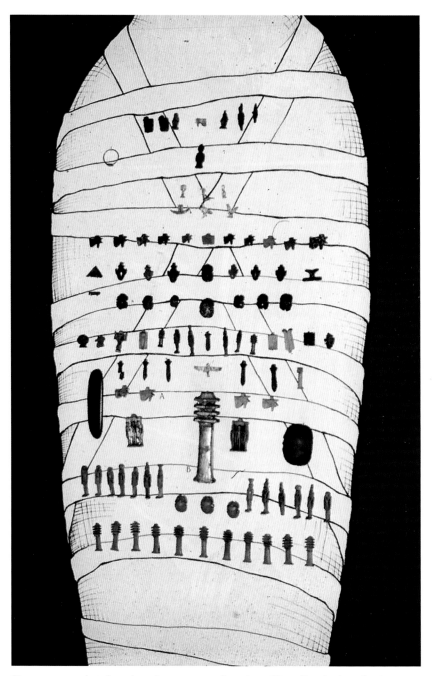

Funerary amulets found on the mummy of a priest, Horudja. Archaeologists very rarely discover a complete set of amulets still in situ on a mummy. This display reconstructs the exact location of each amulet at the time of discovery: most noticeable are the large heart scarab (right, third row from bottom), the adjacent gilded Djed-pillar, and the slate finger (left) for covering the incision through which the viscera were removed from the body. From Hawara. Dynasty 26. Manchester Museum.

heart not to speak against its owner when he faced the Day of Judgement.

Nefert and her family had prepared for her burial in the traditional manner. Long before she was expected to die, they had purchased or commissioned essential tomb goods that would fulfil particular funerary requirements. Other items, such as food, clothing, cosmetics, jewellery and domestic utensils were added to satisfy Nefert's everyday needs in the afterlife. Some of these were specially prepared for the burial assemblage, but Nefert had also instructed her daughters to include favourite possessions that she had enjoyed using and wearing when she was alive.

Mummification

It was now time to transport Nefert's body from the family home to the embalmers' workshop so that it could be prepared for burial. The workshop was known as the *wbt* ('place of purification'), and was supervised by the embalmers. These highly skilled professionals were a special class of priests, and had some connections with medical practitioners. They conducted their work on a commercial basis, and supervised all the physical procedures and religious rituals associated with mummification. However, the man known as the 'cutter', who actually made the incision in the flank of the mummy to remove the viscera, was not himself an embalmer. The unpleasant nature and potential danger of this work (because it gave him direct contact with the corpse) meant that he was regarded as unclean and untouchable. He could never escape from this lowly status, and was always regarded as a social outcast – a member of a group that may also have included convicted criminals.

The Egyptians probably developed the process now known as 'intentional mummification' after a long period of experimentation.[12] It was introduced for royalty and the nobility in *c.*2600 BCE, although the procedure may have originated at a much earlier date. The main aim of mummification was to preserve the body in as recognizable a state as possible so that the deceased's spirit could return at any time, and use the body to partake of the spirit of the food-offerings placed at the tomb.

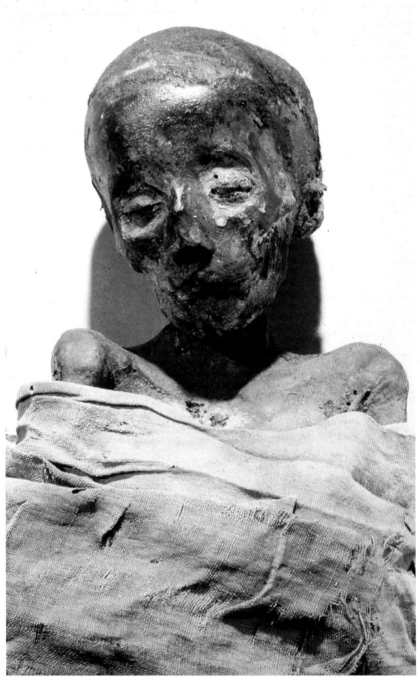

Mummy of a child aged about six years. The body is well preserved; the eyelashes are visible and traces of gilding remain on the face. Unprovenanced. Graeco-Roman Period. From the Stonyhurst College collection, now in Manchester Museum.

During the Middle Kingdom, the middle classes adopted mummification as part of the democratization of religious and funerary beliefs and practices that occurred at that period. It became universal for royalty[13] and the upper and middle classes throughout the pharaonic period, and some people continued to mummify their dead even in the Christian era.

Poor people, however, were always simply interred in shallow graves on the edge of the desert, where the heat and dryness of the sand preserved their bodies (a process known today as 'natural mummification'). Before c.3400 BCE, all Egyptians had been buried in this way, but a change in funerary architecture instigated the need to develop intentional methods of preserving the body. The new type of tomb (which Egyptologists call a *mastaba*-tomb) was used for the upper classes, and had a brick-lined burial chamber. This meant that the body decomposed rapidly because it was no longer directly surrounded by sand. However, funerary beliefs dictated that the body had to be preserved, and so it was essential to find another method of dehydrating the bodily tissues and preventing rapid decomposition.

There is no extant Egyptian account of how mummification was carried out, but presumably the embalmers handed down their oral traditions. However, detailed descriptions have survived in the works of two Greek historians, Herodotus (fifth century BCE) and Diodorus Siculus (first century BCE). These sources, and evidence provided by the mummies themselves, enable us to reconstruct the various stages involved in mummification.[14] Herodotus describes three main methods which were available according to cost. The most expensive method – which members of Nefert's social class would have chosen – involved two main stages: evisceration, and then dehydration of the body by means of natron. In addition, the body was anointed with oils, and sometimes it was coated with resin and treated with plants and plant extracts. According to the ancient literary sources, the procedure lasted seventy days, although modern experiments on dead rats have demonstrated that physical preparation of the body would not have exceeded forty days. The extra days would doubtless have been used for prayers and rituals.

Once the embalmers received Nefert's body from the family, it was placed on a board or platform. The first step was to remove the brain,

Limestone statue of Anubis, the jackal-god associated with mummification and cemeteries. From Saqqara. Dynasty 26. Manchester Museum.

which was usually extracted via the left nostril and a passageway chiselled through the ethmoid bone into the cranial cavity. Using a metal hook, the embalmers then reduced the brain, and scooped it out with a spatula. Since the Egyptians regarded the heart and not the brain as the seat of the intellect and emotions, the brain tissue was considered to be unimportant, and so these fragments were discarded. However, the embalmers were not usually successful in removing the whole brain, and some tissue remained behind in the cranial cavity. Alternative methods of excerebration (brain removal) were sometimes employed; these involved extracting the brain either through the base of the skull or an eye socket.

Next, the viscera were removed through an incision usually made in the left flank. The 'cutter' inserted his hand through this incision and, reaching into the abdominal cavity, he used a special knife to cut free the viscera which he then drew out of the corpse. Making a further incision in the diaphragm, he repeated the process and removed the organs from the chest cavity. According to custom, Nefert's heart was left in place because of its importance as the supposed seat of her personality, and the kidneys also remained *in situ* (although Egyptologists have not identified any religious or philosophical explanation for this). The embalmers then washed out the body cavities with palm wine and spices, and inserted a temporary packing of dry natron, packets of natron and resin, and linen impregnated with resin; these helped to dehydrate the body and prevent the chest wall from collapsing.

The viscera were now dehydrated with a chemical agent. Salt or lime may have been used in some instances, but natron was the most popular choice. A mixture of sodium carbonate, bicarbonate, and some natural impurities, natron occurs in dry deposits in a couple of desert areas of Egypt. Used in its solid, dry state for mummification, it destroyed the body's fat and grease and dehydrated the tissues – a process which successfully arrested bacterial growth and consequent decomposition. During the New Kingdom, the embalmers placed the dehydrated viscera inside the four canopic jars, but other traditions were followed in later times. In Dynasties 21 and 22, the organs were wrapped in four packages and replaced inside the chest and abdominal cavities, while later they were sometimes made into one large parcel and placed on the legs of the mummy.

Following evisceration, the embalmers packed dry natron around the body and inside the bodily cavities, and left it for a period of up to forty days. Then the corpse was removed from the natron and washed with water to remove any residual debris. As the body was still quite pliable, the embalmers were able to straighten it out so that it could be placed in a coffin.

The basic procedures had now been completed, but in order to remove any lingering odours and perhaps to try to deter any insect infestation, the body was anointed with cedar oil and sweet-smelling ointments, and rubbed with cinnamon, myrrh, and other spices. The flank incision was closed either by sewing the edges of the flesh together, or covering them with a metal or beeswax plate. Sometimes, molten resin was poured into the cranial cavity, or it was packed with resin-impregnated linen; the nostrils were also plugged with resin or wax, and finally, a resinous paste was applied to the whole body.

Two gold eye-covers (bottom). Unprovenanced. Roman Period. Three gold tongue plates. From Hawara. Roman Period. The eye-covers were placed over the eyes of the mummy, and the tongue plates inserted in the mouth to provide magical protection for the deceased. Manchester Museum.

The embalmers carefully wrapped Nefert's mummy in linen clothes and bandages; they inserted amulets between the bandage layers, and extended her arms alongside her body. The mummification procedure now drew to a close, and the embalmer, acting in his capacity as a priest, performed a special ceremony which involved pouring a semi-liquid resinous substance over Nefert's mummy, coffin, and her viscera inside the canopic jars.

The Funeral

Once the mummification process was finished, Nefert's family removed the mummy from the embalmer's workshop and took it home. They now had to organize the burial ceremonies so that Nefert could finally be laid to rest. Since various stages of the funeral are depicted in wall-scenes in Theban tombs, it is possible to reconstruct the order of the main events.

Throughout the mummification process, Nefert's family and friends had observed a period of mourning, abstaining from the pleasures of life: they did not bathe, wear fine clothes, or enjoy wine and good food. Now that the mummy had been returned to the house, all the women of the family, together with their relatives and friends, began to mourn outside the home. They rubbed dirt into their faces, tore their dresses to expose their breasts, beat themselves on the forehead, and wailed.

At last, the day of the funeral arrived. Nefert's family and friends, together with professional female mourners engaged to perform the funerary chants, assembled at the family home to escort the body and the associated burial goods to the tomb in the *necropolis* on the West Bank. Leaving the house, situated on the East Bank of the Nile, the mourners boarded a special funerary barque to accompany the mummy on the short journey across the river. Nefert's daughter, Perenbast, and other close female relatives, squatted on the deck, near the brightly painted, flower-strewn coffin which was supported on a bier. These women had torn their dresses and exposed their breasts as a sign of grief; now they bewailed Nefert's death with the traditional eerie cries of mourning. Standing before the bier, the funerary priest burnt incense, recited special prayers, and made offerings on behalf of Nefert's spirit. Another boat which sailed in front of the funerary barque accommodated other female mourners who also sat crying on the deck. A third boat conveyed Nefert's male relatives, while a fourth was filled with servants who carried gifts and bouquets of flowers to leave at the tomb.

Once the boats had moored at the West Bank, the mourners disembarked to begin the final journey to Nefert's tomb, which was cut into the cliffs behind the wide stretch of fertile land where crops were grown and harvested every year. As the procession formed, the funerary barque carrying the coffin was placed on a sledge drawn by two oxen; Nefert's closest male and female relatives walked behind this, lamenting and beating their heads in grief. Distinguished by the panther skin that he wore around his body, the *sem*-priest (a special cleric who supervised the funeral) walked in front of the sledge. He poured a libation on the ground and wafted incense around the coffin. In front of him, another official sprinkled the ground with milk to ease the passage of the sledge, while a short way ahead, a herdsman walked alongside the oxen, urging them onwards with his whip.

239

Slowly, the procession wound its way across the cultivation and then ascended the steep pathway to the rock-cut tomb. Here, in front of the offering-chapel, the funerary officials placed the mummy upright against the entrance, where it was held and supported by a priest wearing a jackal-headed mask to represent Anubis, the god of embalming and the *necropolis*. Perenbast, the chief female mourner, knelt before the mummy, beating her head as a sign of grief; behind her stood a table piled high with food offerings. Four priests waited nearby to perform the funerary rites. One of these carried out the 'Ceremony of Opening the Mouth', touching the face of the mummy with an adze so that the life-force would be restored. Another poured out a libation of water to revivify Nefert, while behind him, the *sem-priest* offered up incense. A lector-priest stood behind this group, holding an unrolled papyrus from which he recited the funerary prayers. He led the main group of male mourners who, followed by the women, beat their foreheads and uttered shrill cries of lamentation.

The burial ceremony concluded with a meal for the mourners at the tomb; this repast closely resembled the banquets the family always enjoyed at home. According to Egyptian belief, the deceased's *Ka* joined the mourners at this funerary feast, and they were all entertained by singers and dancers who had accompanied the funerary procession, and by a harpist who recited special songs which emphasized the joys of eternal existence. Most of these hymns were intended to revive the deceased and make provision for the person's eternal welfare; they also gave the grief-stricken guests some comfort and insight into the meaning of the funerary offerings.

Although most songs emphasized the joys of eternal existence, some (which Egyptologists call *Pessimistic Hymns*) presented a less positive viewpoint. Remarkably, these hymns cast doubts on a major focus of the Egyptians' lives by questioning the existence of an afterlife[15] and whether there was any point in preparing and provisioning a tomb. They claimed that earthly existence was transient and there was no certainty about human life; funerary preparations did not last, and the dead did not return to tell the living what they needed in the next world. Instead, the hymns urged the listeners to enjoy life while they could, because the existence of an afterlife was so uncertain that even a well-provisioned tomb could not guarantee personal survival.

It is possible that these disturbing sentiments were first expressed in literature that dates to an earlier period of economic deprivation and political upheaval, when the Egyptians had reason to question their deepest beliefs and to speculate about the very existence of a hereafter. However, by the New Kingdom, the country was once again powerful and affluent, and these doubts and fears were less evident. During this period, most funerary texts attempted to reject any earlier scepticism, and to reassert a convincing belief in immortality. Nevertheless, tomb-owners evidently considered it advisable to present both viewpoints, probably so that the sceptical version could be aired and rejected. Therefore, some tombs were inscribed with a pessimistic hymn alongside one of the new compositions which gave reassurance about the joys and reality of eternal life.

Generally, songs of lamentation gave mourners the opportunity to confront their deepest fears, and reassured them that neither they nor the deceased tomb-owner would face the ultimate fear – the absolute or 'second death'. The Egyptians dreaded this fate, reserved for the

Reed coffin tied with ropes and a linen strip, containing the naturally mummified body of an infant just under three months of age. X-rays show growth arrest lines in the lower limbs, indicating a period of sustained illness. From Gurob. Dynasty 18. Manchester Museum.

wicked or those who had not made correct burial preparations, because it resulted in complete personal oblivion or a form of semi-existence from which the deceased could not escape.

Nefert's body and its elaborate adornments were finally placed in the burial chamber. The fast-fading bouquets and garlands of flowers brought by the mourners remained on top of the protective nest of coffins which encased the mummy. Nefert's relatives hoped that her burial would remain undisturbed; they prayed that she would attain eternity, and that one day they would be reunited with her in the kingdom of Osiris.

The family had made expensive and meticulous funerary preparations to try to ensure Nefert's afterlife, but they were only too aware that the tomb would probably be plundered before many years had passed. As they and their guests began to leave the tomb and start the descent towards the river, they silently pondered the words of the blind harpist who had entertained them at the funerary banquet. No one admitted it, but the hymns offered little solace; doubts would always remain, and they could not ignore the final advice given in one lament:

'Spend the daily happily,
Do not become weary of it,
Lo, no one can take his possessions with him!
Lo, no one who has departed returns again!'
(Harpist's Song from the Tomb of King Intef. Author's translation]

Appendix

Some Major Archaeological Sites Referred to in this Book

Many Egyptian sites have more than one name; sometimes a site is known by its modern (Arabic), ancient Egyptian, and Classical (Greek or Graeco-Roman) names. In this list, sites are generally arranged under the modern name (this often refers to a village near the archaeological site), and the ancient Egyptian and Classical names (if known) are given in brackets. In some cases, the site is better known by a name other than the modern one, and this is then given in capitals (e.g. *San el-Hagar*; *Eg: Dja'net*; *Cl: TANIS*).

1. Lower Egypt Delta Sites
Alexandria
The chief city and port of the Hellenistic world, Alexandria was founded by Alexander the Great. Important buildings which can still be seen include the Serapeum, which was the centre for the cult of Serapis, and the catacombs of Kom el-Shuqafa (first to second centuries CE).

Damietta
Situated on the east side of the Delta, between the Damietta branch of the Nile and Lake Manzala, this modern town played an important role in medieval times, although very little is known of its earlier history.

Rosetta
Situated on the west side of the Delta at the mouth of the Rosetta arm of the Nile, this modern town has a long history that goes back to at

least medieval times, and probably to antiquity. The famous Rosetta Stone was discovered here at Fort St Julien.

San el-Hagar (Eg: Zau; Cl: SAIS)
This was the capital of the fifth Lower Egyptian *nome* (a geographical and political district). It became the capital of Egypt in Dynasty 26. It was also a religious centre which had temples and the royal tombs of Dynasty 26; the goddess Neith was worshipped here from earliest times.

Samannud (Eg: Tjebnutjer; Cl: SEBENNYTOS)
The capital of the twelfth Lower Egyptian *nome*, this was the home of the Egyptian historian Manetho. It may also have been the capital of the rulers of Dynasty 30. There are remains of the temple of Onuris-Shu (Dynasty 30 and Ptolemaic Period).

Tell Basta (Eg: Per-Bastet; Cl: BUBASTIS)
The capital of the eighteenth Lower Egyptian *nome* in the Late Period, this was the cult-centre of the lioness goddess Bastet; it also became the capital of the kings of Dynasty 22. There are remains of the Temple of Bastet, and of other temples and religious buildings, covering a period from the Old Kingdom to Roman times.

Qantir
The site of Pi-Ramesse (the royal residence of the Ramesside rulers referred to in the Bible as Ramses) is probably near Qantir.

Tell ed-Dab'a (Cl: AVARIS)
To the south of Qantir, the site of Tell ed-Dab'a (probably Avaris, the Hyksos capital) retains evidence of an Aegean presence or influence during the Hyksos Period. In the later New Kingdom, a temple dedicated to Seth was built here.

San el-Hagar (Eg: Dja'net; Cl: TANIS)
This was the main royal residence and *necropolis* during Dynasties 21 and 22. Archaeologists have uncovered the Great Temple of Amun, and also the royal tombs with their magnificent treasure (now in the

Cairo Museum). Construction material was brought here from earlier Ramesside monuments and reused in buildings erected in Dynasty 21. Later, chapels and temples were built here, down to the Graeco-Roman Period.

Tell el-Qasr (Eg: Djedet; Cl: MENDES)

This was the ancient city of Mendes where the *Djed*-column (later associated with Osiris) was worshipped. In the temple, archaeologists discovered the remains of a shrine dedicated by King Amasis; coffins belonging to sacred rams have also been found at the site.

2. Lower Egypt: The Pyramid Area
Heliopolis (Cl.) (Eg: Iunu; Arabic: Tell Hisn)

The capital of the thirteenth Lower Egyptian *nome*, this is now a modern suburb of Cairo. It was the centre of the cult of the sun god, Re-Atum, although this temple no longer survives.

Mit Rahina (Eg: Ineb-hedj ('White Wall'); later, Mennufer; Cl: MEMPHIS)

Little remains of Memphis, the royal residence and capital in the Archaic Period and Old Kingdom, and centre of the first Lower Egyptian *nome*. Archaeologists have uncovered the Temple of Ptah enclosure, and an alabaster sphinx, as well as other religious buildings including the embalming house of the Apis-bulls, a temple of Tuthmosis IV, and other temples dedicated to Hathor and Ptah. In addition, there are tombs of the First Intermediate and Late Periods. The *necropolises* of Memphis included Dahshur, Saqqara, Abusir, Zawiyet el-'Aryan, Giza, and Abu Rawash.

Saqqara

This extensive *necropolis* includes the world's first great stone monument, the Step Pyramid of Djoser (Dynasty 3). There are also pyramids of Userkaf, Isesi, and Unas (all Dynasty 5), and of Teti, Pepy I and Pepy II (all Dynasty 6). The site also includes the royal tombs of the Archaic Period, and officials' tombs from the Old Kingdom onwards, including those of the late New Kingdom courtiers Horemheb, Tia and Maya. There are sacred animal complexes of which the most famous, the Serapeum, was constructed for the Apis-bull burials.

Giza

Egypt's most famous archaeological site, Giza contains the renowned pyramid complexes (Dynasty 4) of Cheops (Egyptian: Khufu), Chephren (Egyptian: Khaefre) and Mycerinus (Egyptian: Menkaure). Chephren's complex is the most complete, with a pyramid, valley building, causeway and mortuary temple. The Great Sphinx is situated near the valley building. The tomb of Queen Hetepheres (Dynasty 4) was discovered near the pyramid of her son, Cheops. There are also extensive cemeteries of *mastaba*-tombs for members of the royal family and senior officials.

Tura (Eg: Royu; Cl: Troja)

The quarries of Tura are situated to the north of Helwan (an outer suburb of Cairo). From pharaonic times down to the Ptolemaic Period, they yielded fine white limestone which was used for the outer casing of pyramids, *mastaba*-tombs, and other important buildings.

3. The Fayoum and Associated Area
The Fayoum (Eg: She-resy)

An important centre in Dynasty 12 and the Graeco-Roman Period, the Fayoum was the location of Lake Moeris (Arabic: Birket Qarun). It was the cult-centre of the crocodile god Sobek (Greek: Suchos), and the royal cemeteries of Dynasty 12 were located here at el-Lahun and Hawara. Greek and Macedonian immigrants settled in the Fayoum during the Graeco-Roman Period.

Hawara

Hawara was the site of the pyramid of Amenemhet III (Dynasty 12) and his mortuary temple (the 'Labyrinth'), as well as cemeteries from the Middle Kingdom to the Graeco-Roman Period. There are temples of different periods, and archaeologists have discovered many Roman Period mummy panel portraits at Hawara.

El-Lahun

This is the site of the pyramid of Senusret II (Dynasty 12), where contemporary royal jewellery belonging to his family was discovered in an associated shaft-tomb.

Kahun (Eg: Hetep-Senusret)

This town accommodated the families of royal workers who built the el-Lahun pyramid. Archaeologists discovered a wide selection of artifacts and the town's archive of papyri, which have provided much evidence about domestic life, crafts, and religion.

Kom Medinet Ghurab (GUROB)

This New Kingdom royal residence town was particularly popular in the reign of Amenhotep III. There are the remains of two temples, cemeteries, and houses.

El-Lisht (Eg: It-towy)

The exact situation of this capital city of Dynasty 12 has never been located, but it was served by the cemeteries at el-Lisht, el-Lahun, and Hawara. The pyramids of Amenemhet I and Senusret I, and non-royal tombs of the Old and Middle Kingdoms were built at Lisht.

4. Middle Egypt
Beni Hasan

The most important Middle Kingdom provincial *necropolis* in Middle Egypt, this served the town of Monet-Khufu. Beni Hasan is the location of large rock-cut tombs belonging to the great provincial rulers of the sixteenth *nome* of Upper Egypt, who lived in Dynasties 11 and 12; south of these are the remains of a rock-cut temple (Speos Artemidos) dedicated to the lioness-goddess Pakhet (Dynasty 18).

El-Ashmunein (Eg: Khmun; Cl: HERMOPOLIS MAGNA)

The capital of the fifteenth Upper Egyptian *nome*, this was the cult-centre of the god Thoth, and the place where a major creation myth originated. The Greeks identified Thoth with their god Hermes, and Graeco-Roman remains at the site include the Temple of Thoth. The *pylon* (gateway) of a temple built by Ramesses II was found to contain over 1,500 decorated blocks brought from dismantled temples of the Aten at Tell el-Amarna.

Tuna el-Gebel

The *necropolis* of the city of Hermopolis Magna, this site also has catacombs filled with ibis and baboon burials which mostly date to the Graeco-Roman Period. Tuna el-Gebel is the location of the tomb of the priest Petosiris (*c*.300 BCE), and others (including that of Isadora) which date to the first centuries CE. There is also a *stela*, one of a group of six erected by Akhenaten (Dynasty 18) to mark the boundary of Tell el-Amarna (Akhetaten) and its environs.

Tell el-Amarna (AMARNA; Eg: Akhetaten)

The capital city built by Akhenaten (Amenhotep IV) in Dynasty 18, this was the cult-centre of the Aten. The remains of temples dedicated to the Aten, courtiers' tombs, and the Royal Tomb (nine kilometres distant, in a remote mountain valley) all provide evidence about Atenism (the worship of the Aten). There is also a workmen's village which accommodated the families of men engaged in building the city.

5. Upper Egypt (North)
Abydos (Eg: Abedju)

Egypt's most important religious city, Abydos was the cult-centre of the gods Khentiamentiu and Osiris. The site had a number of main areas: the royal tombs/cenotaphs of the Archaic Period are situated at Umm el-Ga'ab, there is possibly an early funerary enclosure at Shunet el-Zebib, and there are also tombs that date to the Old, Middle and New Kingdoms and later periods. Abydos is also the location of some famous cultus-temples of Dynasty 19, dedicated to Ramesses I, Ramesses II, and Sethos I (with its associated *Osireion* or 'Cenotaph of Osiris').

Denderah (Eg: Iunet; Cl: Tentyris)

The capital of the sixth *nome* of Upper Egypt, Denderah was the cult-centre of Hathor, where she was worshipped with her husband Horus and son Ihy. A major temple dedicated to Hathor dates to the Graeco-

Roman Period. There are also tombs that date from the Archaic to the First Intermediate Periods.

6. Thebes (Eg: Waset; Cl: Thebai)
(Sites mentioned in the book are indicated in bold text)
This was the capital city of Egypt and its empire during the New Kingdom. Now a major archaeological site, it encompasses the main part of the ancient city on the East Bank of the Nile, and the cemeteries and mortuary temples on the West Bank.

The East Bank
The cultus temple complex of **Karnak**, with centres dedicated to Amun, Montu, Mut and Khonsu, was founded in Dynasty 12, although major additions were made in the New Kingdom, and further work was carried out in later periods. The nearby Temple of **Luxor**, dedicated to Amun's consort, Mut, was built during the New Kingdom and later periods.

The West Bank
Mortuary temples on the West Bank include those built by Mentuhotep Nebhepetre (Dynasty 11) and Hatshepsut (Dynasty 18) at **Deir-el-Bahri**; the **Ramesseum** (Ramesses II) and Qurneh (Sethos I) (both Dynasty 19); and those belonging to Tuthmosis III (Dynasty 18) and Ramesses III (Dynasty 20) at Medinet Habu. Amenhotep III built an extensive complex at **Malkata**: centred round a large lake, the Birket Habu, it included his palace and mortuary temple. There are royal tombs at El-Tarif (Dynasty 11), Dra'abu el-Naga' (Dynasty 17 and early Dynasty 18), and in the **Valley of the Kings (Biban el- Moluk)** (Dynasties 18-20), and the **Valley of the Queens** (Dynasties 19-20). Private (non-royal) tombs, dating from Dynasty 6 to the Graeco-Roman Period, have been discovered at Dra'abu el-Naga', Deir el-Bahri, el-Khokha, Assasif, Sheikh Abd el-Qurna, Deir el-Medina and Qurnet Mura'i. There is also a royal *necropolis* workmen's village at **Deir el-Medina**.

7. Upper Egypt (South)
Iuny; Cl: Hermonthis)
The city included a temple which served the cult of the god Montu. The Bucheum was also located here; this was the burial site of the

Sacred Buchis bulls (Dynasty 30 to Roman Period), the burials of the 'Mother of Buchis' cows, and extensive human cemeteries.

El-Kab (Eg: NEKHEB) Cl: Eileithyiaspolis

Nekheb, a town on the east bank, was a very important predynastic and early dynastic settlement. The local goddess, Nekhbet – the royal patroness of the White Land (Upper Egypt) in predynastic times – was later identified with the Greek goddess Eileithyia. There are temples dedicated to various deities: Nekhbet (New Kingdom), Shesmetet (Ptolemaic Period), Hathor and Nekhbet (Dynasty 18), and a chapel for Re-Harakhte, Hathor, Amun, Nekhbet and Ramesses II (Dynasty 19). The local cemeteries date to the Old, Middle and New Kingdoms: inscriptions in the local tombs of Ahmose Pennekheb and Ahmose, son of Ebana, are a particularly important source for the wars waged against the Hyksos and during early Dynasty 18.

Kom el-Ahmar (Eg: NEKHEN; Cl: HIERACONPOLIS)

Nekhen was situated on the west bank of the river opposite Nekheb. The two places formed the capital of Upper Egypt in predynastic times. The chief god of Nekhen was the falcon Nekheny who was identified with Horus. In the main deposit of votive offerings at the local temple, archaeologists discovered the Narmer Palette, an important artifact which commemorates the unification of Egypt. The site also has extensive predynastic cemeteries, and rock-cut tombs which date from Dynasty 6 to Dynasty 18.

Edfu (Eg: Dbot; Cl: Apollopolis Magna)

This town was the capital of the second *nome* of Upper Egypt. It is the site of tombs of the Old Kingdom and First Intermediate Period, but its most important monument is a temple dedicated to Horus, Hathor of Denderah, and the young Horus. This temple – the best preserved in Egypt – was built and decorated from 237 BCE to 57 BCE, reusing a site where earlier foundations date back to the Old Kingdom. The walls are decorated with important scenes and inscriptions (*The Building Texts*) about temple mythology and the famous 'Sacred Drama', which enacted the conflict between the gods Horus and Seth.

Aswan and Elephantine (Eg: Yebu; Cl: Syere)

In antiquity, the district around modern Aswan, including the island of Elephantine, was the capital of the first Upper Egyptian *nome*. It was an important garrison town and trading centre because of its vicinity to the First Cataract. Monuments that have survived on the island of Elephantine include temples built by Trajan and Alexander II, and the remains of New Kingdom buildings, as well as burials of rams, an animal which was sacred to the local god Khnum. There is also a Nilometer, and archaeological remains of a Jewish colony which flourished here in the Persian Period. Granite quarries to the south of Elephantine were one of Egypt's major sources of building material in pharaonic times. Rock-cut tombs belonging to local governors and officials who lived at Elephantine from the Old to New Kingdoms are located at Qubhet el-Hawa, in the cliffs on the west bank of the river.

Major UNESCO Salvage Operations

The increased water level which resulted from the construction of dams along the Nile in the twentieth century CE threatened many archaeological sites. Prompt action had to be taken, first by the *Archaeological Survey of Nubia* in the early twentieth century, and then by the *UNESCO Salvage Campaign* in the 1960s, in order to rescue some of the monuments and archaeological remains that would be lost forever. Some monuments were removed and rebuilt in an open-air museum at New Kalabsha near Aswan, and at other sites in Egypt; other temples were donated to countries in Europe and the USA as gestures of goodwill for their contributions to the rescue programme. However, the most famous rescue operations were undertaken at Abu Simbel and Philae, where the temples were removed to safe locations near their original sites.

Island of Philae (Eg: Pi-lak)

Once the first dam was built at Aswan in the early twentieth century, this island – situated at the First Cataract – and its ancient temples became submerged for most of the year. Later in the century, plans to build a High Dam at Aswan posed a new threat to these monuments: the rising water levels and construction of a massive lake behind the dam would completely drown the ancient sites. Arrangements were

251

therefore put in place to dismantle the buildings and rebuild them on the neighbouring island of Agilkia. The oldest structures date to Late Period, but the temples (the main one is dedicated to Isis) were mostly built in the Graeco-Roman Period. Ancient cults were still being practised on Philae until they were discontinued by the Roman emperor Justinian (527 CE–565 CE).

Abu Simbel
These two rock-cut temples, built by Ramesses II, were moved in 1964–68 CE, prior to construction of the High Dam, so that they would not be submerged by the waters of Lake Nasser. The Great Temple was built for the worship of Ptah, Amen-Re, Re-Harakhte and the deified Ramesses II, while the Smaller Temple was dedicated to his favourite queen, Nefertari, and the goddess Hathor.

Temples rebuilt at New Kalabsha
Some temples were transported from their original sites and relocated on a promontory near Aswan. These included a rock-cut temple originally located at **Beit el-Wali** which was built by Ramesses II and dedicated to Amen-Re and other gods; and a temple originally situated at **Kalabsha** and dedicated to a local god, Mandulis, which was constructed in reign of the Roman emperor Augustus.

General Geographical Terms
Asia Minor/Western Asia
The region now occupied by Syria and parts of Turkey.

Cataract
There are six cataracts along the Nile; each is formed by a scattering of rocks across the river, and resembles a mountain stream rather than a waterfall.

Delta
The inverted triangle of land which forms the northernmost area of Egypt.

Nile
Originating in central Africa, the White and Blue Niles come together

in the south to create a great river which then flows northwards from the Sudan into Egypt. After a journey of hundreds of miles, the river separates into two main branches; these are channelled through the Delta, and eventually feed into the Mediterranean Sea.

Nile Valley
The course gouged out by the river through southern and middle Egypt, and the land cultivated along its two banks.

Nubia
Extending along the Nile south of ancient Egypt's original border, Nubia comprised the area which is today occupied by southern Egypt and northern Sudan. Primarily because it was a rich source of gold and hard stone, Nubia was colonized by the Egyptians throughout antiquity, although the Nubians reversed this pattern and ruled Egypt for a brief period in Dynasty 25.

Punt
In antiquity, Punt extended inland from the Red Sea coast into the area now occupied by eastern Sudan. The ancient Egyptians went to Punt to trade for incense, which was grown and produced locally.

Syria/Palestine
An area which today encompasses Syria and the coastal and inland regions of the Levant.

Sites Outside Egypt
Byblos
An important sea-port on the Lebanese coast, situated about 25 miles (40 kilometres) north of modern Beirut. Byblos supplied Egypt with timber which came from the city's hinterland.

Khartoum
The capital of modern Sudan, built in 1822 CE by the Egyptian ruler Mohammed Ali, the city is situated on the left bank of the Blue Nile, immediately above its confluence with the White Nile.

Gebel Barkal (Eg: Napata)

During the New Kingdom, Napata was the southernmost city of the Egyptian empire. It reached its zenith in the eighth century BCE when it became the capital of an independent 'Ethiopian' kingdom, ruled over by Piankhy, Shabaka and Taharka who built many fine monuments there. Piankhy and Taharka renewed the great temple to Amen-Re situated at the base of Gebel Barkal ('the sacred mountain') which Egyptian kings of the later Dynasty 18 and Dynasty 19 had founded and extended.

References

Introduction – The Historical and Geographical Setting

1. Baines, J. and Malek, J. (1980) *Atlas of Ancient Egypt*. New York: Facts On File.
2. Bowman, A. and E. Rogan (eds.) (1999) *Agriculture in Egypt: from Pharaonic to Modern Times*. Oxford: Oxford University Press.
3. Brewer, D.J., D.B. Redford, and S. Redford (1994) *Domestic Plants and Animals: The Egyptian Origins*. Warminster: Aris and Phillips.
4. Butzer, K.W. (1964) *Environment and Archaeology. An Introduction to Pleistocene Geography*. Chicago: Aldine Publishing Company.
5. Trigger, B.G., B.J. Kemp, D. O'Connor and A.B. Lloyd (1983) *Ancient Egypt. A Social History*. Cambridge: Cambridge University Press.
6. Adkins, L. and R. Adkins (2000) *The Keys of Egypt: The Race to Read Hieroglyphs*. London: Harper Collins.

Section 1 Inundation
Chapter 1 The Land and its People

1. Kemp, B. (1993) *Ancient Egypt: Anatomy of a Civilisation*. London: Routledge.
2. Butzer, K.W. (1976) *Early Hydraulic Civilisation in Egypt. A Study in Cultural Ecology*. Chicago and London: University of Chicago Press.
3. Winlock, H.E. (1955) *Models of Daily Life in Ancient Egypt from the Tomb of Meket-Re*. Cambridge, Mass.: Harvard University Press.
4. David, A.R. (1996) *The Pyramid Builders of Ancient Egypt*. London: Routledge.
5. Littaeur, M.A. and J.H. Crouwel (1979) *Wheeled Vehicles and Ridden Animals in the Ancient Near East*. Leiden: Brill.

6. Casson, L. (1991) *The Ancient Mariners*. Princeton, N.J.: Princeton University Press.

7. Vinson, S. (1994) *Egyptian Boats and Ships*. Princes Risborough, England: Shire Egyptology.

Chapter 2 Religious Beliefs and Practices

1. Wilkinson, R.H. (2000) *The Complete Temples of Ancient Egypt*. London: Thames and Hudson.

2. Shafer, B.E., A. Arnold, G. Haeny, L. Bell, and R.B. Finnestad (eds.) (1997) *Temples of Ancient Egypt*. Ithaca, N.Y.: Cornell University Press.

3. Reeves, C.N. (2001) *Akhenaten: Egypt's False Prophet*. London: Thames and Hudson.

4. David, A.R. (2002) *Religion and Magic in Ancient Egypt*. Harmondsworth, England: Penguin.

5. Wilkinson, R.H. (1994) *Symbol and Magic in Egyptian Art*. London: Thames and Hudson.

6. Shafer, B.E. (ed.) (1991) *Religion in Ancient Egypt: Gods, Myths and Personal Practice*. London: Routledge.

7. Lesko, L.H. (1994) *Pharaoh's Workers: The Villagers of Deir el-Medina*. Ithaca, N.Y.: Cornell University Press.

8. Pinch, G. (2006) *Magic in Ancient Egypt*. London: British Museum Press.

Chapter 3 Social Customs

1. Kemp, B.J. (1977) The Early Development of Towns in Egypt. *Antiquity* 51: 185-200.

2. Černy, J. (1973) *A Community of Workmen at Thebes in the Ramesside Period*. Cairo: Institut Français d'Archéologie Orientale du Caire.

3. Tooley, A.M.J. (1995) *Egyptian Models and Scenes*. Princes Risborough, England: Shire Egyptology.

4. Uphill, E.P. (1972) The concept of the Egyptian palace as a 'Ruling Machine.' In P.J. Ucko, R. Tringham, and G.W. Dimbleby (eds.), *Man, Settlement and Urbanism*, pp. 721-734. London: Duckworth and Co.

5. Wilkinson, A. (1997) *The Garden in Ancient Egypt*. London: Rubicon Press.

6. Houlihan, P.F. *The Animal World of the Pharaohs* (1996) London: Thames and Hudson.

7. Manniche, L. (1999) *An Ancient Egyptian Herbal*. London: British Museum Press.

Chapter 4 Artisans, Trades and Crafts

1. Nicholson, P.T. and I. Shaw (eds.) (2000) *Ancient Egyptian Materials and Technology*. Cambridge: Cambridge University Press.

2. Crowfoot, G.M. *Methods of Handspinning in Egypt and the Sudan* (1931) Bankfield Museum, 2nd series, 12. Halifax, England: Bankfield Museum.

3. Lucas, A. and J.R. Harris (1999) *Ancient Egyptian Materials and Industries*. Mineola, N.Y.: Dover Publications.

4. Nicholson, P.T. (1993) *Egyptian Faience and Glass*. Princes Risborough, England: Shire Egyptology.

5. Parkinson, R. and S. Quirke (1995) *Papyrus*. London: British Museum Press.

6. Arnold, D. (1997) *Building in Egypt: Pharaonic Stone Masonry*. Oxford: Oxford University Press.

Section 2 Planting
Chapter 5 The Medical Profession

1. Nunn, J. (1996) *Ancient Egyptian Medicine*. London: British Museum Press.

2. David, A.R. (ed.) (1979) *The Manchester Museum Mummy Project: Multidisciplinary Research on Ancient Egyptian Mummified Remains*. Manchester: Manchester Museum.

3. Aufderheide, A.C. (2003) *The Scientific Study of Mummies*. Cambridge: Cambridge University Press.

4. David, A.R. (ed.) (2008) *Egyptian Mummies and Modern Science*. Cambridge: Cambridge University Press. Pb. ed. 2014

5. David, A.R. and E. Tapp (eds.) (1992) *The Mummy's Tale*. London: Michael O'Mara Books.

6. Leitz, C. (2000) *Magical and Medical Papyri of the New Kingdom*. London: British Museum Press.

Chapter 6 The Legal Profession

1. Glanville, S.R.K. (ed.) (1962) *The Legacy of Egypt*. Oxford: Clarendon Press.
2. McDowell, A.G. (1990) *Jurisdiction in the Workmen's Community of Deir el-Medina*. Leiden: Brill.
3. Edgerton, W.F. (1951) The Strikes in Ramesses III's Twenty-ninth Year. *Journal of Near Eastern Studies* 10: 137-145.
4. Goedicke, H. (1963) Was Magic used in the Harem Conspiracy against Ramesses III? *Journal of Egyptian Archaeology* 49: 71-92.
5. Peet, T.E. (1925) Fresh Light on the Tomb Robberies of the 20th Dynasty at Thebes. *Journal of Egyptian Archaeology* 11: 162-164.
6. Robins, G. (1993) *Women in Ancient Egypt*. London: British Museum Press.

Chapter 7 Entertainment and Personal Appearance

1. Manniche, L. (1991) *Music and Musicians in Ancient Egypt*. London: British Museum Press.
2. Fairman, H.W. (1974) *The Triumph of Horus: An Ancient Egyptian Sacred Drama*. London: B.T. Batsford.
3. Foster, J.L. and N.M. Davies (1992) *Love Songs of the New Kingdom: Translated from the Ancient Egyptian*. Austin: University of Texas Press.
4. Vogelsang-Eastwood, G. (1993) *Pharaonic Egyptian Clothing*. Leiden: Brill.
5. Manniche, L. (1999) *Sacred Luxuries: Fragrances, Aromatherapy and Cosmetics in Ancient Egypt*. London: Opus Publishing.
6. Aldred, C. (1971) *Jewels of the Pharaohs*. London: Thames and Hudson.
7. Decker, W. (1993) *Sports and Games of Ancient Egypt*. Cairo: American University in Cairo Press.

Section 3 Harvesting
Chapter 8 Education

1. Simpson, W.K. (ed.) (2003) *The Literature of Ancient Egypt: An Anthology of Stories, Instructions, Stelae, Autobiographies, and Poetry*. New Haven and London: Yale University Press.
2. Lichtheim, M. (1975) *Ancient Egyptian Literature*. Vol.1.

Berkeley and Los Angeles: University of California Press.

3. Lichtheim, M. (1976) *Ancient Egyptian Literature*. Vol.2. Berkeley and Los Angeles: University of California Press.

4. Wente, E. (1990) *Letters from Ancient Egypt*. Atlanta: Scholars Press.

5. Breasted, J.H. (1930) *The Edwin Smith Surgical Papyrus. Volume 1. Hieroglyphic Transliteration with Translations and Commentary*. Chicago: University of Chicago Press.

6. Robins, G. and C.C.D. Shute (1987) *The Rhind Mathematical Papyrus: An Ancient Egyptian Text*. London: British Museum Press.

7. Collier, M. and B. Manley (1998) *How to Read Egyptian Hieroglyphs*. London: British Museum Press.

8. Lichtheim, M. (1980) *Ancient Egyptian Literature*. Vol.3. Berkeley and Los Angeles: University of California Press.

9. Williams, R.J. (1972) Scribal training in ancient Egypt. *Journal of the American Oriental Society* 92: 214-221.

10. Williams, R. J. (1981) The sages of ancient Egypt in the light of recent scholarship. *Journal of the American Oriental Society* 101: 1-14.

Chapter 9 Military Campaigns

1. Schulman, A.R. (1964) *Military Rank, Title and Organisation in the Egyptian New Kingdom*. Berlin: Verlag Bruno Hessling.

2. Kitchen, K.A. (1962) *Suppiluliumas and the Amarna Pharaohs*. Liverpool: University of Liverpool Press.

3. Morkot, R.G. (2000) *The Black Pharaohs: Egypt's Nubian Rulers*. London: Rubicon Press.

4. Nelson, H.H. (1913) *The Battle of Megiddo*. Chicago: University of Chicago Press.

5. Gardiner, A.H. (1960) *The Kadesh Inscriptions of Ramesses II*. Oxford: Griffith Institute.

6. Murnane, W. (1990) *Road to Kadesh: A Historical Interpretation of the Battle Reliefs of Sety I at Karnak*. Chicago: Oriental Institute of the University of Chicago.

7. Kitchen, K.A. (1964) Some New Light on the Asiatic Wars of Ramesses II. *Journal of Egyptian Archaeology* 50: 47-70.

8. *The Epigraphic Survey, University of Chicago, Reliefs and*

Inscriptions at Karnak. 2 vols. (1936) Chicago: University of Chicago Press.

9. Yadin, Y. (1963) *The Art of Warfare in Biblical Lands in the Light of Archaeological Discovery*. London: Weidenfeld and Nicholson.

10. Littauer, M.A. and J.H. Crouwel (1985) *Chariots and Related Equipment from the Tomb of Tutankhamun*. Oxford: Griffith Institute.

11. Landström, B. (1970) *Ships of the Pharaohs, 4000 Years of Egyptian Ship-building*. London: Allen Lane.

12. *The Epigraphic Survey, University of Chicago, Medinet Habu*. 8 vols. (1930-70) Chicago: University of Chicago Press.

13. Edgerton, W. and J.A. Wilson (1936) *Historical Records of Ramesses III*. Chicago: Chicago Oriental Institute.

14. Glanville, S.R.K. (ed.) (1972) *Catalogue of Egyptian Antiquities in the British Museum, Volume 2: Wooden Boat Models*. London: British Museum Press.

15. Jones, D. *Boats* (1995) London: British Museum Press.

Chapter 10 Funerary Customs

1. Taylor, J.H. (2000) *Death and the Afterlife in Ancient Egypt*. London: British Museum Press.

2. Griffiths, J.G. (1980) *The Origins of Osiris and his Cult*. Leiden: Brill.

3. Hornung, E. (1983) *Conceptions of God in Ancient Egypt: The One and the Many*. London: Routledge and Kegan Paul.

4. Griffiths, J.G. (1970) *Plutarch, de Iside et Osiride*. Cardiff: University of Wales Press.

5. Schäfer, H. (1974) *Principles of Egyptian Art*. Translated and edited J. Baines, edited with epilogue by E. Brunner-Traut. Oxford: Oxford University Press.

6. Reeves, C.N. and R.H. Wilkinson (1996) *The Complete Valley of the Kings: Tombs and Treasures of Egypt's Greatest Pharaohs*. London: Thames and Hudson.

7. Ikram, S. and A. Dodson (1998) *The Mummy in Ancient Egypt: Equipping the Dead for Eternity*. London: Thames and Hudson.

8. Hornung, E. (1999) *The Ancient Egyptian Books of the Afterlife*. Translated by D. Lorton. Ithaca, N. Y.: Cornell University Press.

9. Allen, T.G. (1935–60) *The Egyptian Book of the Dead. Documents in the Oriental Institute Museum at the University of Chicago*. Chicago: University of Chicago Press.

10. Ritner, R. (1993) *The Mechanics of Ancient Egyptian Magical Practice*. Chicago: University of Chicago Press.

11. Jones, D. (1990) *Model Boats from the Tomb of Tutankhamun*. Tutankhamun's Tomb series, 9. Oxford: Griffith Institute.

12. Smith, G.E. and W.R. Dawson (1991) *Egyptian Mummies*. London: Kegan Paul International.

13. Harris, J.E. and E.F. Wente (eds.) (1980) *An X-ray Atlas of the Royal Mummies*. Chicago: University of Chicago Press.

14. Cockburn, A., E. Cockburn and T.A. Reyman (1998) *Mummies, Disease and Ancient Cultures*. Cambridge: Cambridge University Press.

15. Lichtheim, M. (1975) *Ancient Egyptian Literature*. Vol.1. Berkeley and Los Angeles: University of California Press.

Appendix

Chronological Table of Egyptian History

Predynastic Period
*c.*5000–3100 BCE

Archaic Period
*c.*3100–*c.*2890 BCE   Dynasty 1
*c.*2890–*c.*2686 BCE   Dynasty 2

Old Kingdom
*c.*2686–*c.*2613 BCE   Dynasty 3
*c.*2613–*c.*2494 BCE   Dynasty 4
*c.*2494–*c.*2345 BCE   Dynasty 5
*c.*2345–*c.*2181 BCE   Dynasty 6

First Intermediate Period
*c.*2181–*c.*2173 BCE   Dynasty 7 (Memphite)
*c.*2173–*c.*2160 BCE   Dynasty 8 (Memphite)
*c.*2160–*c.*2130 BCE   Dynasty 9 (Heracleopolitan)
*c.*2130–*c.*2040 BCE   Dynasty 10 (Heracleopolitan)
*c.*2133–*c.*1991 BCE   Dynasty 11 (Theban)

Middle Kingdom
1991–1786 BCE   Dynasty 12

Second Intermediate Period
1786–1633 BCE   Dynasty 13
1786–*c.*1603 BCE   Dynasty 14 (Xois)

1674–1567 BCE	Dynasty 15 (Hyksos)
*c.*1684–1567 BCE	Dynasty 16 (Hyksos)
*c.*1650–1567 BCE	Dynasty 17 (Theban)

New Kingdom

1567–1320 BCE	**Dynasty 18 (Khary's family)**
1320–1200 BCE	Dynasty 19
1200–1085 BCE	Dynasty 20

Third Intermediate Period

1085–945 BCE	Dynasty 21
945–730 BCE	Dynasty 22 (Bubastis)
817(?)–730 BCE	Dynasty 23 (Tanis)
720–715 BCE	Dynasty 24 (Sais)
715–668 BCE	Dynasty 25 (Ethiopian)

Late Period

664–525 BCE	Dynasty 26 (Sais)
525–404 BCE	Dynasty 27 (Persian)
404–399 BCE	Dynasty 28 (Sais)
399–380 BCE	Dynasty 29 (Mendes)
380–343 BCE	Dynasty 30 (Sebennytos)
343–332 BCE	Dynasty 31 (Persian)

Alexander the Great
332 BCE

Ptolemaic Period
332–30 BCE

Conquest by Romans
30 BCE

Roman Period
30 BCE–fourth century CE